Richard Samans • Jane Nelson

# Sustainable Enterprise Value Creation

## Implementing Stakeholder Capitalism through Full ESG Integration

palgrave
macmillan

Richard Samans
Geneve, Switzerland

Jane Nelson
Cambridge, MA, USA

ISBN 978-3-030-93562-7      ISBN 978-3-030-93560-3    (eBook)
https://doi.org/10.1007/978-3-030-93560-3

# Sustainable Enterprise Value Creation

"While commitment to the principles of stakeholder capitalism is growing, the practice of them is still developing.... That is what makes this book such an important contribution. It is the most extensive treatment to date of the practice and diverse legal and historical traditions of stakeholder capitalism, and it outlines an implementation framework for companies in any industry or country through their corporate governance, strategy, reporting and partnerships. As such, it fills a gap in both scholarship and practice."

—From the Foreword by Klaus Schwab, Founder and Executive Chairman, *World Economic Forum*

"An essential read for all current and future business leaders. We need to redirect capitalism to accelerate global systems transformations to deliver an equitable, net-zero and nature positive world. Jane and Rick expertly take leaders through the practical steps they must take to ensure their businesses continue to create long-term value for all their stakeholders. I look forward to seeing these principles and practices becoming the norm across the corporate world."

—Peter Bakker, President and CEO, *World Business Council for Sustainable Development*

"An insightful and timely book. Stakeholder capitalism can no longer be only a choice but rather must become the floor of competitive practice. A just, inclusive and sustainable future is possible but it will take major reform of investment and corporate practice. All investment must be governed with an ESG lens. And companies must accept responsibility for due diligence for human and labour rights with environmental standards as well as governance with an accountability that embeds these practices in the business model; the human centred approach so ably laid out here. A must read!"

—Sharan Burrow, General Secretary, *International Trade Union Confederation*

"Stakeholder capitalism is about adding value to all stakeholders, as this important book explains in great depth. We need to depart from the assumption that it is zero sum game. Technological advancements have made it possible to serve all stakeholders simultaneously, and it has become good business to develop sustainable solutions for the future. As such, ESG has become core to the strategy of any company, and transparency on ESG has become as important as the traditional financial reporting. Business leadership in this new era is about setting ambitious targets and over-delivering on both to create a sustainable future faster."

—Jim Hagemann Snabe, *Chairman of Siemens and A.P. Moller-Maersk, Vice Chairman, Allianz*

# Foreword

As the world grapples with the climate crisis, growing inequality and pandemic recovery, the need for a more stakeholder-oriented model of business leadership and new models of multistakeholder partnership has never been greater. A vanguard of individuals and institutions is leading the way, and the challenge now is to accelerate and scale action and impact. The growth in interest in stakeholder capitalism and sustainability within the business community in recent years is an encouraging sign that companies are moving in the right direction.

I first wrote about the stakeholder theory of corporate governance as a young business school professor and industry consultant in 1971. I sought to capture the principles and practices that were common, if implicit, in the approach of many companies in Europe and, to a considerable extent, the United States at the time. One of our earliest "calls to action" at the World Economic Forum was the original Davos Manifesto signed in 1973, which outlined the purpose of professional management to serve clients, shareholders, workers and employees, as well as societies, and to harmonize the different interests of the stakeholders.

I had begun my career working in a family-owned industrial company in Germany. These "Mittelstand" firms, and others like them around the world, are typically run according to a broader set of objectives than the maximization of shareholder value. The shift towards shareholder capitalism and the broader financialization of economies was in its infancy then, but the "shareholder versus stakeholder" debate in academia was already in full swing, particularly in the United States where I had spent time in graduate studies. That debate influenced the global spread of shareholder primacy and short-termism in the decades that followed.

So much has changed since then, but the debate continues. I believe the momentum behind stakeholder capitalism is growing, and that history is on its side. By this, I mean that the transformational technological, environmental, geopolitical and socio-economic shifts that are underway in the twenty-first century are compelling corporate boards and management teams to move in this direction. The ground is shifting under their feet. Young generations are more and more eager to have their voice heard, as workers, consumers and investors. Their message is that sustainability and inclusion should be much higher on any corporate agenda. Society, including investors and regulators, is increasingly demanding a more balanced and integrated approach to business value creation, one that consciously strives to optimize both economic and social value through embedding environmental, social and governance (ESG) risks and opportunities in decision-making alongside financial and market ones. This is an approach that the authors call sustainable enterprise value creation.

But while commitment to the principles of stakeholder capitalism and sustainable enterprise value creation is growing, the practice of them is still developing. The current gap between aspiration and commitment, on the one hand, and implementation and results, on the other, must narrow. That is what makes this book such an important contribution. It is the most extensive treatment to date of the practice and diverse legal and historical traditions of stakeholder capitalism, and it outlines an implementation framework for companies in any industry or country through their corporate governance, strategy, reporting and partnerships. As such, it fills a gap in both scholarship and practice. It is relevant for the curricula of business and other professional schools and executive education programmes. It is also an important resource for directors and managers of companies that have taken the step of committing themselves to the principles of stakeholder capitalism and sustainability and aim to be on the leading edge of practice.

The debate about the ultimate purpose of a corporation will certainly continue. Some argue that shareholder and other stakeholder interests are bound to collide and that, in such instances, difficult decisions will have to be made that are likely to sacrifice shareholder or other stakeholder priorities. There is no doubt there can be difficult trade-offs in the short run. But in the long run, any company lives from its "trust capital" and societal "license to operate." Having a stakeholder approach improves both. It is therefore in the interest of shareholders to pursue this trust and license to operate, as it will make the company more profitable. It provides them with more motivated employees, products that customers are willing to pay a premium for and a lower cost of capital. And in either case, the fact that there may be competing interests at play within an enterprise is not a reason to duck the important questions they raise by denying their relevance or indeed materiality. Rather, it is a reason to ensure that the company has prepared the ground as diligently as possible for such situations by installing the kinds of governance processes and management and accountability systems described in this book.

Much of the business community today is ready to move beyond the theoretical debate and proceed with the practical work of embedding stakeholder and sustainability-oriented processes and systems within their firms. They are focusing on fully integrating environmental, social, governance and data stewardship risks and opportunities into their governance and decision-making. And they are making explicit commitments to create long-term, sustainable enterprise value alongside delivering near-term financial results. We certainly see this in the World Economic Forum, where the majority of members of our International Business Council—CEOs and chairpersons of 120 of the largest firms in the world—have committed to implement the Measuring Stakeholder Capitalism metrics that were developed in cooperation with all four of the world's largest accounting firms.

Indeed, one of the book's distinct contributions is the roadmap it describes for the creation of a global baseline standard for ESG and sustainability disclosure, combining and building on the best practices in the market such as the Forum's Stakeholder Capitalism metrics and disclosures. My former colleague, Rick Samans, has been a leading force for this type of convergence and simplification for over a decade, from the time he catalysed the creation of the Climate Disclosure Standards Board, one of many multistakeholder initiatives he shaped as a Managing Director of the Forum. Among these were a number of pioneering global corporate citizenship initiatives in the early to mid-2000s on which he and Jane Nelson collaborated while she was a director of the Prince of Wales International Business Leaders Forum and later the founding director of the Corporate Responsibility Initiative at the Harvard Kennedy School, my alma mater. These initiatives helped to establish the relevance of stakeholder and sustainability considerations for the core business of companies, including their strategy and governance.

Rick and Jane have also been leading contributors to the development of the Forum's role as a platform for innovative multistakeholder initiatives that address complex, systemic challenges no stakeholder has the capacity to solve alone. In fact, I consider the governance gap created by the dominance of shareholder and state capitalism over the past half century to be one of the most important systemic weaknesses facing the world today as we grapple with the challenges posed by inequality, climate change, environmental degradation, declining social cohesion and trust and weak productivity growth. I firmly believe that stakeholder capitalism can help to bridge this gap and be an important part of the solution to these challenges, but only if its principles are translated into rigorous, widespread practice by directors, managers and educators.

This book will give them the running start they need, and it gives me fresh optimism that they can and will succeed.

The World Economic Forum                                    Klaus Schwab
Geneva, Switzerland
August 12, 2021

# Acknowledgements

We have worked together on a variety of projects spanning 20 years, focused on the fields of corporate and global governance, business leadership for sustainable development and public-private partnerships to address complex challenges facing business and society. Both of us have lived and worked in Europe, the United States and Asia, and travelled extensively in Africa, Latin America and the Middle East. During this time, we have learned and benefited immeasurably from the views and experiences of friends and colleagues around the world. While we cannot do justice to acknowledging everyone individually, we are deeply grateful for the many opportunities we've had to learn from and engage with inspiring people from diverse backgrounds, sectors and countries.

The first time we worked together over twenty years ago was to coordinate a series of CEO-level roundtables and publications on business leadership and partnerships in the context of rapid global economic integration. We focused on the role that companies could play working with key stakeholders through their core business activities, far beyond corporate philanthropy, and the growing need for the private sector to address emerging socio-economic and environmental challenges. At the time, Rick was Director of Global Issues at the World Economic Forum and Jane was Director of Policy and Research at The Prince of Wales International Business Leaders Forum. The first joint publication from these efforts was a statement published at the Annual Meeting of the World Economic Forum in 2002, which was hosted in New York in the immediate aftermath of 9/11. Signed by 46 chief executive officers from companies operating in more than 16 different industry sectors and headquartered in 18 countries, it was entitled *Global Corporate Citizenship: The Leadership Challenge for CEOs and Boards*. We are grateful to those ground-breaking CEOs who demonstrated to us what was possible long before ESG and corporate sustainability became mainstream.

Looking back on the evolution of this field since then, we would like to recognize with deep appreciation the pioneering work and support of HRH The Prince of Wales, Klaus Schwab, Mary Robinson, Mark Carney, Paul Polman, Brian Moynihan and Peter Bakker, and that of our late colleagues, John Ruggie and Robert Davies. They all demonstrated remarkable foresight and determined personal leadership over many years on the private sector aspect of governance reform that is required to improve fundamentally the capacity of market economies to generate broad and sustainable progress in living standards. Each stuck their neck out and moved their institutions and networks, thereby moving many others, and they have been a great inspiration to us personally. Such acts of combined moral, intellectual and organizational leadership are rare and deserve to be recognized and celebrated.

We are grateful to the reviewers and the editorial and production teams at Palgrave Macmillan, especially Liz Barlow, Srishti Gupta and Nirmal Kumar, who have provided us with valuable feedback, guidance and encouragement throughout the publication process.

Rick would also like to recognize his colleagues at the Climate Disclosure Standards Board past and present and in particular Lois Guthrie, Mardi McBrien and Paul Simpson for their own determined and inspired leadership—and good judgment—in guiding this small but influential organization so effectively over the past 15 years. Thanks are due as well to CDSB's Board and Technical Working Group members and their institutions for working so collaboratively to lay the groundwork for the actions regulators and international accounting authorities are now taking.

In addition, he would like to express appreciation to his formidable Group of 5 co-facilitators, Veronica Poole and Clara Barby, for their extraordinary knowledge and diligence in driving the convergence of thinking among voluntary standard setting organizations and key accounting and regulatory bodies about the construction of a globally coherent system of corporate sustainability reporting. Thanks are due as well to the World Economic Forum International Business Council project team who made the *Measuring Stakeholder Capitalism* initiative possible, including Maha Eltobgy and other colleagues at the Forum, Lawrence Di Rita and colleagues at Bank of America, and each of the "Big Four" accounting firm teams and corresponding lead partners.

Perhaps most of all, he would like to thank Catherine, Ava and Elijah for enduring the many weekends, evenings and vacation days of a distracted husband and father that were necessary to bring this project to fruition.

Jane would like to thank her colleagues and programme fellows at Harvard Kennedy School, especially Scott Leland, John Haigh, Victoria Groves-Cardillo, Minoo Ghoreishi, Annmarie Basler, Dan Murphy, Matthew Murray, Lisa Dreier, Mark Kramer, Caroline Rees, Beth Jenkins, Lance Pierce, John Sherman, Rachel Davis, David Wood, Steve Lydenberg and Ben Rutledge; her colleagues at Brookings, Homi Kharas, John McArthur, George Ingram and Tony Pipa; and her co-authors on previous books, Ira Jackson and David Grayson, as well as John Elkington, Alison Beanland and Zahid Torres-Rahman, for their many years of friendship and collegiality. Thank you to Ariel Silverman for her research assistance for this book and to many other wonderful students who have taught me so much and greatly inspired me over a decade of teaching.

She is grateful for valuable insights on corporate governance and business leadership gained from her board colleagues and the management teams at Newmont over the past decade, and for the mentorship and support of Noreen Doyle, Bruce Brook, Ronee Hagen, Greg Boyce and Julio Quintana. Likewise, from her experiences learning with fellow advisory council members, colleagues and management teams at other companies and international organizations, especially those at Abbott, AbbVie, Bank of America, Business Fights Poverty, Business for Peace Foundation, Chevron, ExxonMobil, Griffith Foods, the Prince of Wales International Business Leaders Forum, the World Business Council for Sustainable Development, the World Economic Forum and the World Environment Center.

Above all, thank you to dear family and friends—Tony and Libby, Michèle and Scott, Susan, Elizabeth and Ann, Patrick and Jules, Graham and Liz, Ira, Melanie, Dena and David for all your support.

# Contents

# List of Figures

# List of Boxes

# Part I

Sustainable Enterprise Value Creation
and Stakeholder Capitalism

# 1

# Stakeholder Capitalism's Promising Resurgence

Modern civilization is at a crossroads, at a potential inflection point in its historical evolution. The scientific community has advised that the window for decisive collective action to stabilize greenhouse gas emissions and avoid catastrophic impacts on people and the planet will close within a decade. The COVID-19 pandemic has created one of the worst health and socio-economic crises the world has experienced in a century. Inequality is on the rise, and shifts in technology, national politics and international relations are growing in frequency and disruptive force.

No business is immune from these and other major changes. In this dynamic new operating context, no firm's ability to create and sustain value can be taken for granted. There is simply no room for complacency or insularity in management teams and boards.

To this end, business leaders in this new era must look more rigorously beyond their firm's near-term operations and financial results, improving their understanding of how underlying economic, social, political, technological and environmental conditions are evolving and likely to affect their firm's operations and prospects over time. And they must proactively translate this wider appreciation of the drivers of enterprise value into strategies and practices that simultaneously benefit shareholders and other stakeholders, out of a recognition that such synergy is a source of further firm competitiveness and resilience.

This book focuses on the practical actions that all boards of directors and business leaders can take to be better prepared to engage these risks and opportunities more diligently and effectively. It defines a systematic agenda to strengthen board and management processes so that they are better able to

© The Author(s) 2022
R. Samans, J. Nelson, *Sustainable Enterprise Value Creation*,
https://doi.org/10.1007/978-3-030-93560-3_1

generate maximum synergy between business and societal value creation, illustrated by concrete examples of how leading companies are creating long-term enterprise value while contributing to a more just, inclusive and sustainable future for their economies and societies. It outlines specific ways corporate leaders can step up, speak out and act on such issues as addressing climate change, contributing to economic recovery, respecting human rights, reducing inequality, building new skills, responding to pandemics and systemic shocks and ensuring responsible data use and privacy as part of their core business strategy.

The book focuses on four essential areas of business leadership required to create sustainable enterprise value through the rigorous implementation of the principles of stakeholder capitalism and full integration of environmental, social, governance and data stewardship (ESG&D) risks and opportunities. We add a "D" to the familiar "ESG" construct to take account of the rising data intensity of business value creation and its increasingly significant implications for stakeholders and society, as these are not well addressed by current ESG theory or practice.

The specifics of the approach we outline will vary based on industry sector, jurisdiction, size and ownership structure, but these four areas of required action are relevant for every company, everywhere. With the recent resurgence of interest in stakeholder capitalism, firms at the forefront of the movement are implementing reforms in each of these areas:

- **Corporate governance and oversight**: Boards of directors are taking a more integrated approach to governance by strengthening their oversight of environmental, social, governance and data stewardship (ESG&D) risks and opportunities alongside financial and operational ones. They are being more explicit about their duty to stakeholders, including but not only shareholders. They are taking a more proactive role in stewarding corporate purpose, culture, capital allocation and long-term value creation in addition to oversight of short-term risks and performance. And they are adapting their board's organization, composition and stakeholder engagement models to be fit for these purposes.
- **Corporate strategy and implementation**: Leading executive teams and managers are aligning their sustainability strategies with their corporate strategies and their core business targets and incentives. They are strengthening enterprise management of material and salient ESG&D risks and opportunities and investing in innovative science, technology and new business models to drive social and environmental impact. They are developing diverse talent and more inclusive corporate cultures. And they are

undertaking more systematic and transparent engagement with their stakeholders—employees, customers, suppliers, investors, communities and governments.

- **Corporate reporting and accountability**: Leading companies and investors are driving the agenda for a transformation in corporate disclosure and reporting, alongside accountants and standard-setting bodies. They are announcing public goals and targets for their most material ESG&D risks and opportunities and starting to report on their performance against these in a more consistent, transparent and integrated manner as part of their annual reporting cycle to investors. These leaders are recognizing the need for an international sustainability reporting standard and supporting collective efforts to develop one.

- **Corporate partnerships and systemic change**: More companies are acknowledging the need for systems-level change to secure and sustain the vitality and even viability of their operating context. They recognize that challenges such as tackling climate change; developing a well-skilled future workforce; addressing racial and other forms of inequality; reforming tax systems; transforming economic, energy, health and food systems; and achieving the Sustainable Development Goals and the Paris Climate Agreement, all impinge upon their ability to create sustainable enterprise value. And addressing these challenges requires collective action with other actors. Even the largest corporations must build alliances with competitors, other companies, governments and civil society organizations to achieve the type of systems-level transformation that will ensure their future competitiveness and even survival. New models of partnership are essential but often difficult to build and sustain without strong business leadership.

Transformative changes in corporate priorities, behaviours and business models remain the exception rather than the norm in each of these areas, let alone across all of them. Systematic implementation of the principles of stakeholder capitalism and integration of ESG&D risks and opportunities at a practical level by boards, management teams, accountants and investors have a long way to go.

The same can be said of governments and what they are doing to drive transformation in private enterprises and markets. A vanguard is starting to implement the necessary policy, regulatory and fiscal reforms and to shift market signals, such as reforming corporate law and taxation, putting a price on carbon and mandating corporate disclosure of climate risks, inclusion and diversity and human rights due diligence. Yet, major governance gaps and market failures remain in most countries.

The trend, however, is in the right direction. The purpose of this book is to help accelerate and scale this shift towards a more economically, socially and environmentally sustainable model of enterprise value creation by clarifying what it means in practical terms for the leadership of firms.

We begin in Part I by examining the secular forces that are transforming the business context and fuelling the resurgence of stakeholder capitalism as a directional concept. This is followed by a thematic overview of the new business leadership agenda compelled by these mega-trends.

In Part II, we break down this leadership agenda into specific actions in the areas of corporate governance, corporate strategy, corporate reporting and corporate partnerships. We outline priorities and provide examples of good practice and lessons learned in each of these four areas, drawing on the experience of companies that are pioneering change.

The concluding chapter summarizes this practical guide to creating sustainable enterprise value through the full integration of ESG&D risks and opportunities, which is to say the rigorous implementation of stakeholder capitalism. We conclude with a reflection on the mindsets and skill sets that are now required of business leaders and why they will become even more important in the future.

## 1.1   The Imperative for Fundamental Change in Public and Private Economic Governance

Over the past three decades, the forces of market liberalization, globalization, democratization, deregulation and technological innovation have created some of the most fundamental and rapid changes ever experienced on the planet. These changes have measurably improved the lives of several billion people around the globe. Yet, the unparalleled opportunities that have been created for many have been tempered by the persistence of deep-seated structural inequality and economic insecurity for hundreds of millions of people, challenges to social cohesion and growing environmental degradation. Even before the global financial crisis in 2008 and the global COVID-19 pandemic, there was growing awareness of the need to address systemic market failures and governance gaps with the purpose of tackling growing inequality, social unrest, political polarization and nationalism and the relentless march of climate change, alongside other threats to our ecosystem. Today, there can no longer be any doubt. Major changes in public and private governance are needed.

The COVID-19 pandemic has exacerbated these challenges. It has had far-reaching implications for peoples' lives, livelihoods and learning in almost every country.[1] Its impact has been devastating for hundreds of millions of people, both directly and indirectly, as well as for certain industry sectors and millions of small businesses and community organizations. It has widened inequalities and faultlines in our political, social and financial systems while accelerating longer-term technological, geopolitical and socio-economic shifts. Meanwhile, the systemic challenges of climate change and resource insecurity, especially biodiversity and water loss, continue largely unabated and the human and economic costs of racial, gender and other forms of injustice and inequality continue to grow.

Future generations will ask the following questions:

(i) How did leaders in government, business and civil society respond to the global pandemic, climate change, natural disasters, protests around inequality and injustice, and related deterioration of social cohesion and international cooperation in the late 2010s and early 2020s?

(ii) Emerging out of these synchronous crises, did leaders harness the opportunity to strengthen the resilience of essential institutions and systems and build back better towards more just, inclusive and sustainable societies and economies? Or—as happened in the wake of the global financial crisis—did they fail to seize the moment for transformational change?

Over the past few years, countless op-eds, articles and reports have been written, thousands of online meetings, panels and events convened, several major intergovernmental declarations issued, multi-stakeholder coalitions established, and numerous proposals put forward on how to "build back better" from the pandemic. For example, in June 2021, essentially all the world's governments and its leading workers and employers organizations issued a consensus *Global Call to Action for a Human-Centred Recovery That Is Inclusive, Sustainable and Resilient* with a detailed roadmap of policy and other commitments to "build forward better" from the COVID-19 crisis.[2] Earlier that month, G-7 leaders issued a 25-page summit communique entitled *Our Shared Agenda for Global Action to Build Back Better* along with a *Health Declaration* and *Nature Compact*.[3] In 2020, the World Economic Forum and its multi-stakeholder leader-level communities framed the leadership challenge and opportunity as *The Great Reset*, with its founder and executive chairman, Professor Klaus Schwab, arguing that "we need a 'Great Reset' of capitalism that steers the market toward fairer outcomes, ensures that investments advance shared goals, such as equality and sustainability, and harnesses technology to support the public good."[4]

In August 2021, the Intergovernmental Panel on Climate Change (IPCC) released its Working Group I contribution to IPCC's Sixth Assessment Report,[5] which UN Secretary-General, António Guterres, referred to as

> a code red for humanity. The alarm bells are deafening, and the evidence is irrefutable: greenhouse-gas emissions from fossil-fuel burning and deforestation are choking our planet and putting billions of people at immediate risk. Global heating is affecting every region on Earth, with many of the changes becoming irreversible. The internationally agreed threshold of 1.5°C is perilously close. We are at imminent risk of hitting 1.5°C in the near term. … All nations, especially the G20 and other major emitters, need to join the net-zero emissions coalition and reinforce their commitments with credible, concrete and enhanced nationally determined contributions and policies before COP26 in Glasgow.[6]

Although the specific details of the many evolving recommendations and initiatives may vary, there is strong consensus beginning to emerge around the level of ambition and priorities that need to be addressed. Specifically, there is an increasingly unified call for individual, institutional and systemic change to deliver outcomes that are:

- **Just:** This calls for clear and consistent recognition of the dignity and worth of every human being. In turn this requires decision-making by public and private leaders that is morally right and fair, founded on respect for human rights and based on reliable data, analysis and reason. The pandemic has brought into sharp relief the injustice that millions of essential workers, from healthcare to logistics and retail, earn less than a living wage in most countries. And they continue to do so, despite risking their lives to serve others who have much greater economic security and face much less personal risk. The ongoing reality of racial and ethnic injustice in many countries has also become more stark to more people because of the pandemic and following high-profile incidents of intolerance and violence, including brutality against peaceful citizens from law enforcement officers in many countries. Likewise, the structural inequality and injustice of low-income households and communities, and especially women, being the most vulnerable to the risks and costs of public health, environmental and economic crises, and shocks such as the pandemic, technological disruptions, a changing climate and water insecurity. In almost every country, they are far less able to access social safety nets and other services to mitigate these risks and costs, even when such mechanisms exist. Even before the pandemic, there were growing concerns about the challenges of achieving a "just transition" in the shift towards a digital and low-carbon economy. The need to focus on justice and a "just transition" is more important than ever.

- **Inclusive**: This requires concerted public and private sector efforts to include as many people as possible in improved access to social benefits, political participation, economic opportunity and essential goods and services. It calls for a particular focus on those who are most vulnerable or who are currently excluded based on income, gender, race, ethnicity and other types of identity. Closely linked to inequality and injustice is the fact that many people are excluded from access to affordable healthcare and education, to economic opportunities and to having a political voice. The nature and extent of their exclusion is often based on deep-seated structural obstacles and circumstances beyond their own control. The pandemic has made this exclusion even more stark. It has also raised the obstacles that individual households and communities must overcome to achieve greater access and opportunity. Examples include smallholder farmers and micro- or small-scale entrepreneurs who lack access to basic inputs, financing and markets, and racial and ethnic minorities who find it more difficult to finish education, find affordable housing and gain access to financial services and jobs in most countries. Examples also include low-income students who are falling even further behind their contemporaries due to digital exclusion and crowded living conditions. And they include women who are bearing an even heavier burden than normal of caring for children and the elderly while also making up most of the essential workers, and all too often, facing discrimination and harassment at work. Public policies and business models that are intentionally inclusive in their design and implementation are more important than ever.

- **Sustainable**: This requires a public and private sector commitment to achieving development that meets the needs of the present without compromising the ability of future generations to meet their own needs.[7] In particular, strong consensus has been emerging on the need to decouple economic growth from high carbon emissions, the overuse of natural resources, especially water and biodiversity, environmental degradation and pollution, and the exploitation of people. Such decoupling will be essential to tackle the inter-related challenges of poverty, climate change, natural resource scarcity and human insecurity. Despite the slowing of economic activity and growth due to the COVID-19 pandemic, the overall trajectory towards climate-driven catastrophe continues to accelerate and escalate and the number and severity of natural disasters, from wildfires and drought to hurricanes and floods continue, to grow. Many see the global impact of the pandemic as a precursor to the potentially far worse systemic impacts of climate change. Green public policies, new technologies, sustainable financing and infrastructure and more efficient, circular and regenerative business models to achieve a low-carbon or net-zero carbon economy that at the same time create decent jobs are more important than ever.

Just. Inclusive. Sustainable. Readers may ask, "[S]o what is new?" The Universal Declaration of Human Rights has been around since 1948, for example, and there has long been calls for better workers' rights, civil rights and social and environmental justice, years before recent global social movements such as #MeToo, #BlackLivesMatter and #ExtinctionRebellion. In 2011, the UN Guiding Principles on Business and Human Rights were unanimously endorsed by the United Nations Human Rights Council. Likewise, Sustainable Development has been a globally agreed ambition since the UN Conference on Environment and Development in 1992, popularly known as the Rio Earth Summit. It has been given further impetus since 2015, when more than 190 Heads of State signed up to implement both the Sustainable Development Goals in September and the UN Paris Climate Agreement in December of that year.

Over the past two decades, numerous global, national and city-level commissions and reports have explored the types of public policies, laws, regulations and market incentives that are needed to drive towards these goals or to avoid the risks and costs of inaction. Other platforms have identified the priorities for private sector leadership and the actions that corporations, financial institutions, social entrepreneurs and different industry sectors should take to respect human rights, build more inclusive business models and achieve sustainable development.[8] There have been detailed studies on the high economic and health risks of epidemics and pandemics and how to avoid them. There is widespread agreement among policymakers and business leaders in many countries on the crucial role of science, technology, data and innovation in achieving these goals, albeit with some exceptions. There are also many guidelines for actions that can be taken by universities and research groups, nongovernmental organizations, women, youth, labour and indigenous peoples' groups, and civic and community-level leaders.[9]

In short, we largely know what is needed and have known for some time. But despite many individual examples of progress being made, there has been a collective failure to achieve the speed, scale and systemic impact that is required. Business, political and other leaders of society have been too complacent. Most have been too comfortable with the *status quo*. Change has been incremental, at best. Countless projects and initiatives have been launched, but there have been too few system-level changes achieved. Companies have developed new technologies, products, services and metrics, but most of them have not done enough to fundamentally realign their core strategies and business models to achieve measurably beneficial outcomes or to avoid negative impacts on people and the planet. Governments have changed some laws, regulations and market incentives, but too few in too few places. Most of the recovery and stimulus packages after the global financial crisis, for example, failed to incorporate conditions or incentives for more inclusive and green policies and practices, although this gap has been more effectively addressed by pandemic recovery initiatives.

The extraordinary events of 2020 and 2021 have given humanity a "wake-up call" that is impossible to ignore. They have created a universal sense of urgency anchored in a greater sense of human connectedness and common cause, despite the precipitous decline in physical gatherings and travel. More than at any other time in our generation, recent events have highlighted the systemic and structural inequalities and injustices that persist in almost every country. They have made us aware of the synchronous and cascading nature of large-scale humanitarian, economic and natural shocks and crises. Above all, recent events have demonstrated the failure of many of our current institutions and systems to deliver outcomes that are just, inclusive and sustainable. For example, our health systems, food systems, energy systems, social security systems and systems for financial and digital inclusion have all been put under severe strain by the pandemic, high levels of inequality and the climate crisis. Even in the world's wealthiest countries, these critical systems are arguably no longer fit-for-purpose.

Clearly, governments have the ultimate responsibility for enabling their societies to meet these pressing challenges through the necessary changes in public policy and governance.[10] But governments face serious constraints. These range from fiscal constraints and inadequate institutional capacity to lack of political will and debilitating factionalism to corruption, repression and situations of violent conflict. Even in situations of good public governance, the challenges are often too complex and multi-dimensional, and the resources needed to tackle them too distributed and constrained, for governments to act effectively alone.

Business leaders and companies have a crucial role to play. This is especially the case for large, global corporations. Given the scale of their activities and the scope of their networks and relationships, the characteristics of their corporate governance, strategy, reporting and partnerships can impact the lives of millions of people and the planet, both in the immediate and in the long term. Indeed, they are increasingly compelled by *business* logic to act—the logic of sustainable value creation and stakeholder capitalism, which recognizes that many aspects of these challenges are not only social concerns but also material factors in enterprise value creation that need to be fully integrated into strategy formulation and management practice. This is the systemic improvement society requires of private sector governance and management to accompany that which is needed in public governance to secure stronger progress towards a just, inclusive and sustainable future.

## 1.2    The Business Imperative to Translate the Principles of Stakeholder Capitalism into Practice

To be certain, many companies have started to respond over the past two decades. They have established policies and systems to manage and report publicly on their sustainability or environmental, social and governance (ESG) performance alongside their financial and operational performance, and to strengthen mutually beneficial mechanisms for stakeholder engagement. The leaders have also started to work together collectively to agree on shared principles and goals for implementing specific aspects of stakeholder capitalism and for prioritizing ESG&D issues that need to be addressed at a systemic level. But much more work is needed by all companies, even the pioneers, to translate the principles of stakeholder capitalism into rigorous and systematic practice.

### 1.2.1    Firm-Level Policies and Practices

Hundreds of companies are taking actions at the firm level to embed the management of ESG risks and opportunities into their core business operations and supply chains. One of the best barometers for assessing the depth and breadth of a company's sustainability or ESG&D performance and its engagement with and impact on stakeholders is through its public reporting on these. Research by KPMG in 2020 concluded that about 80% of the top 100 companies by revenue in each of 52 countries and jurisdictions surveyed now issue corporate responsibility or sustainability reports, up from about 25% in 2001–2002.[11] KPMG also concludes that 90% or more of the world's 250 largest companies by revenue, as defined by the Fortune 2019 ranking, produce a sustainability report and have been doing so for over a decade. Furthermore, third-party assurance of these reports and their data is also on the rise.[12] In 2021, for example, the Center for Audit Quality found that 95% of S&P companies have detailed ESG information publicly available and that more than half had some form of assurance or verification over their ESG metrics.[13]

The ambition of corporate ESG goals and targets is also increasing. Take climate for example. Leading companies are starting to set targets not only for decreasing the absolute amount and intensity of carbon emissions in their own operations, but also along their supply chains. A growing number is setting even more ambitious science-based targets and commitments to achieve net-zero emissions by or before 2050, in alignment with the Paris Climate Agreement. Likewise, in areas such as water and biodiversity, companies are moving from operational efficiency and management goals within their own "fence" to broader watershed and landscape-wide commitments and to nature-based solutions. A small vanguard of companies is going a step further and making public commitments to environmental and socio-economic practices that deliver regenerative, restorative or net positive solutions that aim to restore and strengthen ecosystems and nature's carrying capacity. These efforts extend beyond the mitigation of negative environmental impacts and externalities. Proactive stakeholder engagement and the achievement of mutual benefit and accountability between a company and its stakeholders are essential in advancing most of these goals.

More companies are also undertaking human rights due diligence to identify, manage, monitor and take accountability for their salient human rights risks. This includes but goes beyond adherence to core and other legally binding labour standards and setting public targets for diversity and inclusion within their own operations and employment practices. Both the COVID-19 pandemic and the climate crisis have highlighted the challenges of inequality and vulnerability within company value chains and the communities where they operate. As a result, leading companies are starting to address issues such as living wages and incomes, accelerated climate action and more holistic approaches to employee well-being. Again, stakeholder engagement and accountability are key. As Professor John Ruggie and his colleagues have noted, "the implementation of human rights due diligence by companies—properly done—brings the concerns and interests of affected stakeholders into greater prominence in corporate decision-making at both the operational and leadership levels, and … it offers a window into what one effective and viable path toward 'stakeholder capitalism' looks like in practice."[14]

Yet, despite the progress being made, in the absence of mandatory disclosure of and accountability for ESG performance, these pioneer companies remain in the minority of the world's estimated 63,000 publicly listed companies and the even larger number of private companies. While plans to implement mandatory disclosure requirements for corporate carbon emissions, human rights due diligence and diversity are being debated in the EU, much work remains for such reporting to become a mainstream driver of change. Equally, although substantial progress was made during 2020 and 2021 towards more commonly agreed ESG metrics, the ongoing absence of a generally accepted global reporting standard means that it is difficult for investors, regulators and other stakeholders to compare even the pioneering corporate reporters at the level of rigour and consistency that is required to drive large-scale transformation, let alone encourage the laggards to make faster progress. The agenda on sustainability target setting and public disclosure is, however, moving in the right direction.

Business innovation for social impact is also gaining momentum. A combination of incumbent companies and start-up entrepreneurs is chasing new business and market opportunities associated with developing new technologies, processes, products, services, financing and business models to meet social and environmental needs. In 2017, for example, the Business and Sustainable Development Commission concluded in its flagship report, "Our research shows achieving the Global Goals in just four economic systems [food and agriculture, cities, energy and materials, and health and wellbeing] could open 60 market 'hot spots' worth an estimated US$12 trillion by 2030 in business savings and revenue."[15] In 2020, the World Economic Forum's report on the *Future of Nature and Business* concluded that 15 transitions in the three socio-economic systems of food, land and ocean use, infrastructure and the built environment, and energy and extractives could deliver US $10.1 trillion of annual business opportunities and 395 million jobs by 2030. The report also added a sobering warning of the severe risks and costs of inaction.[16]

The world's institutional investors are also markedly increasing ESG screening, investment products and corporate engagement activities with a focus on integrating these risks and opportunities into their policies and decision-making. A July 2020 report estimates, for example, "The value of global assets applying environmental, social and governance data to drive investment decisions has almost doubled over four years, and more than tripled over eight years, to $40.5 trillion in 2020," and, "the size of ESG teams at money managers has also grown across the top 30 money managers, by 229% compared with 2017."[17] Analysis by Bloomberg Intelligence predicts, "Global ESG assets are on track to exceed \$53 trillion by 2025, representing more than a third of the \$140.5 trillion in projected total assets under management. A perfect storm created by the pandemic and the green recovery in the U.S., EU and China will likely reveal how ESG can help assess a new set of financial risks and harness capital markets."[18]

Many companies are also making great strides in managing the risks and leveraging the opportunities of digital technology and big data. We are just at the beginning of understanding the opportunities of harnessing digital platforms alongside material and life sciences to address challenges in global health, education, food security, energy, water and digital and financial inclusion. At the same time, we are only in the early stages of understanding and mitigating some of the risks to people and planet posed by these new technologies and the scaled impact of the platforms they enable.

Over the course of 2020 and 2021, thousands of companies have responded to address the humanitarian and economic costs of the COVID-19 pandemic, in addition to focusing on their own business continuity and financial liquidity during the crisis. They have leveraged their core business capabilities, such as occupational health and safety protocols, manufacturing and logistics capacity, marketing and media outreach, as well as their philanthropic donations and volunteering and their voices as policy advocates.[19] Organizations such as the World Economic Forum, Business Fights Poverty, the World Business Council for Sustainable Development, JUST Capital and national chambers of commerce, to name only a few, have established business and COVID-19 response platforms. Their collective goal has been to convene and mobilize the business response to COVID-19, to share good practices and to track performance.

## 1.2.2   Collective Principles and Commitments

Recent collective business leadership has also helped to provide a more solid conceptual foundation for the simultaneous pursuit of business and societal value creation. In 2019, both the World Economic Forum and the US Business Roundtable published seminal statements calling on companies to adopt a set of specific principles in this regard. The Forum's Davos Manifesto refreshed a statement originally published in 1973, and it is outlined in Box 1.1. These statements provide a set of *principles*, although the clear challenge posed by them and addressed in this book is how companies can translate them into systematic *practice*.

**Box 1.1 The Davos Manifesto**

A. The purpose of a company is to engage all its stakeholders in shared and sustained value creation. In creating such value, a company serves not only its shareholders, but all its stakeholders—employees, customers, suppliers, local communities and society at large. The best way to understand and harmonize the divergent interests of all stakeholders is through a shared commitment to policies and decisions that strengthen the long-term prosperity of a company.

(i) A company serves its customers by providing a value proposition that best meets their needs. It accepts and supports fair competition and a level playing field. It has zero tolerance for corruption. It keeps the digital ecosystem in which it operates reliable and trustworthy. It makes customers fully aware of the functionality of its products and services, including adverse implications or negative externalities.

(ii) A company treats its people with dignity and respect. It honours diversity and strives for continuous improvements in working conditions and employee well-being. In a world of rapid change, a company fosters continued employability through ongoing upskilling and reskilling.

(iii) A company considers its suppliers as true partners in value creation. It provides a fair chance to new market entrants. It integrates respect for human rights into the entire supply chain.

(iv) A company serves society at large through its activities, supports the communities in which it works, and pays its fair share of taxes. It ensures the safe, ethical and efficient use of data. It acts as a steward of the environmental and material universe for future generations. It consciously protects our biosphere and champions a circular, shared and regenerative economy. It continuously expands the frontiers of knowledge, innovation and technology to improve people's well-being.

(v) A company provides its shareholders with a return on investment that takes into account the incurred entrepreneurial risks and the need for continuous innovation and sustained investments. It responsibly manages near-term, medium-term and long-term value creation in pursuit of sustainable shareholder returns that do not sacrifice the future for the present.

B. A company is more than an economic unit generating wealth. It fulfils human and societal aspirations as part of the broader social system. Performance must be measured not only on the return to shareholders, but also on how it achieves its environmental, social and good governance objectives. Executive remuneration should reflect stakeholder responsibility.

C. A company that has a multinational scope of activities not only serves all those stakeholders who are directly engaged, but acts itself as a stakeholder—together with governments and civil society—of our global future. Corporate global citizenship requires a company to harness its core competencies, its entrepreneurship, skills and relevant resources in collaborative efforts with other companies and stakeholders to improve the state of the world.

Source: The World Economic Forum, December 2, 2019

During the past few years, several leading global business and investor net-works have set ambitious new requirements and goals for their membership. In December 2020, for example, the World Business Council for Sustainable Development, created at the time of the 1992 Rio Earth Summit and with more than 200 of the world's leading corporations as members, established the following five membership criteria based on sustainability performance. It called on all its members to be able to adhere to or explain their performance in each of these areas by December 2022:

- Set an ambition to reach net-zero greenhouse gas (GHG) emissions, no later than 2050 and have a science-informed plan to achieve it.
- Set ambitious, science-informed, short and mid-term environmental goals that contribute to nature/biodiversity recovery by 2050.
- Declare support for the UN Guiding Principles on Business and Human Rights by having in place a policy to respect human rights and a human rights due diligence process.
- Declare support for inclusion, equality, diversity and the elimination of any form of discrimination.
- Operate at the highest level of transparency by disclosing material sustainability information in line with the Task Force on Climate-related Financial Disclosures (TCFD) and align Enterprise Risk Management (ERM) with environmental, social and governance-related (ESG) risks.[20]

Institutional investors have also increased the ambition and reach of their collective action initiatives, especially on climate change. The Net-Zero Asset Managers Alliance, for example, was launched in December 2020. Governed by a group of six other investor networks, the alliance describes itself as "an international group of asset managers committed to supporting the goal of net zero greenhouse gas emissions by 2050 or sooner, in line with global efforts to limit warming to 1.5 degrees Celsius; and to supporting investing aligned with net zero emissions by 2050 or sooner."[21] As of mid-2021, there were 128 signatories with US $43 trillion in assets under management. Other investor-led climate coalitions established since 2017 include the Net-Zero Asset Owner Alliance, the Paris Aligned Investment Initiative and Climate Action 100+. Investors are also starting to engage in collective action beyond addressing climate change. In 2018, the Investor Alliance on Human Rights was established, with some 170 institutional investors as members,[22] and in 2020, 128 institutional investors came together to endorse a commitment to address systemic racism through their portfolios, corporate engagement and policy advocacy.[23]

In short, companies and investors of all sizes as well as industry sectors and their associations are starting to respond to systemic risks such as the pandemic, climate change, inequality, data privacy and other challenges. They are doing so in a way that aims to balance the interests of employees, communities and other key company stakeholders with expectations regarding financial performance, competitiveness and growth. These bottom-up shifts in behaviour point to a broader shift in corporate governance and management, which has come to be called stakeholder capitalism and framed as a counterpoint to shareholder capitalism. But, while this direction of travel has found expression in principles and a few legal frameworks, it has yet to be defined more specifically and systematically for purposes of practical implementation.

In the absence of such structured practical guidance, stakeholder capitalism remains more an aspiration around which there is growing consensus than the systemic shift in capitalism that leaders of all walks of society have been calling for.[24] This book seeks to help move the stakeholder capitalism movement to this next level from the perspective of what companies themselves can do, both individually and collectively. It aims to provide companies with a practical roadmap for rigorous and widespread practice that will help to reset capitalism in line with the economic, social and political demands it faces in the twenty-first century.

## 1.3    What Stakeholder Capitalism Is and Is Not

Judging from the increasingly lively debate on the topic, the general notion of stakeholder capitalism—a business should be run in the interests of creating long-term value for shareholders AND other key stakeholders—is a contested and often misinterpreted concept. In its most fundamental sense, the concept has a long history and has taken different forms around the world. The contemporary formulation can be traced to US and European management theories that emerged in the 1960s and 1970s,[25] were enshrined in the 1973 Davos Manifesto[26] and have since been refreshed in the updated principles issued by the US Business Roundtable[27] and the World Economic Forum[28] in 2019. These high-profile restatements have generated a new wave of interest and resurrected an old polemic associated most famously with the economist Milton Friedman, who argued against the corporate social responsibility movement of the 1960s and 1970s by asserting in as many words that "the business of business is business."[29]

The best way to improve the clarity and utility of this debate is to define more concretely what stakeholder capitalism is and is not.

### 1.3.1 What Stakeholder Capitalism Is Not

First, stakeholder capitalism is not state-directed capitalism. Quite a number of governments, such as Germany and Japan, have embedded the notion of shared value creation among shareholders and other stakeholders in their own way in their corporate governance statutes and cultures. But in doing so, none is aiming to supplant the role of the board as the ultimate locus of decision-making within firms. These governments are not seeking to substitute their judgements for those of directors and management teams in the strategic decisions and day-to-day running of their firms. There is no *dirigiste* picking of winners and losers by public bureaucrats as far as the allocation of resources and conduct of other aspects of business is concerned.

Second, in the same vein, stakeholder capitalism is not socialism through the back door. It does not hold that shareholder interests should be subordinated to those of other stakeholders, such as employees, or that businesses should do the bidding of governments in providing public goods. Rather, it posits that:

- the corporation, which is a legal construct of society that confers certain privileges such as limited liability and distinct tax treatment, is a vehicle for sustainable enterprise value creation;
- such enterprise value creation is distinguishable from the notion of near-term financial results or stock market valuation; and
- the universe of material contributors to and beneficiaries from enterprise value creation over time is certainly larger than the providers of the firm's financial capital.

Third, just because shareholder capitalism—the view that companies should be run solely in interests of optimizing shareholder returns—is also focused on enterprise value creation does not mean that it is essentially the same thing as stakeholder capitalism. Critics making this argument[30] say that companies run in the sole interests of their shareholders naturally take account of the material role of other stakeholders in creating such value because it is the job of their directors and managers to consider everything that could materially affect the firm's financial performance and share price. If they don't, their share price will suffer, and they will be out of a job. They argue that stakeholder capitalism anchored in sustainable *business* value creation is making a distinction without a meaningful difference. It is old wine in new, more socially presentable, bottles—a public relations exercise.

This argument is flawed. It should be abundantly clear from the long history of shareholders being blindsided (i.e., stock prices of individual firms abruptly crashing) as a result of unforeseen environmental, social and governance lapses that equity and bond markets are not fully efficient. Financial markets are a long way from adequately internalizing material non-financial factors, particularly risks and opportunities that typically play out within a firm over the medium to long term. They do not have perfect information, and neither do the directors and managers within a firm itself, particularly if they are operating within a governance framework that fails to systematically gather and apply actionable information about such medium-term and intangible factors. Just because the process of optimizing enterprise value creation—maximizing discounted cash flows—should *in theory* take account of all financially material considerations, both short and long term, doesn't mean that companies actually do so in practice on a consistent basis. Stakeholder capitalism that is focused on sustainable enterprise value creation is a distinction with a *big* difference, and that difference is practice, which is the topic of this book.

### 1.3.2    What Stakeholder Capitalism Is: Sustainable Enterprise Value Creation

Stakeholder capitalism in *conceptual* terms is the notion of the firm as a social, rather than purely financial, construct, whose purpose is sustainable *enterprise* value creation rather than solely increased profitability and market valuation, which is to say *shareholder* value creation.

*Sustainable* enterprise value creation means generating sustained value for all of the firm's principal stakeholders, including shareholders, employees, customers, suppliers, distributors and communities. This includes creating economic value as well as respecting people's rights, building their human and social capital, and protecting and restoring natural capital, thereby reinforcing the strength of the social and environmental ecosystems in which the firm operates and hence its own performance over particularly the medium to long term. These three aspects—the creation of *sustained* and *shared* direct value for the firm's stakeholders as well as *wider societal* value—are important in their own right, but they are also mutually reinforcing. Together they give effect to the three-dimensional meaning of *sustainable* in this context: value creation that is at once financially, socially and environmentally sustainable.

This definition of sustainable enterprise value creation manifests in clear objective and operational ways within firms that apply it rigorously.

Objectively, sustainable enterprise value creation includes the following *core* elements:

- robust, sustained profitability;
- decent work[31] that includes respect for internationally recognized worker rights and protections and supports compensation that reflects productivity gains and includes an adequate "living" wage;
- respect for human rights more generally[32];
- internalization of significant environmental externalities in the production (through their avoidance and abatement) and sale (through the price) of goods and services; and
- high standards of ethics and governance, including zero tolerance of bribery; avoidance of anti-competitive business practices; and fair payment of taxes in recognition of the vital role public services and administrative capacity play in maintaining a vital business enabling environment and social fabric.

Operationally, it is manifested in the systematic integration of the firm's tangible and intangible, shareholder and other stakeholder, and pecuniary and non-pecuniary dimensions over the medium to long term in its governance processes and management systems. The material aspects of these need to be deliberately understood and consciously weighed in the firm's governance and management. This is because a firm that takes care to steward its assets, investments, key relationships and social licence to operate in a way that produces shared and ongoing rather than narrow and transitory value, and that renews rather than depletes these elements, is more likely to optimize the value of the enterprise to all of its stakeholders, including shareholders, over time. A firm that is not producing fair value to its employees, value chain partners and communities is not likely to sustain a high level of performance over time, because it depends on these assets and relationships. This is especially true today when such intangible, non-pecuniary factors are becoming *more* material to value creation because of corresponding shifts in the underlying business operating context. Such shifts include changes in environmental regulation, consumer and employee attitudes about technology and the collection and application of data, social attitudes regarding discrimination and exclusion, the cost of cybersecurity breaches and insurance coverage, the state of public finances and services in many countries, the extent of precarity, unemployment and inequality in others, and so on.

The practice of stakeholder capitalism is thus the pursuit of sustainable enterprise value creation through the systematic integration of material so-called non-financial factors into the governance, management and reporting of firms. This is what ensures that related risks, opportunities and other considerations are fully internalized in decision-making. The systematic internalization of such factors through the diligent gathering of information and perspectives of the firm's key stakeholders is what helps its board and management team make fully considered judgements about what is best for the firm's capacity to sustain the creation of shared value over time. Simply put, stakeholder capitalism is about good governance—the application of greater rigour and wider due diligence in the running of a firm that is particularly important in today's changing context.

The bottom line of stakeholder capitalism is that increases in shareholder value, particularly when interpreted in the extreme as the near-term stock price and earnings per share performance, may be a necessary condition, but it is certainly not a sufficient condition for fulfilment of the fundamental purpose of the firm: shared and sustained improvement in the value of the enterprise to all of its key stakeholders, including but not limited to its providers of capital.

The concept and narrative of stakeholder capitalism has gained—or more accurately re-gained—prominence in recent years, notably with the reissuance of the Davos Manifesto and Business Roundtable's Statement of the Purpose of a Corporation as well as recent related EU initiatives, including its 2014 Non-Financial Reporting Directive,[33] Action Plan for Financing Sustainable Growth[34] and its recent Sustainable Corporate Governance Initiative, which received broad-based support during public consultations and appears likely to result in important changes in the near future.[35] Yet, these are not novel notions. Stakeholder capitalism is not new. It has existed in various forms and business cultures for decades, even centuries, even if the term was not explicitly used.

### 1.3.3  Stakeholder Capitalism's Diverse Historical and Legal Tradition

As outlined earlier, a stakeholder-oriented economic model is not new. In the UK, for example, corporations enjoying limited liability and tradable shares were originally restricted to those chartered by the Crown or an Act of Parliament, in principle to carry out a specific public interest activity like building a bridge or university.[36] This practice evolved over time to extend to enterprises with a perceived quasi-public purpose such as promoting Great Britain's economic interests abroad through the establishment of large trading companies in specific regions, early examples being the Company of Merchant Adventurers in 1553 and the East India Company, chartered in 1600. The then-private Bank of England's 1694 charter made clear that its purpose was "to promote the public good and benefit of our people."

Wider access by private companies to limited liability and the trading of shares was extended only in the mid-nineteenth century through passage of the Joint Stock Companies Act of 1844 and Limited Liability Act of 1855. But maximizing shareholder return was not the centrepiece of companies' objectives or directors' duties during the nineteenth century.[37] Beginning in the early twentieth century, however, growth in the influence of investors combined with favourable jurisprudence helped to enshrine shareholder primacy as the dominant paradigm of corporate governance in the UK.[38] The 2006 Company Act sought to meld these divergent traditions. It embedded a shareholder primacy reading of directors' responsibilities into law but also indicated that they should "have regard" for the interests of other stakeholders. This ill-defined compromise formulation has come to be called *enlightened shareholder value*, but it has spawned endless debate about what it means in practice and in the event of litigation.

In the US, in the first half of the twentieth century, leading companies very publicly declared their commitment to weigh the interests of multiple stakeholders. Henry Ford famously declared: "*There is one rule for the industrialist and that is: make the best quality goods possible at the lowest cost possible, paying the highest wages possible.*" In 1929, General Electric's chairman and president stated that they were running the company on the basis of a stakeholder theory of corporate governance without naming it as such:

> If you will pardon me for being personal, it makes a great difference in my attitude toward my job as an executive officer of the General Electric Company whether I am a trustee of the institution or an attorney for the investor. If I am a trustee, who are the beneficiaries of the trust? To whom do I owe my obligations? My conception of it is this: That there are three groups of people who have an interest in that institution. One is the group of fifty-odd thousand people who have put their capital in the company, namely, its stockholders. Another is a group of well toward one hundred thousand people who are putting their labour and their lives into the business of the company. The third group is of customers and the general public. Customers have a right to demand that a concern so large shall not only do its business honestly and properly, but, further, that it shall meet its public obligations and perform its public duties— in a word, vast as it is, that it should be a good citizen.
>
> Now, I conceive my trust first to be to see to it that the capital which is put into this concern is safe, honestly and wisely used, and paid a fair rate of return.

Otherwise, we cannot get capital. The worker will have no tools. Second, that the people who put their labour and lives into this concern get fair wages, continuity of employment, and a recognition of their right to their jobs where they have educated themselves to highly skilled and specialized work. Third, that the customers get a product which is as represented and that the price is such as is consistent with the obligations to the people who put their capital and labour in. Last, that the public has a concern functioning in the public interest and performing its duties as a great and good citizen should. I think what is right in business is influenced very largely by the growing sense of trusteeship which I have described. One no longer feels the obligation to take from labor for the benefit of capital, nor to take from the public for the benefit of both, but rather to administer wisely and fairly in the interest of all.[39]

Similarly, Johnson & Johnson's Credo, approved in 1943, the year before the company transitioned from family to public ownership, and still in force today, states explicitly that its responsibility is to those using its products and services, employees, communities and stockholders in that order, stating at the end: "When we operate according to these principles, the stockholders should realize a fair return."[40] In the 1950s, Sears CEO Robert E. Wood argued that shareholders' long-run profit could be enhanced by satisfying the needs and expectations of other stakeholders.[41] General Motors' 1964 annual report also reflected "a company recognizing the value being created by and for all its stakeholders."[42] This was the prevailing mindset in the American business community during the era of so-called managerial capitalism dating from the 1940s to the 1970s. These decades were a period of high growth and broadly rising prosperity in the US, suggesting at a minimum that a stakeholder capitalism corporate culture is not inconsistent with robust industrial competitiveness and economic growth, notwithstanding the counter-narrative that arose with the ascendance and continuing dominance of the shareholder primacy doctrine in the decades since.

Europe, Asia and Latin America have had a long and more durable tradition of companies being managed in the interests of long-term enterprise value creation for the benefit of all stakeholders. The important role played by family-controlled shareholder foundations and holding companies has certainly contributed to continental Europe's distinct long-term, patient-capital corporate culture. There are over 3000 such foundations across Scandinavia, Germany and Switzerland. These account for a third of the GDP of Sweden and over half of the market capitalization of the Copenhagen Stock Exchange as well as significant share of the German and Swiss corporate communities.[43] Germany's strong base of medium-sized, family-owned industrial "Mittelstand" firms also fits within this management tradition. Although foundation-owned firms have many features in common with family businesses, they are distinguished by an additional and irrevocable commitment to the continuation of the company, that is, to sustainable *enterprise* value creation. As such, studies have shown that foundation-owned companies tend to have even longer time horizons than family-owned firms, which have been found to have longer time horizons than external investor-owned firms.[44]

Asia and Europe also have corporate governance legal frameworks and customary practices which embed many of the features of stakeholder capitalism. In Japan and elsewhere in East Asia, for example, the company and its stakeholders often perceive of themselves implicitly as akin to a family. The Japanese system has been described as

> being based on 'community logic' against the US system which is based on 'market logic'. In the UK and USA the tendency has been for the market to operate freely and in recent times for the state to pick up the social consequences, for example in unemployment pay and national assistance. In Japan, the tendency has been to regard it as preferable to prevent and delay potential tears in the social fabric and for government to act to mitigate the effects of any changes that cannot be avoided. This seems true at both company and national level and what it boils down to is belief that 'the family' comes first. Put another way, the fabric of society should not be wantonly or carelessly torn and if necessary, the state should step in to prevent it. … Of course, profit matters and is essential for survival, but to the Japanese it is not all that matters—even in these days when the importance of 'shareholder value' has become a sort of religion elsewhere.[45]

Owing to this cultural context as well as a tendency towards extensive industrial and bank cross-shareholdings or their equivalent (e.g., South Korea's chaebol groups), corporate governance in Northeast Asia leans towards cooperation and consensus building among stakeholders—that is, the integration of multiple stakeholder interests into corporate decision-making, whether formally or implicitly, as well as a tendency to conceive of the corporation as ultimately a social rather than essentially financial construct. Indeed, for years, foreign investors have complained about the subordination of shareholder interests, sometimes vociferously. But while attitudes and practices have been changing in this respect, Northeast Asian corporate governance continues to exhibit a strong stakeholder capitalism ethos.

In South and Southeast Asian countries as well as Latin America, family-owned or family-controlled businesses dominate the corporate landscape.[46]

Approximately 85% of firms in the Asia-Pacific region are family-owned, including in China.[47] McKinsey has estimated that the share of family-owned businesses among the largest multinational firms in the world could increase from 15% to 40% from 2015 to 2025, mainly as a result of the rising number of large family firms in the Asia-Pacific.[48] In India as well, a tradition of large corporate family-owned firms prevails and there is a widespread use of company groups, often in the form of pyramids with a wide basis in many different activities and companies. In Asian and other emerging market firms, a family-centric governance model tends to be strongly preferred over the Western "professional" non-family governance model.[49]

Thus, the corporate governance culture of most of the world is geared towards the long-term sustainability of the company and preservation of the stakeholder relationships supporting this purpose, which is to say stakeholder capitalism. It is no wonder that directors and executives from outside the US and UK are often befuddled by the debate over stakeholder capitalism there. They have been running their firms according to these precepts for decades. At least in this important respect, the Anglo-American system has some catching up to do, even if Asia continues to catch up in other aspects of good corporate governance.[50] More precisely, given their own historical tradition of managerial capitalism, the US and UK have some important rebalancing to do in order to correct their overshooting in the direction of the primacy of shareholder interests during the past generation.

Much of this international consensus outside the US and UK is rooted in law, although for the most part these corporate governance codes remain at a high level, articulating mainly the duty of directors towards the corporation rather than a particular stakeholder such as shareholders. But even in the US, the stakeholder perspective on corporate governance has influenced jurisprudence if not statutory law. In the case of Paramount Communications v. Time Inc. in 1989, the state of Delaware's Chancery Court allowed Time Inc.'s directors to reject Paramount's takeover offer even though that offer maximized shareholders' financial value. In that influential case, the pure shareholder primacy argument was rebuffed by the court.[51] In the case of Credit Lyonnais Bank N.V. v. Pathe Communications Corp. (1991), the Chancery further promoted a stakeholder model on the basis that directors do not owe duties to any single interest group but to the corporation as a whole and "the community of interests that the corporation represents."[52] By 2000, 25 US states had amended their General Corporation Laws to incorporate aspects of the stakeholder concept, with most of the states expressly permitting directors to take into account the interests of stakeholders in their decision-making.[53]

One country that has a very specific statutory basis for a stakeholder approach to corporate governance is Germany. Its Stock Corporation Act, Codetermination Act and Corporate Governance Code formally frame a system of stakeholder participation in company decision-making or more precisely of employee participation. Large companies have a management board and supervisory board. For companies with more than 2000 employees, half of the members of the supervisory board are elected by the employees. For firms with between 500 and 2000 employees, the workers select one-third of the supervisory board.[54] Management boards of large firms are required to have a director for labour affairs. In addition, works councils are required in which

> [e]mployees participate in discussions and decisions about all matters pertaining to conditions of employment. … The works council also has rights of co-determination in the case of dismissals, in the field of employees' vocational training, and in the case of grievances. In bigger companies, there must also be a small economic committee. This does not have rights of co-determination but rights to information—and these are extensive, including information on: the economic and financial situation of the company; the production and sales situation; the investment programme; rationalization projects and closures; organizational changes, including mergers; proposed changes in method. The idea behind the works councils is that co-determination, that is the right to participate in decisions (about matters that affect them, plus getting crucial background information about the enterprise), should promote trust, cooperation, and harmony. What actually seems to happen is that this helps improve the whole network of relationships between employer and employee, because the mere existence of a formal right to be consulted ensures that informal discussions occur. And the supply of information forms the background for participation at board level.[55]

It remains to be seen whether other countries will move to enshrine stakeholder capitalism more explicitly and specifically into their corporate governance statutes and if so how.

In a related development, some jurisdictions have begun to examine whether to create or expand a statutory basis for public-benefit or so-called Fourth Sector enterprises, returning in a sense to the original British approach to chartering public-purpose corporations.

Economies typically have three sectors: the public sector, the private sector and the non-profit sector (civil society non-governmental organizations). But in some jurisdictions,[56] there is an emerging fourth sector combining market-based approaches of private companies with the social and environmental aims of the public and non-profit sectors. Organizations in this sector, often referred to as for-benefit enterprises, come in a wide variety of models, from mission-driven businesses, social enterprises and sustainable businesses to cooperatives, benefit corporations and faith-based enterprises, among others.[57]

For-benefit or public-purpose corporations are arguably the ultimate expression of stakeholder capitalism. They have been growing in number and size in recent years in the US, UK and elsewhere[58] in response to perceived limitations of the shareholder primacy laws and practices in those jurisdictions. But while several countries have adopted new corporate forms and other legal and regulatory reforms in recent years to recognize for-benefits, the Fourth Sector Group, an organization dedicated to advancing the sector, has observed:

> These are still quite nascent and only serve the needs of a very narrow range of for-benefit organizations. For most part, for-benefits are not recognized as a legally distinct class of entities. Thus, when for-benefit-minded entrepreneurs set out to create a new entity to realize their goals, they are typically forced to choose a for-profit or non-profit path, or resort to creating a complicated hybrid structure if they can find (and afford) the right legal advice. This often leads to them having to sacrifice their visions and accept burdensome trade-offs. This challenge is beginning to be addressed as for-benefit enterprises become better understood. As their potential for driving economic, social, and environmental progress is seen, the fourth sector will become more formalized and distinguished in law, complementing existing sectors while enabling for-benefits to drive sustainability and equity alongside profit.[59]

In sum, stakeholder capitalism is already practised and anchored in law around the world to a very considerable extent, albeit in different forms. But even in those jurisdictions where it is not well rooted, a change in public statute, corporate charter or ownership structure is not required to run a business according to these precepts. Rather, this can be achieved through a clear understanding of the concept, an appreciation of the drivers of its rising relevance and a commitment to practical implementation by the board and management team based on emerging good practice. There is no inherent barrier to joining the growing movement of companies across sectors and regions taking practical steps to respond to this new business leadership imperative.

This volume is intended to serve as a conceptual and practical resource for this new generation of business leadership, an exposition of the why, what and how of stakeholder capitalism and sustainable enterprise value creation. This introductory chapter has defined these concepts and provided a brief overview of their varied historical and legal manifestation around the world. Chapter 2 examines the recent shifts in the operating context of business that are driving the practice of corporate governance and management further in this direction, irrespective of legal and cultural context. Chapter 3 provides an overview of the five main thematic elements of an agenda to implement the principles of stakeholder capitalism diligently within a firm in order to enhance its capacity to generate shared and sustained enterprise value. Chapters 4, 5, 6 and 7 provide a more detailed, functional view of this action agenda: a practical guide for the conduct of boards, management teams, corporate reporting and strategic partnerships with outside organizations and constituencies to address systemic weaknesses in the social and economic context in which the firm operates, respectively.

## Notes

1. Zahid Torres Rahman and Jane Nelson. *Business and COVID-19: Supporting the most vulnerable.* Business Fights Poverty with Harvard Kennedy School, Corporate Responsibility Initiative. 2020. https://businessfightspoverty.org/protecting-the-most-vulnerable-a-business-response-framework/. See also: Business Fights Poverty, COVID Response Centre. https://businessfightspoverty.org/covid-19-response-centre/
2. *Global Call to Action for a Human-Centred Recovery from the COVID-19 Crisis that is Inclusive, Sustainable and Resilient,* Resolution of the 109th International Labour Conference, International Labour Conference, June 17, 2021.
3. *Our Shared Agenda for Global Action to Build Back Better,* Carbis Bay G7 Summit Communique, June 13, 2021, https://www.g7uk.org/
4. Klaus Schwab. "Now is the time for a 'great reset'." World Economic Forum Agenda. June 3, 2020. https://www.weforum.org/agenda/2020/06/now-is-the-time-for-a-great-reset/. See also: Klaus Schwab with Peter Vanham. *Stakeholder Capitalism: A Global Economy that Works for Progress, People and Planet.* Wiley, 2021.
5. The Intergovernmental Panel on Climate Change (IPCC). The Working Group I contribution to the Sixth Assessment Report, *Climate Change 2021: The Physical Science Basis.* August 2021. https://www.ipcc.ch/assessment-report/ar6/
6. Statement by UN Secretary-General, António Guterres on 9 August 2021. "Secretary-General Calls Latest IPCC Climate Report 'Code Red for Humanity', Stressing 'Irrefutable' Evidence of Human Influence". https://www.un.org/press/en/2021/sgsm20847.doc.htm

7. The term sustainable development and this definition were coined by the World Commission on Environment and Development, popularly known as the Brundtland Commission after its Chair, former Norwegian Prime Minister, Gro Harlem Brundtland, in its 1987 report, *Our Common Future*.
8. Examples of seminal reports and initiatives in this area include:

    (a) Ongoing work by long-standing business-focused organizations such as:

    The World Business Council for Sustainable Development (WBCSD). https://www.wbcsd.org/
    The United Nations Global Compact. https://www.unglobalcompact.org/
    Business for Social Responsibility. www.bsr.org
    Business Fights Poverty. https://businessfightspoverty.org/
    (b) The two-year initiative of the Business and Sustainable Development Commission. http://businesscommission.org/
    (c) The World Economic Forum's *Global Corporate Citizenship Initiative* from 2002 to 2006 and, more recently, the Forum's ongoing systems leadership platforms. https://www.weforum.org/platforms/
    (d) The five-year *Business as a Partner in Development Initiative* led by UNDP, the World Bank Group and the Prince of Wales Business Leaders Forum from 1995 to 2000. Reports included:

    Jane Nelson. "Business as Partners in Development: Creating wealth for countries, companies and communities." 1996.
    Jane Nelson. "Building Competitiveness and Communities: How world class companies are creating shareholder value and societal value." 1998.

9. See, for example: The "major groups" engaged with the UN's Sustainable Development Goals https://sustainabledevelopment.un.org/mgos
10. See, for example, Richard Samans, *Level-Up Economics: Beyond the Wealth of Nations*, Institute for New Economic Thinking Working Paper, January 2020. https://www.ineteconomics.org/research/research-papers/level-up-economics-beyond-the-wealth-of-nations; Samans, R. 2021. Financing human-centred COVID-19 recovery and decisive climate action worldwide: International cooperation's twenty-first century moment of truth, ILO Working Paper 40 (Geneva, ILO). https://www.ilo.org/global/publications/working-papers/WCMS_821931/lang--en/index.htm; and World Economic Forum, *The Inclusive Growth and Development Report 2017*, http://reports.weforum.org/inclusive-growth-and-development-report-2017/?doing_wp_cron=1645528337.6849899291992187500000
11. *The Time Has Come*, The KPMG Survey of Sustainability Reporting 2020. KPMG Impact, 2020.
12. Ibid.
13. Center for Audit Quality, "S&P 500 and ESG Reporting," August 9, 2021. https://www.thecaq.org/sp-500-and-esg-reporting/

14. John G. Ruggie, Caroline Rees and Rachel Davis. *Making "Stakeholder Capitalism" Work: Contributions from Business and Human Rights.* Working Paper No. 76. Corporate Responsibility Initiative, Harvard Kennedy School. November 2020. https://www.hks.harvard.edu/sites/default/files/centers/mrcbg/files/CRI_WP76.pdf

15. Business and Sustainable Development Commission. "Better Business Better World" January 2017. http://businesscommission.org/

16. World Economic Forum in collaboration with AlphaBeta. The Future of Nature and Business. New Nature Economy Report II. 2020. https://www.weforum.org/reports/new-nature-economy-report-ii-the-future-of-nature-and-business

17. Sophie Baker. Global ESG-date driven assets hit $405 trillion. Pensions & Investments. July 2, 2020. https://www.pionline.com/esg/global-esg-data-driven-assets-hit-405-trillion

18. Bloomberg Intelligence. ESG assets may hit $53 trillion by 2025, a third of global AUM. February 23, 2021. https://www.bloomberg.com/professional/blog/esg-assets-may-hit-53-trillion-by-2025-a-third-of-global-aum/

19. Zahid Torres-Rahman and Jane Nelson. *Business and COVID-19. From Response to Rebuilding Better: Creating a more inclusive and resilient future for those most impacted by COVID-19.* Business Fights Poverty and Harvard Kennedy School, Corporate Responsibility Initiative. May 2020. https://businessfightspoverty.org/articles/covid-19-response-centre/

20. WBCSD. WBCSD Raises Bar for Sustainable Business Leadership, 26 October 2020. https://www.wbcsd.org/Overview/News-Insights/General/News/New-membership-criteria

21. Net Zero Asset Managers Initiative. https://www.netzeroassetmanagers.org/#

22. The Investor Alliance for Human Rights, "About the Investor Alliance for Human Rights." An initiative of ICCR. https://investorsforhumanrights.org/about

23. Racial Justice Investing. https://www.racialjusticeinvesting.org/about

24. Firms signing up to stakeholder capitalism principles are facing greater scrutiny and criticism with respect to their implementation. See, for example, Bebchuk, Lucian A. and Tallarita, Roberto, Will Corporations Deliver Value to All Stakeholders? (August 4, 2021). Available at SSRN: https://ssrn.com/abstract=3899421 or https://doi.org/10.2139/ssrn.3899421; and *Financial Times*, "A Whistleblower Who Calls ESG a Deadly Distraction," August 13, 2021; and a rebuttal to these criticisms, Martin Whitaker and Peter Georgescu, "Don't believe the cynics: Done right, stakeholder capitalism is what America needs," *Fortune*, August 18, 2021. https://fortune.com/2021/08/18/stakeholder-capitalism-business-roundtable-corporate-purpose-just-capital/

25. See discussion and citations in the corporate governance section of Chap. 2.

26. https://www.weforum.org/agenda/2019/12/davos-manifesto-1973-a-code-of-ethics-for-business-leaders/

27. Business Roundtable, *Statement on the Purpose of a Corporation*, 2019, https://s3.amazonaws.com/brt.org/BRT-StatementonthePurposeofaCorporationOctober2020.pdf

28. World Economic Forum, *Davos Manifesto 2020: The Universal Purpose of a Corporation in the Fourth Industrial Revolution*, December 2019, https://www.weforum.org/agenda/2019/12/davos-manifesto-2020-the-universal-purpose-of-a-company-in-the-fourth-industrial-revolution/

29. Milton Friedman, "The Social Responsibility of Business is to Increase Profits," *The New York Times Magazine*, September 13, 1970. http://umich.edu/~thecore/doc/Friedman.pdf

30. See in particular Bebchuk, Lucian A. and Tallarita, Roberto, "The Illusory Promise of Stakeholder Governance" *Cornell Law Review*, December 2020, SSRN: https://ssrn.com/abstract=3544978 or https://doi.org/10.2139/ssrn.3544978

31. The International Labour Organization (ILO) has defined and its tripartite constituents of governments, employers and workers have endorsed the Decent Work Agenda. Decent work as defined by the ILO is captured in four strategic objectives: fundamental principles and rights at work and international labour standards; employment and income opportunities; social protection and social security; and social dialogue and tripartism. These objectives hold for all workers, women and men, in both formal and informal economies; in wage employment or working on their own account; in the fields, factories and offices; in their home or in the community. See, for example, https://www.ilo.org/global/topics/decent-work/lang%2D%2Den/index.htm; and https://web.archive.org/web/20071223160432/http://www.ilo.org/global/About_the_ILO/Mainpillars/WhatisDecentWork/lang%2D%2Den/index.htm

32. UN Guiding Principles on Business and Human Rights, https://www.ohchr.org/documents/publications/guidingprinciplesbusinesshr_en.pdf

33. https://ec.europa.eu/info/business-economy-euro/company-reporting-and-auditing/company-reporting/corporate-sustainability-reporting_en

34. https://www.unpri.org/sustainable-financial-system/explaining-the-eu-action-plan-for-financing-sustainable-growth/3000.article

35. See https://ec.europa.eu/info/law/better-regulation/have-your-say/initiatives/12548-Sustainable-corporate-governance/public-consultation_en

36. New Economics Foundation, *Shareholder Capitalism: A System in Crisis*, 2017, p. 5.

37. Andrew G. Haldane, "Who Owns a Company?", Speech to University of Edinburgh Corporate Finance Conference, May 22, 2015, p. 6.

38. See, for example, Haldane, *op. cit.* pp. 6–8 for a brief summary of this evolution.

39. Address of Owen D. Young, January 1929, quoted in SEARS, THE NEW PLACE OF THE STOCKHOLDER (1929) 209. For a fuller discussion, see:

E. Merrick Dodd, Jr., *For Whom Are Corporate Managers Trustees?, Harvard Law Review*, Vol. 45, No. 7 (May, 1932), pp. 1145–1163, http://www.jstor.org/stable/1331697

40. http://www.jnj.ch/fileadmin/user_upload/Downloads/JnJ_Credo_english.pd. For historical context, including minutes of the board discussion approving the Credo, https://www.kilmerhouse.com/2013/12/the-writing-of-our-credo

41. Hummels, H. (1998) Organising Ethics: A Stakeholder Debate, *Journal of Business Ethics*, 17, 1403–1419.

42. Martin Whittaker, "From Shareholder Primacy to Stakeholder Capitalism," *Just Capital*, August 22, 2019.

43. Prophil, Presentation entitled "The European Model of Shareholder Foundations: An Inspiration for Entrepreneurs," 2017, http://www.step-lausanne.org/wp-content/uploads/2015/08/STEP-05092017-Presentation-Lausanne-ALB-5septembre.pdf

44. Steen Thomsen, Thomas Poulsen, Christa Borsting and Johan Kuhn, "Industrial Foundations as Long-term Owners," *Corporate Governance International Review*, Wiley, 2018; 26:180–196.

45. Jonathan Charkham, *Keeping Better Company: Corporate Governance Ten Years On*, Oxford, 2005, pp. 110–111.

46. See OECD, Survey of Corporate Governance Frameworks in Asia, 2017, https://www.oecd.org/daf/ca/OECD-Survey-Corporate-Governance-Frameworks-Asia.pdf

47. See, for example, EY Family Business Yearbook. 2014. *Family Business in Asia-Pacific: Facts and Figures.* Available at: http://familybusiness.ey.com/pdfs/page-72%2D%2D-73.pdf and Annie Koh, "Why Family Firms Will Continue to Propel Asia's Growth," Duke Corporate Education Insights, December 2017, https://www.dukece.com/insights/why-family-firms-continue-propel-asias-growth/

48. Asa Bjornberg, Heinz-Peter Elstrodt and Vivek Pandit, "The Family-Business Factor in Emerging Markets," *McKinsey Quarterly*, December 1, 2014.

49. Chung, C. N., & Luo, X. R. 2013. Leadership succession and firm performance in an emerging economy: Successor origin, relational embeddedness, and legitimacy. *Strategic Management Journal*, 34(3): 338–357.

50. See, for example, OECD assessment *op. cit.* at 12.

51. Steve Letza, Xiuping Sun and James Kirkbride, "Shareholding Versus Stakeholding: a critical review of corporate governance," *Corporate Governance*, Blackwell, Volume 12 number 3, July 2004, p. 253.

52. Sullivan, D. P. and Conlon, D. E., "Crisis and Transition in Corporate Governance Paradigms: the Role of the Chancery Court of Delaware," *Law and Society Review*, 1997, Volume 31, 713–763.

53. Van der Weide, M. E., "Delaware's New Mandate in Class Action Settlements: Expanding the Scope and Intensity of Settlement Review," *Delaware Journal*

*of Corporate Law*, 1996, Vol. 20, 496–534. See also Stoney, C. and Winstanley, D., "Stakeholding: Confusion or Utopia? Mapping the Conceptual Terrain, Journal of Management Studies," 2001, Vol. 38, 603–626.

54. Seibt, Christoph H. and Kulenkamp, Sabrina, "Corporate governance and directors' duties in Germany: overview." *Thomson Reuters Practical Law*, June 1, 2020.

55. Charkham, *op. cit.*, pp. 38–39.

56. See, for example, Paul C. de Bernier, Michael Lebovitz, Tareah E. Ikharo and Stephanie M. Hurst, "A Primer on Public Benefit-Focused Corporate Models in California and Beyond," Mayer Brown, June 10, 2020, https://www.mayerbrown.com/en/perspectives-events/publications/2020/06/the-benefit-corporation-a-primer

57. This description is drawn from the materials of the Fourth Sector Group, an advisory and advocacy organization established to promote the concept and practice: https://www.fourthsector.org/

58. See, for example, HEC, "France Reaches Out to Mission-led Companies," June 5, 2018, https://www.hec.edu/en/news-room/france-reaches-out-mission-led-companies

59. Fourth Sector Group, *Op. cit.*

# 2

# The New Business Operating Context of the 2020s

In the twenty-first century, the business community is facing fundamentally new and more complex risks and opportunities. In this chapter, we first outline some of the most substantial shifts under way, most of which have been accelerated or exacerbated by the humanitarian and economic costs of the COVID-19 pandemic. We then outline the associated growing materiality of environmental, social, governance and data stewardship (ESG&D) issues and recent changes in corporate governance and corporate responsibility in response to these changes. We conclude by making the case for a more integrated approach to governing and managing businesses.[1]

We argue that in today's context, only by systematically integrating ESG&D considerations into core governance, management and disclosure practices can firms effectively implement the principles of stakeholder capitalism and consistently deliver sustainable enterprise value for shareholders and other stakeholders alike. Such integrated corporate governance, management and disclosure are the practical essence of stakeholder capitalism, the walk that accompanies the talk. In addition, corporate partnerships to drive system-level change are often necessary to overcome some of the systemic weaknesses or risks in their enabling environments that individual companies are unable to address effectively on their own.

© The Author(s) 2022
R. Samans, J. Nelson, *Sustainable Enterprise Value Creation*,
https://doi.org/10.1007/978-3-030-93560-3_2

## 2.1     Systemic Shifts and Shocks

Over the past two decades, the technological, environmental, geopolitical and socio-economic context in which major companies operate has changed fundamentally. This fourfold transformation is giving birth to a new phase of industrial development and global economic integration that have been described as the Fourth Industrial Revolution[2] and Globalization 4.0,[3] respectively. It is also contributing to more severe and systemic shocks and crises. The trajectory of these major transformations will depend in large measure on how well governance at multiple levels—corporate, governmental and international—adapts. For companies, they are changing the nature of value creation, risk and societal expectations in ways that challenge the traditional conception of both corporate governance and corporate responsibility.

### 2.1.1     Technological

Economic activity has become much more knowledge intensive and geographically integrated as the digital economy and globalization have taken hold over the past two decades. It will become even more so as the next phase of automation, connectivity and market integration unfolds over the next 20 years. The massive scale and exponential speed of technological change and the growing convergence between digital, physical and biological technologies are creating fundamentally new risks and opportunities for companies in every industry sector. These secular forces are transforming corporate value creation and competitive advantage, making them increasingly dependent upon intangible capital formation, particularly innovation, talent development and branding. These usually require investment over a sustained period, a considerably longer time span than that required for two value creation strategies that have been in vogue for the past generation: aggressive cost-cutting including through outsourcing and offshoring; and overuse of leverage, share buybacks and financial engineering.

In today's economy, for many industries the time to market and agility in response to changes in customer requirements are increasingly important sources of competitive advantage. Combined with threats to supply chain resilience caused by the pandemic, these have begun to induce a reshoring and reintegration of production as automation reduces the share of labour in the total cost of production. In particular, the ongoing digitalization of economic activity is reshaping industries and in some cases blurring the lines between them, creating new risks alongside enormous opportunities for value creation and intense competitive pressures on companies to make the investments in technology and people needed to stay ahead of such disruption. Mobile connectivity and cloud computing, machine learning and big data, ubiquitous sensors and the internet of things, robots and virtual reality, and additive manufacturing and nanotechnology are disrupting business models in virtually every industry and service sector.

This disruptive change has a long way to run. The World Economic Forum's Digital Transformation of Industry initiative estimated that it has the potential to generate upwards of $100 trillion of value for industry and society over a decade's time.[4] The biotechnology revolution—particularly recent advances in the sequencing and manipulation of genes—is likely to create an additional large wave of disruptive value creation across multiple industries over the coming decade or two. A third disruption—an energy revolution—may not be far behind; the vertiginous decline in the cost of renewable energies and solar energy in recent years could be a harbinger.[5]

Advances in these three technology domains—digital, biotechnology and energy—are accelerating and intertwining. They are likely to reinforce each other over the next decade or two in ways that transform business models in nearly every industry. These shifts remain at an early stage, but clearly the COVID-19 pandemic has accelerated the first of these tectonic forces—digital—and may prove to have a similar impact on the second, biosciences. Its stimulative effect on the digital economy has taken the form of big increases in remote working, digital conferencing, e-commerce, e-learning, the digital consumption of entertainment, e-medicine, automated package delivery and logistics and more. Many of these changes in production and consumption appear likely to endure well beyond the public health crisis, with a profound and lasting impact on supply chains and distribution channels.

Thus, innovating to anticipate and adapt to technological change is likely to be the central value creation imperative of this new era for nearly every industry. After a generation of outsourcing and offshoring and a decade of extraordinarily low interest rates, most companies have passed the point of diminishing returns from creating value primarily through cost efficiencies and leverage. These strategies are not likely to be major sources of sustained enterprise value creation in the years to come. Instead, investment in the hardware and software of innovation, including particularly the skills, creativity and motivation of the people who drive and apply it, is poised to be the most important driver of competitive advantage. The *sine qua non* of business leadership in the 2020s will therefore be the ability to rally the firm around a strategy to increase investment, particularly in intangibles such as innovation, workforce development and empowerment, and customer personalization and brand loyalty.

### 2.1.2    Environmental

In the years since the UN Paris Agreement on climate change was agreed in 2015, there has been a major shift in social attitudes, energy markets, regulatory agendas and consumer and investor preferences with respect to the need to take urgent action on addressing climate change. These trends are accelerating, galvanized by a dramatic increase in climate-related, extreme weather events in many countries over the past five years and by evermore compelling scientific and economic evidence of the costs of inaction. The IPCC's 2021 report provides the starkest warning to date that climate change is widespread, rapid and intensifying.[6] These trends require companies to think more deliberately and strategically about the risks and opportunities that climate change and an energy transition towards net-zero carbon emissions by 2050 pose to their current operations and future strategies from the perspective of both mitigation and adaptation. Indeed, both regulators and investors are rapidly moving to require firms to integrate climate change considerations into corporate governance, strategy, risk management and disclosure, in recognition that related physical and transitional risks can have major implications for corporate performance, even the viability of some companies and industries.

The Network for Greening the Financial System (NGFS), for example, is a network of central banks and financial supervisors that aims to accelerate the scaling up of green finance and develop recommendations for central banks' role in addressing climate change. Established in December 2017, NGFS had 95 members as of June 2021, including the world's largest central banks. Among other actions, it has encouraged "all companies issuing public debt or equity as well as financial sector institutions to disclose in line with the Task Force on Climate-related Financial Disclosures (TCFD) recommendations." As of late 2020, support for the TCFD had grown more than 85% over a period of 15 months, reaching more than 1500 organizations globally, including over 1340 companies with a market capitalization of $12.6 trillion and financial institutions responsible for assets of $150 trillion.[7] In addition to voluntary initiatives and commitments, the European Union and the US Securities and Exchange Commission (SEC), among other regulators, are starting to establish requirements for mandatory disclosure by corporations and financial institutions on their climate strategies and metrics.

As a result of these regulatory, investor and business leadership initiatives, a new corporate best practice has emerged. It is a public commitment by companies and institutional investors to achieve a net-zero "science-based" emissions target by 2050 and to begin implementing within the next few years specific strategies and pathways consistent with this goal. As of mid-2021, over 1700 companies worldwide had committed to set emissions reduction targets grounded in climate science through the Science Based Targets initiative (SBTi).[8] Some 715 of these firms have adopted the high ambition 1.5 °C target set by the Paris Agreement.

As for investors, the United Nations-sponsored Net-Zero Asset Owner Alliance and the Net-Zero Asset Managers Initiative have convened institutional investors representing US $6.6 trillion and US $43 trillion in assets under management respectively to commit collectively to transition their investment portfolios to net-zero GHG emissions by 2050 in line with the 1.5 °C target set by the Paris agreement.[9] Political jurisdictions, both national and regional, are also setting net-zero targets, including such major actors as the European Union,[10] China,[11] the US,[12] Japan and South Korea. These shifts in policy and regulation are bound to intensify the pressure on the corporate sector to move more rapidly in the direction set by these first-mover business and investor coalitions.

In summary, the legal and political ground is rapidly shifting under companies with respect to environmental stewardship. While climate change has been the "game changer" in terms of putting environmental issues more firmly on the boardroom and executive agenda, other environmental issues are also rising in terms of their materiality and importance. They include the related and escalating challenges of water insecurity, biodiversity loss and a growing public backlash against pollution, ranging from a severe deterioration in air quality in certain cities to plastics in the ocean.

### 2.1.3   Geopolitical

The growing multipolarity of international relations and return of overt great power rivalry are contributing to the ongoing plurilateralization of the world economy—the fragmentation of international trade and investment driven until recently by regional trade agreements but increasingly shaped by geopolitical frictions. Uncertainty and complexity are on the rise, requiring multinational firms to take a more deliberate approach to assess such risks, including the threat of finding themselves caught in the middle of trade, investment and migration disputes or technological competition between major countries and trading blocs. Some countries are instituting new barriers to cross-border flows of investment, natural resources, people and data, reflecting a decline in trust among nations and the tendency of international rule-making to lag changes in the world economy.

Industrial policies of various sorts are on the rise around the world related to the increased economic and national security stakes countries perceive in the "winner-take-all" scaling effects of new digital technologies and business models. Investment screening, procurement requirements and export restrictions are on the rise, as is competition among regional preferential trading arrangements, all of which contributes to rising complexity and political sensitivity in running global supply chain and sales operations. The deterioration in Great Power relations and logjam within the WTO's negotiating and adjudicatory functions are a clear sign that geopolitical factors are likely to remain a topic requiring strategic and operational agility by companies.

## 2.1.4   Socio-economic

As automation and globalization have increased economies of scale and industrial restructuring, income inequality and worker insecurity have risen in many countries. These trends have combined with longstanding racial and ethnic inequalities, the disproportionate impact on low-income households of the global financial crisis and COVID-19 pandemic, and rising tensions over migration to fuel a popular perception in many countries that their economies are not sufficiently benefiting the citizenry at large. These frustrations and the protests, civil unrest and political polarization to which they have contributed are a warning sign that the social consensus underpinning open, pro-growth economic policies and capitalism itself has eroded considerably, as has trust in corporations, which tend to be the agent and public face of economic disruption.

As governments struggle to respond to these socio-economic and political challenges, companies are faced with rising expectations regarding their role in contributing to the general welfare of their workers and communities. There are growing expectations that this role needs to include but go beyond respecting workers' rights in the company's own operations and supply chain and supporting host communities through contributions to charities and schools. Companies are increasingly being called upon to commit themselves and press governments to respect human rights, protect civil rights and address social injustice and structural inequity more generally.

In addition, while digital technologies offer many benefits to society, they also pose new challenges to human rights and to the social contract, from the use of mass surveillance technologies and large-scale collection and sale of other personal data to the growing need to tackle misinformation, disinformation and hate speech. As such, companies that produce or use these technologies are under growing pressure to demonstrate that they understand and are mitigating the corresponding risks to their workers, customers and the public at large, including those that might lead them to become complicit in human rights abuses or violations of local social norms.

In a climate of increased social fragility and diminished trust, a lapse by an individual company, such as an incident relating to customer data privacy, corruption, labour rights or environmental pollution, is more likely to escalate into a crisis, potentially to the point of threatening a firm's very existence. This is particularly the case if a company already suffers from a deficit of trust because of a perceived track record of insensitivity to or degradation of the social context in which it operates.

## 2.1.5    Systemic Shocks and Crises

Systemic shocks and crises that cause substantial losses and disruption for millions of people are clearly not new. The enormous humanitarian and economic toll of two World Wars and the Great Depression are obvious examples. Yet, resulting from the transformational shifts outlined in this section, the frequency, speed and in some cases the scale of natural, humanitarian and economic or financial crises and system-level shocks have increased over recent decades. In most cases a natural or humanitarian crisis leads to substantial financial and job losses and these in turn further aggravate human suffering. Consider the following:

**Epidemics and pandemics:** A prescient 2019 report by the World Economic Forum noted, "On the 100th anniversary of the 1918 influenza pandemic, it is tempting to believe the world has seen the worst epidemics. However, with increasing trade, travel, population density, human displacement, migrations and deforestation, as well as climate change, a new era of the risk of epidemics has begun. The number and diversity of epidemic events has been increasing over the past 30 years, a trend that is only expected to intensify. ... Outbreaks and epidemics are also causing more economic damage when they occur."[13] Thus, we cannot assume the COVID-19 pandemic is a once-in-a-lifetime, black swan event.

**Natural disasters:** Countries around the globe are experiencing unprecedented droughts, heatwaves, wildfires, floods, hurricanes and other climate-related extreme weather events. The associated humanitarian crises, economic costs and enterprise risks are continuing to grow, in size and severity. Research by both scientists and practitioners highlights increasing concerns. According to Aon's 2019 annual Weather, Climate and Catastrophe Insight Report, "The decadal period from 2010–2019 marked the costliest in the modern record for global natural disasters on a nominal and inflation-adjusted basis. Total direct economic damage and losses tallied USD 2.98 trillion. This was USD 1.1 trillion higher than the previous decade. … It is impossible to know precisely what the next decade will bring. If loss trends are a guide, however, then it is expected that there will continue to be larger and costlier events on a global scale."[14]

While the world's attention is rightly focused on addressing the COVID-19 pandemic, the potential widespread humanitarian, economic and environmental costs of climate change and climate-related shocks cannot be underestimated and need to be mitigated and adapted for immediately, not left to some future date. As Aon conclude in their 2020 Weather, Climate and Catastrophe Insight Report:

> Perhaps the biggest takeaway from 2020 was the recognition of how concurrent events can have major global implications. These 'compounded' or 'connected extremes' will provide critical learning opportunities for better planning as the world becomes increasingly complex and faces growing or emerging risks. 2020 also highlighted topics such as the protection gap to address the underserved, increasingly vulnerable populations, the need for additional investment around risk mitigation strategies to navigate new forms of volatility, and the growing influence from climate change on daily life.[15]

## 2.2 The Growing Materiality of ESG&D Risks and Opportunities

The trends outlined above are increasing the materiality of ESG&D issues for corporations in almost every industry sector. While the specifics differ depending on industry and circumstances, ESG&D risks and opportunities are having a growing impact on the financial condition or operating performance of companies through their effect on the ability of firms to create and sustain new economic value, manage risks and preserve existing value, and meet societal expectations and evolving social norms and values that relate to the firm's social licence to operate. This shift in the relative weight of so-called non-financial factors in the creation and maintenance of enterprise value is increasingly requiring boards to think beyond the traditional segmented logic of shareholder primacy and corporate responsibility.

## 2.2.1 Creating and Sustaining Value

Healthy profits remain the *sine qua non* of corporate performance. But in this new context issues that were previously considered secondary or even ancillary matters for CEOs and boards—the province of the firm's stakeholder relations, philanthropy and information technology departments—have become more important determinants of a firm's capacity to create and sustain economic value. They therefore merit full integration into the core oversight, strategy formulation, risk management, performance evaluation and public reporting duties of boards and executive teams.

Climate change, water, biodiversity and other aspects of environmental stewardship, for example, are increasingly material economic factors in a world in which related technology, regulation and physical impacts are changing within the space of years and sometimes months. The same is true for the management of the key source of competitive advantage in the Fourth Industrial Revolution: intangible assets and particularly people. The continuous cultivation of the talent, motivation and diversity of a firm's workforce and of its intellectual property, including new technologies, process innovations and data, are central to value creation in this new era.

Considerations related to people, planet and innovation, including the protection and value-added application of company data, must therefore figure more prominently in capital allocation and other core management decisions going forward. The increased significance of these value creation factors implies a growing need to better understand the trade-offs between investment in new capacity and capabilities and rationalization of existing operations and assets. Doing a better job of investing for future growth while delivering current operational efficiency and excellence implies a lengthening of investment time horizons beyond the depreciation schedules of capital equipment and typical return-on-investment timelines of cost-cutting, restructuring and outsourcing strategies. These will clearly remain important elements in the ability of companies to create value, but for company success to be sustained over time and shared with key stakeholders, boards and executive teams will need to pay careful attention to the full range of shifts outlined in the previous section to ensure that capital is properly allocated to longer-term investments in new products, skills, markets and productive capacity.

## 2.2.2   Managing Risks and Preserving Value

Effective stewardship of the firm's environmental, social, governance and digital footprint is also increasingly important for value preservation. It therefore must figure more prominently in enterprise and operational risk management as well.

An important part of the risk these factors pose is reputational. As such, they are just as crucial to the maintenance of trust as traditional governance issues such as ethics, transparency and board independence. The reputational damage resulting from a customer data breach, environmental disaster, corruption scandal or human rights abuse can be substantial and enduring. In many cases, however, reputational damage is only part of the cost a company will incur. Failure to manage ESG&D risks effectively can result in a combination of safety risks, other physical and supply chain risks, litigation and regulatory risks, and risks to employee morale and the ability to attract and retain the best talent. In addition, failure to anticipate changes in technology or environmental regulation can result in serious transition risk for companies in certain industries, potentially to the point of threatening their long-term viability if they are not able to adapt with new products, services and business models.

Thus, the growing materiality of ESG&D factors for both value creation and preservation creates an imperative for them to be integrated fully into the theory and practice of corporate governance, strategy, capital allocation, risk management, reporting and performance evaluation and remuneration. In the new environmental, social, geopolitical and technological context of the 2020s, these factors are not only ethical or constituent relations matters. They are fundamental to the exercise of fiduciary duty in the disposition of corporate resources.

### 2.2.3   Addressing Changing Societal Expectations, Norms and Values

Finally, the growing materiality of ESG&D issues is also a manifestation of important changes in the social license to operate of firms in the 21st century. Societal expectations of corporations are shifting, as popular concern about automation, trade, climate change, inequality, immigration, corporate ownership of personal data, corruption and other issues rises. These broader trends, compounded by the legacy of the global financial crisis, have produced a deficit of trust in corporations in many countries,[16] as well as growing debate about whether they contribute sufficiently to the ultimate purpose of economies, which is to produce the broad-based gains in living standards that come from inclusive economic growth.[17]

These social pressures are likely to mount further as technology continues to increase economies of scale, disrupt industries and, other things being equal, shift the distribution of national income in the direction of owners of capital and away from labour. The OECD reports that there has been a significant such shift in the past two decades within advanced economies, although with considerable variation between countries, industries and skill cohorts of workers.[18] This distributional shift and hollowing out of the middle class in many countries has been driven by not only technological change but also public policy and corporate strategy choices, and it is contributing to the drop in public support for open markets and to the polarization of politics more generally in some countries.

Thus, there is a larger social and political economy rationale for boards of directors and executive management teams to ensure that their firms are creating sustainable value and not just maximizing short-term profit through cost efficiencies and rent extraction and that they are properly addressing new risks that have grown out of the changed technological, environmental, geopolitical and social context of their operations. Business leaders must recognize that the long-term viability of their companies as engines of value creation is in no small part a function of the viability of the societies and economies in which they operate. In other words, companies are stakeholders themselves in the health of their social, policy and economic enabling environment. They have an intrinsic, material stake in both the social cohesion of the jurisdictions in which they have significant operations and the capacity of public institutions therein to deliver basic public services and ensure the fair and efficient functioning of markets.

In summary, ESG&D risks and opportunities are becoming more material to the ability of companies across industry sectors to create and sustain value, manage risks and preserve value, and address changing societal expectations, norms and values. Failure to understand and manage these factors effectively is likely to result at best in lost business opportunities and at worst serious deterioration in financial and operational performance as well as reputational standing and relationships with key stakeholders from investors and regulators to employees and customers. In extreme cases, it could threaten the firm's viability as a going concern.

## 2.2.4    The Material Consequences of Getting It Wrong or Failing to Act

Some companies and industry sectors are already learning the hard way that failure to treat their material ESG&D issues as important corporate governance and strategy considerations can result in the rapid deterioration of investor, employee and societal trust, heightened financial and operational risks, and impairment of value.

Consider the escalating business risks and costs associated with climate change, for example. Companies are facing substantial physical, operational, financial and transitional risks resulting from the impact of extreme weather events or failures to adequately address the impact of climate change on their business. These include significant short-term costs as well as risks to long-term profitability and even viability for some companies, especially but not only those in the utilities, insurance and financial services, energy, food, beverages and agriculture, and tourism sectors. In 2020, S&P Global estimated that "more than 40% of the world's largest companies have sites at high risk from the physical impacts of climate change—that's wildfires, water stress, heatwaves and hurricanes among others. For US companies this rises to almost 60%."[19] A 2019 study by Ceres cited the following climate-related business risks and costs, all of which are likely to have increased substantially since the research was undertaken:

- *Physical risks:* In 2017, 73 companies on the S&P 500 publicly disclosed a material effect on earnings from weather events and over 90% of these companies disclosed the effect on earnings was negative.
- *Supply chain risks:* Supply chain disruptions due to climate risk increased 29% from 2012 to 2019.

- *Litigation risks:* More than 100 cases had been filed in the US on climate change impacts as of May 2019.
- *Regulatory risks:* The number of climate change regulations had grown to 1500 globally, up from 72 in 1997.[20]

Another increasing risk and cost for business is the challenge of avoiding and responding to breaches in data privacy. The 2021 ForgeRock Consumer Identity Breach Report, for example, offers sobering evidence of the increased business risks and costs of cyberattacks on consumer data following the large-scale digital migration of consumers, workers and students that occurred during the COVID-19 pandemic, when the amount of time that people spent online was estimated to have doubled.[21] Among their findings was evidence of a 450% increase in breaches containing usernames and passwords in 2020, totalling 1.48 billion breached or compromised records in the US alone.[22] They found that while healthcare was the most targeted sector, accounting for 34% of all breaches, the technology sector paid the highest aggregate cost of recovery at US $288 billion, with more than 1.6 billion records stolen.[23] In 2020, the so-called Solar Winds hack alone breached hundreds of government agencies and large corporations at an estimated cost of as much as $100 billion.[24] While it is the mega-breaches and cyberattacks on well-known consumer brands that make the headlines, small and medium-sized companies can be devastated by the financial and reputational costs of a data breach.

Increased public awareness of the human costs and abuse of people's rights associated with sexual harassment and misconduct in the workplace offers another example of the growing financial, reputational and operational costs faced by companies that fail to strategically address this issue. Over the past decade, the #MeToo movement has played a crucial role in raising awareness, mobilizing activism, influencing corporate cultures and policies, starting to shift legal and regulatory reforms, and increasingly holding both companies and culpable senior executives to account. As *Fortune* magazine noted in an article on the Conference Board's 2019 edition of the CEO Succession Practices report, "Among the 18 non-voluntary CEO departures, 5 were related to personal conduct and #MeToo allegations. That's especially noteworthy given that only one CEO between 2013 and 2017 was fired as a result of personal conduct unrelated to performance, according to the Conference Board. Overall, the trend is proof that the #MeToo movement has reached the boardroom."[25] This is just the tip of the iceberg in terms of the costs to employee morale and trust, lost productivity, litigation, shareholder derivative lawsuits and reputational harm that companies are starting to face as a result of failure to address long-standing human rights, inclusion and diversity issues that had not been given the prominence and importance they deserve at the board level.

These brief examples of the growing materiality to companies and their boards of climate risk management, consumer and employee data stewardship, and respecting human rights are just three key examples of the need for greater board oversight of ESG&D issues. More broadly, research by Bank of America Merrill Lynch released in September 2019 found that "15 out of 17 (90%) bankruptcies in the S&P 500 between 2005 and 2015 were of companies with poor Environmental and Social scores five years prior to the bankruptcies" and "major ESG-related controversies during the past six years were accompanied by peak-to-trough market capitalization losses of $534 billion for large US companies. Loss avoidance is key for portfolio returns over time."[26]

An analysis of US proxy voting trends on environmental and social issues from 2000 to 2018 further illustrates the point of growing materiality. As a commentary by the Managing Editor of ISS Analytics states:

> the reality is that investor voting behaviour among owners of U.S. companies has changed significantly—perhaps almost revolutionarily—over the past two decades. … Proxy voting policies are becoming more complex, as investors continue to add to the list of factors they consider in their review and analysis of governance practices, including board independence, board accountability, diversity, myriads of executive compensation factors, shareholder rights, and environmental and social factors. Based on our analysis, the most significant change in investors' voting behaviour pertains to environmental and social issues, as these issues are earning record levels of support in recent years.[27]

The Bank of America and ISS Analytics research are just two of a growing number of studies from the financial, consulting and academic communities to make the case for the growing materiality of ESG&D issues and for integrating them into corporate governance. The specific issues and the materiality of the risks and opportunities that they present to a company will vary based on industry sector, jurisdiction and circumstances, but no large company or its board is immune to this trend. The Sustainability Accounting Standards Board (SASB), now part of the Value Reporting Foundation, has undertaken an extensive consultation process with major corporations and investors over the past decade to identify the subset of ESG issues most relevant for financial performance in each of 77 industry sectors, with the goal of helping companies in these sectors to disclose the most financially material sustainability information to their investors.[28] The Global Reporting Initiative is also developing sustainability reporting standards for 40 sectors, starting with those that have the highest impact on people and the planet.[29] As outlined in detail in Chap. 6, concerted efforts are underway to achieve a comprehensive global baseline of sustainability-related disclosure standards that provide investors and other capital market participants with information about companies' material sustainability-related risks and opportunities.

Thus, the business case for full integration of ESG&D factors into the core governance, strategy and reporting functions of firms has been growing stronger and is increasingly accepted in principle. However, stakeholder capitalism and sustainable enterprise value creation remain a long way from supplanting the doctrine of shareholder primacy and narrow, near-term optimization of financial performance in practice, particularly in the US and UK but also in other important segments of global business and financial markets. The next section describes the journey traveled thus far, placing stakeholder capitalism's promising resurgence in historical, legal and cross-cultural context.

## 2.3 The Evolution of Corporate Governance and Corporate Responsibility Since the 1970s

### 2.3.1 Corporate Governance

The paradigm of shareholder value maximization as the paramount fiduciary responsibility of boards of directors gained prominence in the US during the 1970s. It was influenced by two seminal articles and the academic research underpinning them. First was Milton Friedman's *New York Times Magazine* article of 1970, "The Social Responsibility of Business Is to Increase Its Profits," challenging both the theory and practice of corporate social responsibility.[30] Second was the 1976 *Journal of Financial Economics* article "Theory of the firm" by Michael Jensen and William Meckling.[31] This view was also supported by business leaders and organizations such as the Business Roundtable (BRT), which issued its first Principles of Corporate Governance in 1978. From its origins in the US, the shareholder primacy concept has driven the practice of corporate governance and the legal interpretation of fiduciary responsibility in a growing number of other economies, gaining additional traction in the late 1980s and 1990s during the era of large-scale economic liberalization, globalization and privatization.

As discussed in Chap. 1, different ownership structures and corporate governance models in European and Asian countries have tempered the spread of shareholder primacy, such as two-tier boards with an explicit governance role for labour and foundation ownership structures. Likewise, in a variety of jurisdictions, such as the UK, Australia, India and South Africa, the legal concept that directors owe their duty to the company rather than to the shareholders has become more clearly articulated as a result of seminal reviews and revisions to corporate governance codes. The OECD's Principles of Corporate Governance, first published in 1999 and most recently revised in 2015, now provide guidance on responsibilities to both shareholders and other stakeholders and are increasingly used as an international benchmark including by the G20, Financial Stability Board and World Bank.

This trend reflects decades of scholarship focused on developing a theory or set of theories around the role of stakeholders in corporate governance.[32] Most researchers trace the origins of this line of intellectual inquiry and the use of the term "stakeholder" in the context of corporate governance to the Stanford Research Institute in the early 1960s, where a working group was examining the question of who should have a say in formulating a company mission. Their discussions resulted in a basic diagram and methodology for stakeholder needs assessment.[33] In 1971, Hein Kroos and Klaus Schwab published the German book *Moderne Unternehmensführung im Maschinenbau* (*Modern Enterprise Management in Mechanical Engineering*) arguing that the management of a modern enterprise must serve not only shareholders but all stakeholders (*die Interessenten*) to achieve long-term growth and prosperity.[34] And R.E. Freeman developed the concept further in his 1984 *Strategic Management: A Stakeholder Approach*. Referring to the social, economic and environmental shifts in the business context of the day he argued: "Our current theories are inconsistent with both the quantity and kinds of change that are occurring in the business environment of the 1980s. […] A new conceptual framework is needed."[35]

Today, even in the countries where it is most deeply rooted, the paradigm of shareholder value maximization is under rising pressure from dramatic changes in the underlying operating context of businesses. This corporate governance reset is being driven not only by the recent pandemic and economic crises but also by the secular increase in ESG&D materiality described in this chapter and the lessons learned from decades of corporate scandals resulting from serious lapses in attention to such factors. The ability to be profitable and deliver measurable value for shareholders in the near term remains essential and is a particularly strong focus of influential activist investors. But an expanding combination of leading CEOs, investors, regulators, activists and academics are calling for companies also to make an explicit and measurable commitment to harmonize the needs of all key stakeholders and demonstrate that their strategies are fit for the purpose of delivering long-term as well as short-term value.

In 2017, an article by Professors Joseph Bower and Lynn Paine in *Harvard Business Review* made the compelling assertion, "Most CEOs and boards believe their main duty is to maximize shareholder value. It's Not."[36] The authors make a strong case for moving to a "company centred" versus "shareholder centred" approach to corporate governance, with guidance on the changing role of boards, including setting the business purpose of their company. Research by a growing number of other management and legal academics reinforces these ideas of companies having a broader corporate purpose than maximizing shareholder value and a changed role for boards of directors as a result.

As outlined in other chapters, many of the world's largest asset owners and managers are also increasing their focus on long-term value creation and ESG stewardship as part of their analysis of, engagement with and investment in major corporations. The evolution over the past few years of the annual corporate governance letter sent to CEOs by BlackRock's Larry Fink is one example, which explicitly calls on CEOs and boards to take responsibility for focusing on strategy aligned to long-term value creation, for understanding and ensuring oversight of the company's purpose and role in society, and for assessing and reporting on climate-related financial risks.

Legal scholars and practitioners have also contributed to the shifting paradigm. In 2019, for example, Martin Lipton of the law firm Wachtell, Lipton, Rosen & Katz issued a commentary entitled "It's Time to Adopt the New Paradigm." Based on a 2016 paper prepared for the World Economic Forum, he outlines "a reconception of corporate governance as a collaboration among shareholders, managers, employees, customers, suppliers, and the communities in which corporations operate."[37] This law firm is not alone, and many others are issuing guidance to their clients on the evolving practice of a stakeholder-oriented approach to corporate law and governance. In recent years, the American, European and International Bar Associations, among others, have also provided guidance to companies and their boards on the legal implications of respecting human rights and addressing other ESG&D issues.

Business leadership groups are also becoming more active in the debate. In August 2019, 181 CEO members of the BRT signed a new Statement on the Purpose of a Corporation, committing to leading their companies for the benefit of all stakeholders—customers, employees, suppliers, communities and shareholders. As the BRT comments, "Each version of the document issued since 1997 has endorsed principles of shareholder primacy—that corporations exist primarily to serve shareholders. With today's announcement, the new Statement supersedes previous statements and outlines a modern standard for corporate responsibility."[38] In making this statement, the BRT, among other business organizations, is committing to a clearer alignment between the concepts and the practices of corporate governance and corporate responsibility. Also in 2019, in preparation for its 50th anniversary Annual Meeting in Davos, the World Economic Forum issued its Davos Manifesto 2020: The Universal Purpose of a Company in the Fourth Industrial Revolution, updating its earlier 1973 Davos Manifesto.

These developments indicate that the paradigm of shareholder value maximization is shifting and leading to the convergence and effective integration of corporate governance with corporate responsibility.

## 2.3.2   Corporate Responsibility and Citizenship

The related fields of corporate responsibility and corporate citizenship have also evolved substantially over the past two decades—and in a similar direction. During this period, they have transformed from being focused almost solely on corporate philanthropy and basic compliance with the law to concentrating primarily on:

- How companies identify and manage the ESG risks and opportunities that are most relevant to their core business strategies, operations and performance and that are most salient to people and the planet.
- How companies measure, report and account for their performance in relation to these ESG risks and opportunities to key stakeholders, including but not only shareholders.

In 1999, at the World Economic Forum Annual Meeting in Davos, the late UN Secretary-General Kofi Annan called on business leaders, "individually through your firms, and collectively through your business associations—to embrace, support and enact a set of core values in the areas of human rights, labour standards, and environmental practices."[39] This led to the creation of the UN Global Compact, today the world's largest voluntary initiative based on CEO commitments to uphold a set of 10 universal principles in the above areas and anti-corruption.

In 2002, we co-authored a World Economic Forum report entitled *Global Corporate Citizenship: The Leadership Challenge for CEOs and Boards*. The report was written for a task force of 46 chief executive officers from a diverse range of countries and industry sectors, and it was developed in partnership with the Prince of Wales International Business Leaders Forum. Working closely with the CEOs, we identified three key leadership challenges and a framework for action. We summarize these here, in part to recognize some of the early business pioneers, most of whose companies continue to play a leadership role today in driving more just, inclusive and sustainable growth.[40] In addition to recognizing some of the pioneers of stakeholder capitalism, we re-state this three-pronged leadership statement because it remains not only relevant but more important than ever in today's world. The 46 CEOs signed the following statement:

* First and foremost, **our companies' commitment to being global corporate citizens is about the way we run our own businesses.** The greatest contribution we can make to development is to do business in a manner that obeys the law, produces safe and cost-effective products and services, creates jobs and wealth, supports training and technology cooperation and reflects international standards and values in areas such as the environment, ethics, labour and human rights. To make every effort to enhance the positive multipliers of our activities and to minimize any negative impacts on people and the environment, everywhere we invest and operate. A key element of this is recognizing that the frameworks we adopt for being a responsible business must move beyond philanthropy and be integrated into core business strategy and practice.
* Second, **our relationships with key stakeholders are fundamental to our success inside and outside our companies**. Being global corporate citizens requires us to identify and work with key stakeholders in our main spheres of influence: in the workplace, in the marketplace, along our supply chains, at the community level and in public policy dialogue. Our key stakeholders will vary based on our particular circumstances, but for most of us our employees, customers and shareholders are of fundamental importance, together with host communities and governments and a growing variety of civil society organizations.
* Third, **ultimate leadership for corporate citizenship rests with us as chief executives, chairmen and board directors.** Although it is essential that we assign clear responsibilities, resources and leadership roles to our managers for addressing these issues on a day-to-day basis, ultimate responsibility rests with us. While specific definitions, approaches and issues may differ according to industry sector, location of operations, size and type of company ownership, we believe the Framework for Action provides a template for leadership that is relevant for all companies, industry sectors and

countries. Some of us will use the terminology of corporate citizenship, others of corporate social responsibility, ethics, triple-bottom-line or sustainable development, but we believe the core principles and actions required are the same. First, provide leadership. Second, define what it means for your company. Third, make it happen. Fourth, be transparent about it.[41]

Building on the 2002 statement, in 2008 another task force of CEOs working with the World Economic Forum, Business for Social Responsibility (BSR), Harvard Kennedy School, AccountAbility and the International Business Leaders Forum focused on the role of business in working collectively beyond their own operations and supply chains to help strengthen public governance. This group outlined specific actions that companies could take as good corporate citizens to strengthen the broader enabling environment in which business operates. Examples ranged from joint efforts to help governments build capacity to deliver public goods such as health, education and training, to tackling corruption at the national level, as well as bringing a business voice to strengthen global governance frameworks. The report was one of the first of its kind that outlined a clear roadmap for building mutually reinforcing links between corporate responsibility and citizenship, corporate governance and public governance.[42]

Also, in 2008, in a seminal article in *Foreign Affairs* magazine, the World Economic Forum's Founder and Executive Chairman Klaus Schwab wrote,

> A new imperative for business, best described as global corporate citizenship, must be recognized. It expresses the conviction that companies not only must be engaged with their stakeholders but are themselves stakeholders alongside governments and civil society. International business leaders must fully commit to sustainable development and address paramount global challenges, including climate change, the provision of public health care, energy conservation, and the management of resources, particularly water. Because these global issues increasingly impact business, not to engage with them can hurt the bottom line. Because global citizenship is in a corporation's enlightened self-interest, it is sustainable.[43]

In 2011, further impetus came from work by Professor Michael Porter and Mark Kramer, who working with Peter Brabeck, the former CEO of Nestlé, among others, coined the term "Creating Shared Value" to describe how companies can create both economic and social value by reconceiving products and services, redefining productivity in the value chain and improving their operating environment.[44] In the same year, the UN Guiding Principles on Business and Human Rights, authored by Professor John Ruggie, were unanimously endorsed by the UN Human Rights Council. [45] And, in the lead up to 2015, a core group of business leaders from diverse countries and industry sectors played a role in the consultations and negotiations that resulted in the Paris Agreement on climate change and the Sustainable Development Goals (SDGs).[46]

In recent years, such voluntary leadership and commitments by a small number of CEOs and boards have grown substantially. More companies are taking an approach to corporate responsibility and citizenship that is focused on identifying and managing the material ESG&D risks and opportunities in their core business operations and business relationships. As outlined elsewhere, a key driver has been the growing focus on ESG&D issues by many of the world's largest asset owners and managers, from sovereign wealth funds, pension funds and insurance companies to other institutional investors. The signatories of the UN Principles for Responsible Investment, for example, have grown from 100 in 2006 to over 4000 in 2021 and together accounted for some US $120 trillion in assets under management as of mid-2021.[47]

Today, the focus by a growing number of large companies on integrating material ESG&D risks and opportunities into their core business strategies, operations, supply chains and policy dialogue is more important and relevant than ever. To be effective and sustained, board-level engagement and oversight is required. A lack of clarity and consistency of terminology and metrics remains a challenge for many companies, investors and other stakeholders. These practices are variously described as corporate responsibility, corporate citizenship, corporate social responsibility, corporate sustainability, ESG, triple bottom line, creating shared value, inclusive business models and total societal impact, to name some of the more common terms used. Linked to the challenge of different terminology and approaches, there are a plethora of different measurement and ranking systems that are being used by companies, investors and other stakeholders to evaluate and compare business commitments and performance on ESG&D issues. Yet, in all cases, the attention of leading companies, shareholders and other stakeholders is increasingly focused on the issues that are most material to the company and most salient to people and the environment.

## 2.4    Stakeholder Capitalism: From Principles to Practice

Thus, profound changes in the operating context of companies are aligning the interests of shareholders and other stakeholders more closely by increasing the financial materiality of the stewardship of ESG&D risks and opportunities. This has the potential to usher in a new phase of capitalism—stakeholder capitalism—which shifts market economies beyond the managerial capitalism of the 1950s–1970s and the financial capitalism of the 1980s–2010s, a hallmark of which has been the pre-eminence of shareholder value and the segmentation and *de facto* subordination of environmental, social and broader value chain stewardship issues.

Stakeholder capitalism holds promise for both shareholders and society at large. By better internalizing factors that influence value over time, it could generate stronger and more resilient financial returns for the ultimate owners of companies: people with retirement and other saving accounts intended to fund medium- to long-term family needs. At the same time, it could accelerate progress towards the broader aspirations of society, such as combating climate change, reducing inequality and advancing sustainable development through the fulfilment of the Sustainable Development Goals.

As outlined earlier, the principles of stakeholder capitalism have recently been restated in the World Economic Forum's refreshment and republication of its 1973 corporate governance manifesto and the Business Roundtable's statement of corporate purpose, as well as in national regulations and frameworks, such as the revised UK Corporate Governance Code and the UK Stewardship Code 2020 and the 2020 additions to the French Civil and Commercial Codes, among others. But realizing the potential for sustainable enterprise value creation articulated by these principles will require companies to translate them into practice. They must do so by transcending the traditional segmentation of shareholder and stakeholder considerations—exemplified by the concepts of shareholder primacy and corporate responsibility—by integrating them.

Integrated corporate governance, strategy and reporting depart from the mindset and associated practices of shareholder primacy and corporate social responsibility, which have regarded ESG&D factors as primarily non- or prefinancial matters. Instead, it takes a holistic view of shareholder and wider stakeholder interests by systematically internalizing ESG&D considerations into the firm's strategy, resource allocation, risk management, performance evaluation and disclosure policies and processes. It does so not for ethical or political reasons, although these are crucial factors that must also be fully considered by firms, but out of a recognition that in the twenty-first century, strong and sustained value creation beyond the near term is increasingly dependent upon a rigorous understanding and active management of these considerations as part of the core governance and strategy of the firm.

If stakeholder capitalism is to be more than an optimistic vision, it will require this integration to become better defined in operational terms and translated into practices that are widely adopted by boards and management teams in five key areas:

1. Align governance, strategy and capital allocation with the key drivers of shared and sustainable value creation
2. Internalize material ESG&D risks and opportunities into enterprise risk management and innovation
3. Reinforce preparedness and resilience to crises and systemic shocks
4. Recognize that the firm is a stakeholder itself in the vitality and resilience of its operating context and partner with other stakeholders to address relevant systemic challenges therein
5. Integrate financial and material non-financial information in mainstream internal and external reporting

Chapter 3 elaborates on these five elements, providing a *thematic* overview of the leadership agenda required to implement diligently the principles of stakeholder capitalism within a firm. In Part II, Chaps. 4, 5, 6 and 7 provide a *practical* guide, a more detailed look at what this leadership agenda means in *functional* terms for the firm with reference to existing examples of good practice: for governance and the role of boards; for strategy and management and the role of the C-suite; for reporting and communications with investors in particular; and for broader system-level engagement, including particularly partnership with other stakeholders to address weaknesses in the underlying economic and societal operating context.

This is an agenda to assist business leaders who subscribe to the precepts of sustainable enterprise value creation and stakeholder capitalism to adapt their firm's governance, management, reporting and partnerships to the new business operating context of the 2020s through the systematic integration of ESG&D considerations. The extent to which this integration is achieved in practice has an increasingly important bearing upon the performance, licence to operate and resilience of companies, whether they are publicly, privately or state owned. Accordingly, this business leadership agenda is relevant for consideration by any company and its stakeholders regardless of jurisdiction, ownership structure or business model. It is a call to action and practical resource for firms seeking to keep pace with changing economic circumstances and social expectations—to "walk the talk" of stakeholder capitalism. For business to maintain the public's trust and stakeholder capitalism to be more than an optimistic vision, boards and management teams must integrate these principles and practices across industry sectors and countries. Such integration is central to the art of business leadership in this new era—the key to creating long-term sustainable enterprise value for shareholders and other stakeholders alike.

## Notes

1. This chapter has been drawn from an earlier white paper, Richard Samans and Jane Nelson. *Integrated Corporate Governance: A Practical Guide to Stakeholder Capitalism for Boards of Directors*. World Economic Forum, June 2020.
2. World Economic Forum, "The Fourth Industrial Revolution, by Klaus Schwab", https://www.weforum.org/about/the-fourth-industrial-revolution-by-klaus-schwab
3. World Economic Forum. *Globalization 4.0: Shaping a New Global Architecture in the Age of the Fourth Industrial Revolution*. White Paper, 2019, http://www3.weforum.org/docs/WEF_Globalization_4.0_Call_for_Engagement.pdf
4. World Economic Forum. *Digital Transformation of Industry Initiative Executive Summary*. World Economic Forum in collaboration with Accenture, May 2018. http://reports.weforum.org/digital-transformation/wp-content/blogs.dir/94/mp/files/pages/files/dti-executive-summary-20180510.pdf
5. See, for example, International Renewable Energy Agency, *Renewable Power Generation Costs in 2019*, IRENA, June 2020. https://www.irena.org/-/media/Files/IRENA/Agency/Publication/2020/Jun/IRENA_Power_Generation_Costs_2019.pdf and Bloomberg New Energy Finance, *New Energy Outlook 2020*, https://www.statkraft.com/globalassets/0/.com/newsroom/2020/new-energy-outlook-2020.pdf
6. The Intergovernmental Panel on Climate Change (IPCC). The Working Group I contribution to the Sixth Assessment Report, *Climate Change 2021: The Physical Science Basis*. August 2021. https://www.ipcc.ch/assessment-report/ar6/
7. Task Force on Climate-related Financial Disclosures, TCFD 2020 Status Report, October 2020. Page 2. https://www.fsb.org/2020/10/2020-status-report-task-force-on-climate-related-financial-disclosures/
8. See https://sciencebasedtargets.org/companies-taking-action

9. These figures are as of June 2021. For updated figures on participants, see the Net Zero Asset Owner Alliance, https://www.unepfi.org/net-zero-alliance/ and the Net Zero Asset Managers Initiative, https://www.netzeroassetmanagers.org/#

10. European Commission, "State of the Union: Commission raises climate ambition and proposes 55% cut in emissions by 2030", 17 September 2020. https://ec.europa.eu/commission/presscorner/detail/en/IP_20_1599

11. The New York Times, "China in Pointed Message to the U.S., Tightens its Climate Goals," September 22, 2020. https://www.nytimes.com/2020/09/22/climate/china-emissions.html

12. The White House, "Executive Order on Tackling the Climate Crisis at Home and Abroad". January 27, 2021. https://www.whitehouse.gov/briefing-room/presidential-actions/2021/01/27/executive-order-on-tackling-the-climate-crisis-at-home-and-abroad/

13. World Economic Forum in collaboration with the Harvard Global Health Institute (2019) Outbreak readiness and business impact: Protecting Lives and Livelihoods across the Global Economy. http://www3.weforum.org/docs/WEF%20HGHI_Outbreak_Readiness_Business_Impact.pdf

14. Aon (2020) Weather, Climate and Catastrophe Insight. 2019 Annual Report.

15. Aon (2021) Weather, Climate and Catastrophe Insight. 2020 Annual Report

16. Edelman, "2018 Edelman Trust Barometer", 2018, https://www.edelman.com/sites/g/files/aatuss191/files/2018-10/2018_Edelman_Trust_Barometer_State_of_Business.pdf

17. See, for example, World Economic Forum, The Inclusive Growth and Development Report 2017 http://www3.weforum.org/docs/WEF_Forum_IncGrwth_2017.pdf and The Inclusive Development Index 2018, 2018, https://www.weforum.org/reports/the-inclusive-development-index-2018

18. Organisation for Economic Co-operation and Development, "Labour share developments over the past two decades: The role of technological progress, globalisation and 'winner-takes-most' dynamics", Economics Department Working Papers No. 1503, 2018, http://www.oecd.org/officialdocuments/publicdisplaydocumentpdf/?cote=ECO/WKP(2018)51&docLanguage=En

19. S&P Global, "The Big Picture on Climate Risk". Webinar, February 11, 2020. https://www.spglobal.com/marketintelligence/en/events/webinars/the-big-picture-on-climate-risk

20. Ceres. *Running the Risk: How Corporate Boards Can Oversee Environmental, Social and Governance (ESG) Issues.* November 2019. https://www.ceres.org/resources/reports/running-risk-how-corporate-boards-can-oversee-environmental-social-and-governance

21. ForgeRock. *2021 ForgeRock Consumer Identity Breach Report. The Year of the Great Digital Migration: How Usernames and Passwords Found Their Way Into the Crosshairs of Attackers.* https://www.forgerock.com/resources/view/122965273/analyst-report/forgerock-consumer-identity-breach-2021-report.pdf

22. Ibid. Page 2.
23. Ibid. Page 3.
24. Gopal Ratnam. "Cleaning up SolarWinds hack may cost as much as $100 billion", January 11, 2021. https://www.rollcall.com/2021/01/11/cleaning-up-solarwinds-hack-may-cost-as-much-as-100-billion/
25. Lambert, Lance, "#MeToo Pushes CEO Firings to a 15-Year High", Fortune Magazine, 6 November 2019.
26. Bank of America Merrill Lynch. ESG Matters—US, 10 reasons you should care about ESG, 23 September 2019.
27. Papadopoulos, Kosmas, "The Long View: US Proxy Voting Trends on E&S Issues from 2000 to 2008", Harvard Law School Forum on Corporate Governance and Financial Regulation blog, 31 January 2019.
28. Value Reporting Foundation, Sustainable Accounting Standards Board (SASB) Standards. https://www.sasb.org/standards/download/
29. Global Reporting Initiative. *GRI Sector Program—Revised list of prioritized sectors.* Approved by the Global Sustainability Standards Board (GSSB) on 19 November 2020. https://www.globalreporting.org/media/mqznr5mz/gri-sector-program-list-of-prioritized-sectors.pdf
30. Friedman, Milton, "The Social Responsibility of Business Is to Increase Its Profits", The New York Times Magazine, 13 September 1970.
31. Jensen, Michael and William Meckling, "Theory of the Firm: Managerial behavior, agency costs
    and ownership structure", Journal of Financial Economics, vol. 3, no. 4, October 1976, pp. 305–360.
32. For an overview of this literature, see, for example, Steve Letza, Xiuping Sun and James Kirkbride, "Shareholding Versus Stakeholding: a critical review of corporate governance," *Corporate Governance*, Blackwell, Volume 12, Number 3, July 2004, pp. 242—262; and John McVea and R.E. Freeman, "A Stakeholder Approach to Strategic Management," Darden Graduate School of Business Administration, University of Virginia, Working Paper 01—02, 2001. file:///C:/Users/SRI/Downloads/SSRN-id263511.pdf as well as R. E. Freeman et al., *Stakeholder Theory: The State of the Art*, The Academy of Management Annals, June 2010. https://www.researchgate.net/publication/235458104_Stakeholder_Theory_The_State_of_the_Art
33. R.F. Stewart, J.K. Allen, J.M. Cavendar: The Strategic Plan, LRPS report no 168, Long Range Planning Service, Menlo Park, Stanford Research Institute, 1963. For further background on the context on the discussions that led to this initial work, see, for example, R. E. Freeman, Harrison, J., Wicks, A., Parmar, B., & de Colle, S. (2010). *Stakeholder theory: The state of the art.* Cambridge, UK: Cambridge University Press; and Braun, Robert, (2019) *Corporate Stakeholder Democracy: Politicizing Corporate Social Responsibility*, Central European University, pp. 58–59.

34. http://www3.weforum.org/docs/WEF_KSC_CompanyStrategy_Presentation_2014.pdf

35. Freeman, R. E. (1984) *Strategic Management: A Stakeholder Approach*. Boston: Pitman, p. 5.

36. Bower, Joseph and Lynn Paine, "The Error at the Heart of Corporate Leadership", Harvard Business Review, May–June 2017.

37. Lipton, Martin, Wachtell, Lipton, Rosen & Katz, "It's Time to Adopt the New Paradigm", Harvard Law School Forum on Corporate Governance and Financial Regulation blog, 11 February 2019, https://corpgov.law.harvard. edu/2019/02/11/its-time-to-adopt-the-new-paradigm. See also World Economic Forum, "The New Paradigm: A Roadmap for an Implicit Corporate Governance Partnership Between Corporations and Investors to Achieve Sustainable Long-Term Investment and Growth", a document prepared for the International Business Council of the World Economic Forum by Martin Lipton of Wachtell, Lipton, Rosen & Katz, 2 September 2016.

38. Business Roundtable, "Business Roundtable Redefines the Purpose of a Corporation to Promote 'An Economy That Serves All Americans'", 19 August 2019, https://www.businessroundtable.org/business-roundtable-redefines-the-purpose-of-a-corporation-to-promote-an-economy-that-serves-all-americans

39. United Nations, UN Secretary-General, "Kofi Annan's address to the World Economic Forum in Davos", 1 February 1999, https://www.un.org/sg/en/content/sg/speeches/1999-02-01/kofi-annans-address-world-economic-forum-davos

40. World Economic Forum and the Prince of Wales International Business Leaders Forum. "Global Corporate Citizenship: The Leadership Challenge for CEOs and Boards." 2002. https://www.griequity.com/resources/integraltech/GRIMarket/WEFCEOglobalcorpcitizenship.pdf

    The CEOs who signed the statement came from the following companies (in alphabetical order): ABB; Abbott Laboratories; Abril Group; Accenture; Anglo American; Anglovaal Mining; Aramex International; Arthur D. Little; Artoc Group; Ayala Corporation; Bajaj Auto; The Boots Company; Budimex; Carlson Companies; The Coca-Cola Company; Codelco Chile; Deloitte; Deutsche Bank; DHL; Diageo; EDF; Empresas Polar; FleetBoston (Now Bank of America); Infosys Technologies; ING Group; Lafarge; McDonald's Corporation; Merck & Co.; MTR Corporation; Organizações Globo; Phillips-Van Heusen (PVH) Corporation; PwC; Renault; Rio Tinto; Royal Ahold; S.C. Johnson; Siemens AG; Statoil; Thames Water; Transnet; UBS AG; WMC Resources; and Xenel Industries.

41. Ibid.

    These three leadership challenges are taken verbatim from page 2 of the World Economic Forum and the Prince of Wales International Business

Leaders Forum. "Global Corporate Citizenship: The Leadership Challenge for CEOs and Boards." 2002.

42. World Economic Forum, Business for Social Responsibility, Harvard Kennedy School Corporate Responsibility Initiative, AccountAbility and International Business Leaders Forum, Partnering to Strengthen Public Governance: The Leadership Challenge for CEOs and Boards, 2008, https://www.bsr.org/reports/BSR_Davos08_Leadership-Challenge.pdf

43. Schwab, Klaus, "Global Corporate Citizenship: Working with Governments and Civil Society", Foreign Affairs, January/ February 2008, https://www.foreignaffairs.com/articles/2008-01-01/global-corporate-citizenship

44. Porter, Michael and Mark Kramer, "Creating Shared Value: How to reinvent capitalism—and unleash a wave of innovation and growth", Harvard Business Review, January–February 2011.

45. "UN Guiding Principles on Business and Human Rights", https://www.shift-project.org/un-guiding-principles

46. See, for example, the We Mean Business Coalition, https://www.wemeanbusinesscoalition.org/about/

47. UN Principles for Responsible Investment, "About the PRI", https://www.unpri.org/pri/about-the-pri

# 3

# Business Leadership Priorities for Implementing Stakeholder Capitalism

We have argued in Chap. 2 that major shifts in the drivers of enterprise value creation, risk management and societal expectations have substantially increased the financial materiality of environmental, social, governance and data stewardship (ESG&D) issues. This new materiality is compelling companies to transcend the traditional, segmented logic of shareholder and stakeholder considerations—exemplified by the concepts of shareholder primacy and corporate social responsibility—by integrating them, which is to say by systematically internalizing material ESG&D risks and opportunities into corporate governance, strategy, management and reporting.

Such integration is required to give practical effect to the principles and values of stakeholder capitalism. It is how companies implement and institutionalize their commitment to deliver sustainable enterprise value creation—how they "walk the talk" of stakeholder capitalism.

Business leaders who are pioneering this reset of enterprise value creation within their firms are implementing a wide variety of approaches. They are combining new governance, business and financing models with innovations in the way they invest in new technologies, markets and their people alongside more diverse and integrated approaches to risk management, stakeholder engagement, talent development, incentives and reporting. The specifics vary, based on different industry sectors, ownership and operating models, and on geographic reach, but this change agenda boils down to five key priorities:

© The Author(s) 2022
R. Samans, J. Nelson, *Sustainable Enterprise Value Creation*,
https://doi.org/10.1007/978-3-030-93560-3_3

1. Align governance, strategy and capital allocation with the key drivers of sustainable enterprise value creation
2. Internalize material ESG&D risks and opportunities into enterprise risk management and innovation
3. Reinforce preparedness and resilience to crises and systemic shocks
4. Recognize that the firm is a stakeholder itself in the vitality and resilience of its operating context and partner with other stakeholders to address relevant systemic challenges therein
5. Integrate financial and material non-financial information in mainstream reporting

Each of these leadership priorities is necessary, but not sufficient on its own. Success will be determined by the dynamic interaction between them and the agility and ability of boards and executive teams in working with key stakeholders to shape not only their own strategy and operating environment, but also the vitality and resilience of the broader system in which they operate and in which they themselves are stakeholders.

This chapter provides a *thematic* overview of this business leadership agenda[1]—a holistic picture of the *priority actions* business leaders need to embrace to respond effectively to both the current crisis and the secular forces reshaping our economies, societies, geopolitics and environment in the twenty-first century. Most of these leadership priorities touch on more than one corporate function and team, and hence Chaps. 4, 5, 6 and 7 in Part II present a *functional* view of this agenda, breaking it down into specific recommended practices, including best-practice illustrations of leading companies, for corporate governance and oversight, strategy and capital allocation, disclosure and accountability, and partnerships with other stakeholders. Specifically, Chap. 4 presents what full integration of ESG&D considerations means for board processes, practices and composition. Chapter 5 does the same for the C-suite and its responsibilities for strategy, resource allocation and other relevant executive practices. Chapter 6 provides a practical agenda to adapt corporate reporting to stakeholder capitalism: how firms should work with their accountants and auditors to strengthen accountability to investors and other stakeholders through construction of a disclosure "stack" having an integrated annual report as its foundation. And Chap. 7 interprets what heightened ESG&D materiality means for the role of companies as stakeholders themselves within a broader system—as actors with a material interest in and the ability to positively influence in concert with others the basic health of the social and economic ecosystems in which they operate.

## 3.1 Align Governance, Strategy and Capital Allocation with the Key Drivers of Sustainable Enterprise Value Creation

The ultimate purpose of a business is the creation of sustainable enterprise value for its shareholders and other stakeholders. This is the fundamental axiom of stakeholder capitalism, as expressed in the principles issued by the World Economic Forum (WEF) and Business Roundtable as well as various corporate governance statutes around the world. The first step in aligning a business with these principles is to rigorously test its business model, strategy and resource allocation priorities against them.

"Sustainable" takes on new meaning in a decade characterized by a deadly pandemic that has disrupted business continuity for millions of companies, dangerous climate change that poses existential risks to many businesses, so-called de-globalization that is challenging current business models and supply chains, and the technological disruption of the Fourth Industrial Revolution which is creating new risks and opportunities for every industry sector. In the midst of such change, boards and executive teams are re-examining old assumptions and taking the time to consult with key internal and external stakeholders to sharpen their shared understanding of the larger and longer-term social purpose their business model serves and how it benefits people, especially those producing and consuming its goods and services and their communities. Such an exercise in defining corporate purpose can be unifying and inspiring for the board, management, employees, suppliers and communities. It can also help to place consideration of the firm's governance, strategy and resource allocation priorities into wider and longer-term context, leading to more coherent decision-making on priorities for near-term performance and operational excellence.

Corporate strategy and capital allocation should also be tested against the firm's conception of its ultimate purpose and its commitment to sustainable enterprise value creation. The aim should be to ensure that they properly balance near-term returns and distributions to shareholders with investments in long-term competitiveness and growth opportunities, including increasingly important intangible drivers of value. These include research and innovation, employee well-being and empowerment, talent development, brand loyalty, corporate culture, and stakeholder relationships and public trust.

What is long-termism? An April 2020 report, *Tone at the Top: The Board's Impact on Long-Term Value* by Russell Reynolds Associates and Focusing Capital on the Long Term (FCLTGlobal) provides a useful summary:

> It is how boards and executives think and act in regard to the practice of applying a long-term approach to business and investment decision-making, including focusing on key elements of performance such as competitive advantage, long-term objectives and a strategic plan matched with clear capital allocation priorities. It stands in contrast to short-termism, or a continued focus on quarterly or other near-term performance issues and is increasingly in demand from stakeholders who want a fundamental rethink around how companies operate and create value.[2]

Consensus among leading investors and companies on the need for a greater board focus on long-termism has been gathering momentum for several decades, especially since the global financial crisis. Collective initiatives such as Focusing Capital on the Long Term, the Embankment Project for Inclusive Capitalism and the Aspen Institute's Business and Society programme on Long-Term Capital, among others, are developing important insights, tools and metrics to support boards and executive teams in driving long-term investment.

In 2017, the International Business Council of the World Economic Forum created *The Compact for Responsive and Responsible Leadership: A Roadmap for Sustainable Long-Term Growth and Opportunity*.[3] Signed by 145 major companies from 35 countries, the Compact commits firms to:

- Ensure the board oversees the definition and implementation of corporate strategies that pursue sustainable long-term value creation
- Encourage the periodic review of corporate governance, long-term objectives and strategies at the board level as well as clear communication between corporations, investors and other stakeholders about the outcomes
- Promote meaningful engagement between the board, investors and other stakeholders that builds mutual trust and effective stewardship and promotes the highest possible standards of corporate conduct
- Publicly support the adoption of the compact and implement policies and practices within the organization that drive transformation towards adherence to long-term strategies and sustainable growth for the benefit of all stakeholders

The overall aim of the Compact is to provide guidance for governance and investor relations practices to balance short- and long-term business practices. It has led to a body of work and related community on Active Investor Stewardship, with the goal of building a set of tools for stronger and more long-term focused investor-corporate relationships.[4]

Work by these and other initiatives continues to focus on two important enablers of long-termism. First is a growing body of empirical research and evidence to support the business case for boards to engage proactively with management on maintaining a long-term commitment to capital allocation while executing on shorter-term imperatives. Second are collective efforts that combine survey work, legal analysis and accounting methodologies to develop common metrics and reporting practices for long-term-oriented boards and investors.

For example, in 2017, research by the McKinsey Global Institute in cooperation with FCLTGlobal found compelling evidence that companies deliver superior results when executives manage for long-term value creation and resist pressures to focus excessively on meeting quarterly earnings expectations.[5] Using a dataset of 615 large- and mid-cap US publicly listed companies from 2001 to 2015, they created a five-factor Corporate Horizon Index (CHI) based on investment, earnings quality, margin growth, quarterly management and earnings-per-share growth. After controlling for industry characteristics and company size, their findings showed that companies classified as "long term" outperformed their shorter-term peers on a range of key economic and financial metrics. Specifically, they concluded that over the 14-year period, long-term firms:

- Exhibited stronger fundamentals and delivered superior financial performance
- Continued to invest in sources of growth, for example, R&D, even in difficult times
- Added more to economic output and growth, including job creation

Their findings for the period studied included evidence that

companies that operate with a true long-term mindset have consistently outperformed their industry peers since 2001 across almost every financial measure that matters. The differences were dramatic. Among the firms we identified as focused on the long term, average revenue and earnings growth were 47% and 36% higher, respectively, by 2014, and market capitalization grew faster as well. The returns to society and the overall economy were equally impressive. By our measures, companies that were managed for the long term added nearly 12,000 more jobs on average than their peers from 2001 to 2015. We calculate that

U.S. GDP over the past decade might well have grown by an additional $1 tril-lion if the whole economy had performed at the level our long-term stalwarts delivered—and generated more than five million additional jobs over this period.[6]

Despite this evidence, pressure on CEOs, CFOs and their teams to make decisions and take actions that bolster short-term, quarterly earnings con-tinue to be high. Their research also found "that 61% of executives and direc-tors say that they would cut discretionary spending to avoid risking an earnings miss, and a further 47% would delay starting a new project in such a situation, even if doing so led to a potential sacrifice in value. We also know that most executives feel the balance between short-term accountability and long-term success has fallen out of whack; 65% say the short-term pressure they face has increased in the past five years."[7]

Despite the progress made by leading companies over the past five years to integrate long-term goals into their strategy, capital allocation frameworks and incentives, investor pressure on companies to meet quarterly earnings targets and other short-term performance goals continues to be high. Boards and executive teams must continue to deliver short-term performance while demonstrating a compelling strategy for creating long-term value; however, more research is needed on the business benefits of long-termism and integra-tion of ESG&D risks and opportunities into core business goals and perfor-mance metrics.

For example, current accounting and reporting practices have not fully addressed the challenge of measuring and reporting the value of intangible assets.[8] As a result, there is still a significant discrepancy between market capi-talization and reported assets, on the order of two-to-one. This means that around 50% of market capitalization is effectively unaccounted for, creating a skewed view of an organization's ability to create long-term value. A central aspect of a firm's intangible capital is its human capital, the talent and engage-ment of its people, and this has long been an area of underinvestment by companies as well as governments. As outlined further in this book, other types of capital such as natural capital and social capital and other aspects of ESG&D performance are also key components of a firm's non-financial and intangible capital. As such, they need to be more rigorously understood, mea-sured and accounted for, with board oversight.

In their 2019 report, *Predicting Long-Term Success for Corporations and Investors Worldwide*, FCLTGlobal reviewed long-term performance in terms of Return on Invested Capital (ROIC), focusing on the large publicly traded companies in the MSCI All Country World Index (AWCI), which represents

85% of the global investable opportunity set.[9] They concluded that using Total Shareholder Return (TSR) rather than ROIC would have produced similar, if slightly weaker, results. Their analysis identified the following range of factors associated with the long-term health of companies:

- **Factors associated with higher long-term value creation:** Greater fixed investment; higher research quotient (RQ); greater board gender diversity; higher sales growth; and greater long-term investor presence.
- **Factors associated with lower long-term value creation:** Overdistribution of capital; ESG controversies; providing short-term guidance; and leverage ratio.[10]

There is obviously no simple 'one-size-fits-all' approach, and appropriate capital allocation will vary depending on factors such as industry, strategy, risk tolerance and growth profile. However, all companies should be engaged in ongoing, rigorous dialogue and analysis on how best to achieve long-term value creation while delivering short-term performance. Leading firms, for example, are reviewing performance targets and capital allocation plans through both a long- and a short-term lens as well as aligning director and executive compensation more closely to long-term success and investing more time in reviewing corporate culture and talent development beyond the executive team. They are allocating more dedicated time to strategy discussions and retreats to work through corporate purpose, its long-term value drivers and how these translate into immediate strategic and resource allocation priorities. And, as part of this process they are engaging with and learning from external perspectives to better understand long-term risks, disrupters and opportunities, speaking not only with key institutional investors but also with other stakeholders.

## 3.2 Internalize Material ESG&D Risks and Opportunities in Enterprise Risk Management and Innovation

The financial costs and loss of stakeholder trust stemming from failure to identify and address material ESG&D risks can reverse years of advances in market value and, in some cases, threaten a firm's very existence, especially if accompanied by high litigation and remediation costs and/or fines and increased regulatory oversight. These include risks relating to climate change;

corruption and financial crime; human rights and labour practices; and one of the most important drivers of innovation today, the collection, application and stewardship of data. Equally, failure to identify and invest in ESG&D-related business opportunities can undermine current and future innovation, productivity, revenue growth and competitiveness.

In this book, we have added "D," data stewardship, to the commonly used acronym, "ESG," environmental, social and governance issues, as we argue that it needs to be given a higher profile in the context of disruptive and widespread digitalization and the Fourth Industrial Revolution. In essentially every industry, the value-added application of data generated in the production and consumption of goods and services represents one of the most dynamic areas of new value creation today. And yet the way a company collects, applies and stores such data can have profound social externalities—that is, broader human impacts—either positive or negative. For example, lapses in the security of personal and other sensitive data or poor judgement in the deployment of algorithms in the workplace or the design of products and services sold to customers can backfire severely on firms, destroying trust, customer and employee loyalty and brand value. These stewardship considerations are similar in nature and potential material impact to the traditional areas of non-financial corporate performance and risk which have been characterized since at least 2004 as "ESG" factors.[11] In short, given the increasingly digital nature of economic activity and business value creation in the mid-twenty-first century, which has accelerated and scaled even further during the COVID-19 pandemic, it is time to update this construct by appending to it a "D" for data stewardship: ESG&D.

Material ESG&D risks and opportunities need to be integrated directly into core business strategy, goal setting and operations as well as internalized into broader enterprise risk management frameworks. In its 2018 report, *Enterprise Risk Management*, the World Business Council for Sustainable Development cooperated with the Committee of Sponsoring Organizations of the Treadway Commission (COSO) to release guidance for applying enterprise risk management approaches to ESG-related risks.[12] In addition to broad frameworks, there is a growing need for more topic-specific and technically rigorous guidance for companies desiring to strengthen their focus on specific ESG&D issues that represent the most material risks and opportunities to their business.

Following are examples of some of the most authoritative governance frameworks and tools that have been created for use by companies on the key ESG&D topics, which are relevant to most businesses regardless of industry sector, jurisdiction or ownership model. In addition, most strategic consulting and advisory firms, as well as a plethora of niche ESG&D consulting firms and non-profit organizations have or are developing guidance on corporate governance and management frameworks across a wide range of ESG&D risks and opportunities. Boards and executive teams wishing to internalize ESG&D factors into their firm's efforts to create and preserve value through diligent risk management and responsible innovation should ensure that their firms apply these frameworks and management systems or their equivalent.

Although the following sections are framed under the pillars of ESG&D, it is important to note that there are systemic linkages and feedback loops between each of these pillars. Many environmental challenges and negative externalities that are the heart of the "E," for example, create risks not only for the planet, but also for people and for human rights and livelihoods. Climate change is obviously an existential environmental risk, but also a massive financial and economic risk for business and for economies, and a threat to human rights and to millions of people's health and safety, livelihoods and living incomes. Corruption offers another cross-cutting example. While it is viewed as a key issue under "G," it not only creates legal, financial and reputational risk to companies and undermines good governance and economic growth, but also often facilitates environmental degradation and over-exploitation of natural resources, and it tends to increase inequality and undermine efforts to improve access to essential services, especially for the most vulnerable and excluded populations. Similar cross-cutting examples can be found for most other "E," "S," "G" and "D" issues. As such, leading companies need to understand each of these individual risks and opportunities in depth, which requires specific technical or professional expertise, as well as the linkages between them and how they either reinforce or undermine each other in the broader value chains and systems in which the company is operating. Understanding systems dynamics and complexity has become a key leadership imperative for responsible business and sustainable enterprise creation.

## 3.2.1 Environmental: The "E" in ESG&D

The over-riding environmental risk, and associated financial and resilience risk, facing most companies is the climate crisis. There are also business opportunities for those companies that set ambitious net-zero carbon emissions targets and invest in effective mitigation and adaptation strategies, technologies, processes and business models.

There are a growing number of governance and management frameworks to guide boards and executive teams in addressing climate change. Most notably, the Financial Stability Board's Industry Task Force on Climate-Related Financial Disclosures (TCFD) established a corporate governance framework in 2015 in respect of climate change that has begun to be adopted by companies and investors around the world.[13] As outlined in other chapters, the TCFD recommendations call on companies to report on how they are addressing climate change through their governance, strategy, risk management, and metrics and targets. The Climate Disclosure Standards Board (CDSB) and Sustainability Accounting Standards Board (SASB) have produced a joint TCFD Implementation Guide[14] and related set of Good Practices[15] for the reporting of climate-related performance and risk in mainstream corporate reports in line with the TCFD framework.

In 2019, the World Economic Forum issued a set of climate governance principles for boards of directors. Developed in collaboration with PwC, these are designed to help increase directors' climate awareness, embed climate issues into board structures and processes and improve navigation of the risks and opportunities that climate change poses to business.[16] In 2020, the Centre for Climate Engagement at Cambridge University, together with the World Economic Forum, established the Climate Governance Initiative to accelerate and scale the implementation of these principles by boards around the world. By providing a compass to enable more effective climate governance within companies, this framework provides boards with the right tools to make the best possible decisions for the long-term resilience of their organizations.

There is also growing urgency and momentum for companies in all industries, but especially the large carbon emitters, to establish science-based targets and plans to reach net-zero greenhouse gas (GHG) emissions, no later than 2050. Companies are increasingly required by regulators and investors to set and disclose annual progress towards an absolute and/or intensity GHG reduction target. Initiatives such as CDP, GRI and SASB provide frameworks for companies to measure and report on their GHG emissions. This is a step all organizations can take to increase both their internal operating efficiency and the pace at which society is implementing the goals set by the United Nations Paris Agreement.[17] Yet, while many current corporate commitments are important steps forward, they are not commensurate with the scale and urgency of the climate crisis. Best practice is now defined in terms of science-based targets,[18] aligning companies' GHG emission reduction targets with the well-below-2 °C and 1.5 °C emissions scenarios recommended by the scientists of the Intergovernmental Panel on Climate Change (IPCC) and enshrined in the Paris Agreement.

The increasingly urgent need for companies to understand and improve the management and governance of climate-related risks and opportunities has been the key driver in ensuring that environmental issues have become a boardroom topic across industry sectors. It is, however, not the only one. Depending on the industry sector, boards and management teams also need to be asking the same types of questions around their company's policies, strategies, risk management processes and targets for tackling other material environmental issues, such as water insecurity, nature loss in terms of biodiversity loss and land use trade-offs, and pollution, such as air, water and land pollution.

In all these areas, as with mitigating and adapting to climate change, there is a growing expectation that large companies will move beyond focusing only on improvements in their own operations and supply chains, although these remain crucial, to also addressing the more complex and systemic challenges associated with negative environmental externalities.

In the case of water, for example, companies are being called on not only to be responsible managers of fresh water in their own activities, but also stewards of the watersheds or river basins where they operate, and even advocates for water security, more broadly. As such, in addition to establishing plans and targets to mitigate negative environmental, social and economic impacts of their water usage and discharges and to improve the efficiency and other aspects of operational performance associated with water management in their own operations and supply chains, they are also establishing partnerships to address system-level water challenges.[19]

Over the past decade, there has been a growing focus on the linkages between biodiversity loss, land use systems and the unsustainable business models and policies that currently underpin global and local food systems. As the World Resources Institute and others have stated, "If today's levels of production efficiency were to remain constant through 2050, then feeding the planet would entail clearing most of the world's remaining forests, wiping out thousands more species, and releasing enough greenhouse gas emissions to exceed the 1.5 °C and 2 °C warming targets enshrined in the Paris Agreement—even if emissions from all other human activities were entirely eliminated."[20]

Companies operating at all stages of food and beverage value chains, as well as in the many other industries that rely extensively on the extraction and development of natural resources, from energy and mining to packaging, construction and even consumer electronics, need to focus not only on understanding their full impact on natural capital and establish strategies to minimize nature loss that is directly caused by their own operations but also take more ambitious steps to support regenerative or net positive approaches that contribute to nature and biodiversity recovery. As with other major operational and systemic environmental challenges, while there are costs in failing to act, there are also business opportunities in developing new technologies, products, services and business models to find solutions. The 2020 report, *The Future of Nature and Business*, provides some of the most rigorous empirical evidence to date on both the costs and opportunities and guidance on the best ways for companies to take action.[21]

There is also an urgent imperative to tackle the substantial growth in waste of non-biodegradable materials and products such as plastics, batteries, electronic devices and computers, glass and metals, which are increasing the need for landfills and creating pollution on land, in fresh water and the ocean. Leading companies are recognizing that they must move beyond traditional reduce, reuse and recycle approaches in their own operations, although these remain important, to develop new technologies and system-level circular economy models within larger systems such as industrial parks, cities, global supply chains and industries more broadly.[22] The World Economic Forum's Platform for the Circular Economy, the Ellen MacArthur Foundation and the Global Battery Alliance are three of a growing number of initiatives that provide useful guidance for companies that aim to be leaders in this area.

### 3.2.2    Social: The "S" in ESG&D

Effectively addressing the "S" in ESG&D requires a company to respect human rights, including the letter and spirit of labour standards, and to address the most salient risks that its operations and business relationships pose to people and their right to be treated with dignity. Almost all people-focused issues considered to be part of "S," such as diversity, inclusion and equity, minimum wages, living wages and pay ratios, and health, safety and well-being, are strengthened if a company builds on a strong foundation of the corporate responsibility to respect human rights and people's dignity.

Respect for labour standards is often a legal obligation. Many of the International Labour Organization's Conventions and Recommendations have been implemented by countries in national law and regulation.[23] Moreover, the ILO has identified eight "fundamental" Conventions in its Declaration on Fundamental Principles and Rights at Work (1998) covering: freedom of association and the effective recognition of the right to collective bargaining; the elimination of all forms of forced or compulsory labour; the effective abolition of child labour; and the elimination of discrimination in respect of employment and occupation. The ILO's 187 member countries have an obligation, by virtue of their membership in the organization, to work towards realizing these fundamental rights even if they have yet to ratify them. As of 2019, there were 1376 national ratifications of these Conventions, representing 92% of the possible number of ratifications.

The United Nations Guiding Principles on Business and Human Rights (UNGPs) have become the authoritative global standard on business and human rights.[24] They were developed over five years by a team led by Professor John Ruggie, the UN Secretary-General's Special Representative on Business and Human Rights, through extensive research, pilot projects and about 50 consultations around the world, engaging governments, business, civil society, the legal profession, academics and international organizations. In June 2011, they were unanimously endorsed by the United Nations Human Rights Council. The UNGPs clearly state that "all companies everywhere have a responsibility to respect human rights, which means to avoid having negative impacts on them and to address such impacts where they do occur. This responsibility applies to their own operations and to all their business relationships, including those throughout their value chain."[25] Over the past decade, they have been "increasingly incorporated or reflected in law, regulation, judicial and administrative decision-making, public policy, multistakeholder norms, commercial and financial transactions, the practices and policies of leading companies, and the advocacy of civil society."[26]

Boards and management teams should have oversight on the policies, due diligence processes, stakeholder engagement and remediation mechanisms their company has in place to respect human rights. Importantly, they should understand the human rights risks that are most salient to the people who are affected by the company's operations and business relationships and not only those that are material to the company, in terms of its own legal, financial, operational and reputational risks. The UK's Equality and Human Rights Commission has prepared *Business and Human Rights: A Five-Step Guide for Company Boards*, which provides useful guidance for boards on implementing the UNGPs.[27]

Increasingly there is an expectation that in addition to managing human rights risks within the company's own operations and value chain relationships, businesses should also understand the risks to people that result from their business models and the systems in which they are operating more broadly and should aim to use their leverage, which "refers to the ability of a business enterprise to effect change in the wrongful practices of another party that is causing or contributing to an adverse human rights impact."[28] There is also growing awareness of the links between respecting human rights and addressing environmental challenges, leading to a focus on topics such as climate justice.[29]

In addition to individual company policies and due diligence practices to respect human rights, a variety of industry-sector initiatives have evolved over the past decade that are focused on defining standards that companies operating in that sector should adhere to in respecting human rights. These are particularly prevalent and important in high-risk sectors such as oil, gas and mining, agriculture, apparel and other consumer goods manufacturing, tourism, financial services and information and communications technology. Extensive guidance also exists on specific issues, such as labour practices, employee health and safety, tackling discrimination and harassment and improving inclusion and diversity, community relations, indigenous peoples' rights, consumer and product safety and living wages. Boards should be aware of the collective initiatives relevant to their company and industry and understand if and how their company is adhering to these industry-wide or issue-specific standards.

Preventing discrimination and harassment based on race, religion, nationality, gender, sexual orientation, disability, age and other personal traits and characteristics is a key component of respecting human rights. There is also a growing imperative for boards and executive teams to be more proactive in addressing ways in which their company's corporate culture, behaviours, social norms and incentives are either promoting or impeding more diverse, inclusive and equitable working environments, value chains and communities.

Also relevant to the "S" in ESG&D is the importance of training and skills development, especially investments made by companies in the new types of skills and capabilities needed for the future in the Fourth Industrial Revolution. Corporate commitments to create employment opportunities, improve livelihoods and wealth generation and develop products and services that directly address social needs are other areas where businesses can make a vital contribution to improving the quality of people's lives and their opportunities to build assets and economic security. Finally, there is the role that companies can play to support local communities, build social capital and help to address broader social issues through their corporate social investments and philanthropy, product donations, employee volunteering and policy advocacy activities.

### 3.2.3   Governance: The "G" in ESG&D

Key governance issues include the composition and quality of a company's governing body and its committees, the rigour and transparency of its stakeholder engagement mechanisms, the systems it has in place to ensure strong risk management and oversight, and the company's policies, standards, audit processes and performance in areas such as ethics compliance and integrity, anti-corruption, anti-competitive behaviour and compliance with myriad laws and regulations in different countries.

An area of growing focus for many global companies is how to ensure a more holistic and systemic approach to tackling corruption that includes but goes beyond compliance to build a corporate culture of ethics and integrity. Useful guidance for boards is provided by the World Economic Forum Partnering Against Corruption Initiative (PACI), launched in 2004 in partnership with Transparency International and the Basel Institute on Governance.[30] The platform is CEO-led and focuses on public-private cooperation, responsible leadership and identifying and promoting technology advances in tackling corruption, through its Tech for Integrity programme.

In 2020, PACI endorsed an *Agenda for Business Integrity*. Developed by the Forum's Global Future Council on Transparency and Anti-Corruption, this framework is aimed at providing guidance to companies on achieving the following four pillars of leadership action in tackling corruption and strengthening integrity and transparency, all of which have implications for board oversight:[31]

* Commit to ethics and integrity beyond compliance
* Strengthen corporate culture and incentives to drive continuous learning and improvement
* Leverage technologies to reduce the scope of corruption
* Support collective action to increase scale and impacts

Another area of growing focus in the "G" of ESG&D is the increase in requests from investors and other stakeholders for greater transparency and public disclosure on corporate lobbying activities with governments and, where relevant, corporate political contributions to politicians and their parties. Increasingly, this includes requests for information on the company's financial and in-kind contributions to trade and industry associations, research institutions and non-profit, policy advocacy organizations. In an era of political polarization and growing mistrust among citizens about the relationships between regulators and the companies that they regulate, the board of directors needs to understand and provide oversight on the nature and range of the company's relationships with politicians, governments and policy advocacy organizations.

### 3.2.4  Data Stewardship: The "D" in ESG&D

Over the past several years, it has become increasingly clear across a wide range of industry sectors that company data protection and use are far more than technical or operational matters. They are first order strategic considerations that pose major—potentially existential—risks as well as important opportunities for competitive advantage. Accordingly, directors and management teams need to ensure that they have the skills and processes in place to perform these rapidly evolving dimensions of fiduciary and executive responsibility diligently.

#### Cybersecurity

In 2017, the World Economic Forum issued a first-of-its-kind resource to support boards of directors and CEOs to take action on cybersecurity and cyber resilience: *Advancing Cyber Resilience: Principles and Tools for Boards.*[32] Developed in collaboration with the Boston Consulting Group and Hewlett Packard Enterprise, the report is the product of an extensive process of collaboration and consultation that distilled leading practice into a framework and set of tools that boards can use to smoothly integrate cyber risk and resilience into business strategy so that their companies can innovate and grow securely and sustainably.

The Forum has since released a second resource aimed at corporate leadership teams more broadly, entitled *The Cybersecurity Guide for Leaders in Today's Digital World.* Produced by the Forum's public-private Centre for Cybersecurity,[33] the guide charts the key tenets of how cyber resilience in the digital age can be formed through effective leadership and design. From the steps necessary to think more like a business leader and develop better standards of cyber hygiene through to the essential elements of crisis management, it offers a practical cybersecurity playbook for business leaders.

## Artificial Intelligence (AI) and Machine Learning

As AI increasingly becomes an imperative for business models across industries, corporate leaders and boards will be required to identify the specific benefits this complex technology can bring to their businesses as well as address concerns about the need to design, develop and deploy it responsibly. Striking the right balance will lead to sustainable businesses in the Fourth Industrial Revolution, but failing to design, develop and use AI responsibly can damage brand value, risk customer backlash and lead to litigation and financial costs. Board members of all companies are responsible for stewarding their companies through the current period of unprecedented technological change related to AI, and its attendant societal impacts.

A practical set of tools can empower board members in asking the right questions, understanding the key trade-offs and meeting the needs of diverse stakeholders, as well as considering and optimizing approaches such as appointing a Chief Values Officer, Chief AI Officer or AI Ethics Advisory Board. The Forum has produced a board toolkit, *Empowering AI Leadership*.[34] Developed by its Centre for the Fourth Industrial Revolution, this framework was established in consultation with over 100 stakeholders. It is designed to help boards be responsible stewards of their companies' deployment of AI by more deeply understanding this transformational technology, asking the right questions, balancing trade-offs, meeting the needs of diverse stakeholders and formulating innovative governance approaches.

## Data Collection, Management and Use

Business models in virtually every industry are becoming more data intensive. Companies are routinely accumulating and applying a large amount of personal and commercially sensitive data via their interaction with customers, suppliers, employees and others. Optimizing the collection, management and use of such data is an increasingly important value creation driver; however, it also poses new material risks that boards cannot assume will be mitigated solely through compliance with regulatory requirements. A leading example of a company effort to formalize a stronger degree of data stewardship to maintain the trust of stakeholders and mitigate risk above and beyond regulatory compliance is Mastercard's framework of six principles for responsible data management. Its survey research suggests that an organization committing to these principles would help drive trust with upwards of 90% of individuals.[35]

## 3.3 Reinforce Preparedness and Resilience to Crises and Systemic Shocks

Company directors and executives need to understand and provide oversight on enterprise-level or specific operational, financial, reputational and regulatory ESG&D risks that their company or a particular business unit, project or product needs to address and mitigate. They also have an increasingly crucial role in ensuring their company's ability to respond to and be resilient in recovering from short-term or prolonged external crises and systemic shocks.

The reach and impact of these systemic risks and shocks range from global crises such as the COVID-19 pandemic and the 2008–2009 financial crisis to regional or location-specific currency crises, conflict and extreme weather events or other natural disasters, a growing number of which are exacerbated by a changing climate. Despite obvious differences between the types of crises and between locations and industry sectors, they share the common characteristic of being systemic in terms of their impact and beyond the control of any individual company to prevent.

The key question for any company is how well is it prepared to respond to such crises and how resilient is it in terms of its ability to survive the immediate aftermath and to recover, either by rebounding or by fundamentally changing and adapting, over the medium and longer term? Three key areas of focus that all boards and executive teams should consider are improving preparedness, responding to and managing the immediate crisis and strengthening recovery and future resilience.

### 3.3.1 Improving Preparedness

The ability of a company to respond to and recover from an acute or systemic crisis is obviously determined by a variety of external factors beyond the company's control. At the same time, the effectiveness of any response and recovery process also depends on the rigour and scope of the company's risk management systems and its crisis preparedness processes, combined with an adaptive and engaged corporate culture and the quality of leadership at both the executive and operational levels of the company. Boards should provide oversight and support to management in the following areas.

## Undertake Scenarios, Stimulations and Stress-Testing

As an ongoing process, boards and management teams need to undertake more regular and sophisticated scenario analysis, horizon-scanning activities and crisis management simulations and planning to better understand the likelihood and potential impact of systemic risks resulting from technological, environmental, geopolitical and socio-economic changes. Linked to this, they need a better understanding of the potential systemic risks to their company resulting from stress on key systems such as financial services, trade and supply chains and energy and health systems. Such understanding is needed at both global and enterprise level as well as operationally, especially in high-risk locations.

The practice of regulatory-led "stress-testing" has become common in the financial sector following the global financial crisis and more recently is being explored as an approach to assess business resilience in the face of climate-related risks.[36] This approach could be applied more widely as an internal corporate governance and management tool to help boards and management assess their company's preparedness and resilience for different types of crisis and system-level shocks. Key pillars of the organization's preparedness that should be assessed include governance and leadership structures and key components of operational, financial, technological and cultural resilience.

## Developing Crisis Succession Plans for Key Executives and Mission Critical Operators

Rigorous succession planning remains crucial at any time but deserves targeted board attention as part of crisis management and contingency planning. Chair and CEO succession plans are obviously essential, but boards also need to ensure there are succession plans in place and optionality for other members of the executive team and for "mission critical" roles and functions at the operating levels of the company. These are the leaders who will be essential in responding to and recovering from a crisis, especially in situations where peoples' safety and well-being are at stake or where business continuity is being challenged, either immediately or over a prolonged period. Alongside other executives, the human resource function has a critical place at the table on crisis preparedness and planning, and relevant Board Committees should review mission critical roles as well as executive succession plans on an ongoing basis.

## Reviewing Deployment Options for Emergency Response Assets and Relationships

In addition to crisis leadership planning, companies should have plans in place at both corporate and operating levels for essential assets that may need to be rapidly deployed and key stakeholder relationships that may need to be mobilized in the event of a crisis. Needs obviously vary based on the industry and location, but in all cases there is usually a need to consider internal asset deployment and stakeholder communications as well as external efforts. From an internal perspective, the company needs to understand how essential physical and financial assets can either be moved or be adapted to respond to a crisis as well as exploring alternative or back-up supply and distribution networks.

Companies that have products, services, digital platforms or physical logistics networks that are particularly important at times of a natural or man-made humanitarian disaster have an additional responsibility to understand and plan how these can best be deployed in a crisis. Leaders in the pharmaceutical, consumer goods, transport and logistics and information technology industries have long-standing experience in the latter, usually with board oversight. All companies, however, should review their assets and stakeholder relationships with a view to internal and external crisis response.

## 3.3.2    Responding to and Managing the Immediate Crisis

No matter how well prepared a company is, crises will happen—both acute, short-term crises affecting a particular location, business unit or key leader and more prolonged, systemic crises affecting the entire company. Boards need to be equipped to immediately respond to these. Sometimes the board or a senior non-executive director will be required to step directly into an executive role, but more often such crises require the board to support its senior management team.

The need to distinguish clearly between the roles of management and the board is probably greatest at the time of crisis management. Management teams will be working under intense pressure and time constraints, putting crisis response teams in place, implementing and often adapting existing crisis management plans, engaging with key stakeholders from employees, customers, suppliers and shareholders to communities and governments, depending on the crisis, and making a multitude of decisions, some of them mission critical. The board should be available to offer support, especially in the case of mission critical decisions, but not overload management with constant demands for information or meetings. Having said that, the following areas are important for boards to consider in most crisis situations, especially more systemic shocks.

## Put People First

This is crucial in a natural disaster or humanitarian crisis, but also relevant in a sustained economic or financial crisis. A key question is how is the company ensuring the immediate safety and well-being of people in its operations and value chain? Depending on the type of crisis, what are the health, safety, financial and job implications for employees, customers, suppliers (especially small businesses) and people in the company's local communities? After addressing immediate health and safety considerations, how are the livelihoods and incomes of the company's stakeholders being affected—both by the crisis itself and by the decisions the company is having to make in terms of business continuity and financial liquidity? What can the company do on its own to support its employees and other stakeholders who are adversely affected, and what type of government support and social welfare or safety nets can the company access or advocate for on behalf of these people? Linked to the above, how effectively are the CEO and management communicating with key stakeholders?

In response to the COVID-19 pandemic, for example, leading World Economic Forum representatives and members, including Klaus Schwab, Founder and Executive Chairman, Bank of America CEO Brian Moynihan, Siemens and Maersk Chairman Jim Snabe and Royal DSM Chairman Feike Sijbesma, called on their peers to support a set of "Stakeholder Principles" to manage the economic impacts from the public health emergency and work towards economic recovery. These outline a set of principles and commitments that business leaders and boards should make to their employees, ecosystem of suppliers and customers, end consumers, governments and society, and shareholders in helping them to respond to the crisis and build future resilience.[37]

The Forum has also produced additional guidance on Workforce Principles for the COVID-19 Pandemic.[38] Business Fights Poverty and the Corporate Responsibility Initiative at Harvard Kennedy School have developed a set of toolkits and hosted webinars on how companies can support the most vulnerable people among their employees, workers, customers, small business partners and communities in response to this global humanitarian and economic crisis.[39] Many national business associations and other corporate responsibility leadership groups have also activated their members to support people adversely affected by the pandemic.

## Support Critical Functions and Operations for Business Continuity

In some crises, business continuity will be impossible or seriously constrained, even if the company is not facing a liquidity crisis. In others, the focus will be on maintaining as much functional and operational capacity as possible to ensure that safe and if possible productive and profitable operations can continue. Questions that need to be addressed include: the effectiveness of plans to ensure that mission critical leadership and operational roles are sustained and given the support they need; understanding the extent of disruption in the company's key supply chains and its own ability to supply customers and what flexibility and optionality is available to address these; how effectively is the company engaging and where possible partnering with key suppliers and customers to resolve bottlenecks and shortfalls; and what, if any, are the trade restrictions and implications the company must address?

## Provide Oversight of Financial Risks and Resilience

Closely intertwined with business continuity is the obvious risk of financial liquidity and other financial challenges. At times of crisis, the board and management team need to review their current capital allocation strategies and priorities, as well as their engagement with key investors and regulators. For example, should they be stopping share buyback programmes, reviewing dividends and/or postponing capital projects? Are there opportunities to increase or at least maintain cost discipline? How proactively are the CEO and CFO engaging with investors? What actions should be taken to revise business plans and change operating and financial forecasts and guidance to the market? How can this be presented in a way that addresses the immediate crisis while also outlining longer-term resilience and recovery potential if possible? Are there crisis-related risks from activist shareholders or potential hostile takeover bids? From a compliance perspective, what, if any, are different financial reporting and disclosure requirements to be met in the immediate aftermath of a crisis and how is the company working with its auditors and legal advisers on addressing these? Are there tax implications and/or government support funds and incentives that can be accessed to help address immediate financial losses and manage ongoing risks?

### 3.3.3  Strengthening Recovery and Future Resilience

The length of time, intensity and global scope of a crisis management situation will obviously vary depending on the nature of the crisis and how systemic it is. As soon as possible, however, the board and management team should be reviewing medium and longer-term recovery plans and discussing lessons learned to strengthen the company's resilience for the future.

#### Start Reviewing Recovery Options and Strategy as Early as Possible

Boards should stay focused on the company's strategy and be ready to support management as they implement ramp-up options if business activities have been slowed or shut down due to a crisis. More importantly, following a crisis there may need to be changes or even a transformation in the company's policies and operating procedures, risk management systems, capital allocation priorities and even its core business strategy. Specific markets or industries may have changed fundamentally, and there may be new risks and opportunities emerging for the company as a result. After transitioning out of a crisis management phase there is a unique opportunity for the board and management team to review and where needed to either refresh or transform each of the above areas.

#### Build Future Operational, Cultural, Financial and Technological Resilience

Linked to the above, crises nearly always provide useful lessons for improving risk management and stakeholder engagement. More broadly, they often point to the need and opportunity to strengthen a company's resilience, its ability to respond to and recover from future crises. Even in the absence of a crisis, the nature of the technological, environmental, geopolitical and social shifts underway is placing a greater premium on the concept and practice of resilience as a crucial and more strategic element of effective risk management. Research by a variety of practitioners and academics points to the need for boards and management to review resilience through the combined lenses of operational, cultural, financial and technological capabilities and abilities to withstand systemic risks and shocks.

Building long-term and trusted relationships with external stakeholders is another important element in building resilience. At times of crisis, these relationships can be key to the company and its employees, customers, business partners and communities being able to respond and recover. And they usually need to be built over time. As previously outlined, applying the concept of "stress-testing" to these different aspects of resilience offers potential. Likewise with boards and management jointly undertaking scenario analysis and crisis simulation exercises. In the same way that boards are taking a more proactive role in engaging in strategy and long-term value creation discussions with management, there is a need for more systematic board-level discussions around strengthening business resilience.

## 3.4    Recognize the Firm Is a Stakeholder Itself in the Vitality and Resilience of Its Operating Context

Recent events, from the COVID-19 pandemic to trade policy shocks to social protests over inequality and discrimination to changes in energy and financial regulation related to climate change, illustrate that companies have a very material stake in the basic health of their operating context—in the essential functioning of the societies and economies in which they operate. Major disruptions therein can have a serious, even existential, impact on businesses. Even though principal responsibility for these matters often resides in public institutions and authorities, company practices and operations can have an important influence, either positive or negative.

Four critical dimensions of the way in which firms guided by the principles of stakeholder capitalism need to think seriously about their shared stewardship of the social and economic context in which they operate are as follows: the capacity of people in the firm's communities to absorb and manage economic change; the payment of taxes and capacity of public institutions to provide public goods on which all societal actors, including companies, depend; the extent of structural inequality and injustice and adequacy of existing public and private responses to address these; and the relevance of the firm's core competencies and resources to support national governments in implementing their priority commitments to the Sustainable Development Goal (SDG) and Paris Climate Agreement.

### 3.4.1   Collective Investment in Human Capital and a Just Transition

One of the principal weaknesses, even failings, of corporate and public governance during the past generation has been an underappreciation of and underinvestment in the human costs of rapid economic change. A new dimension of corporate governance and leadership requiring attention from boards and executive teams is the need to identify salient just-transition risks related to automation, restructuring, climate change abatement or other plans to move to a low carbon economy. This challenge is likely to intensify in the Fourth Industrial Revolution as automation spreads, global markets become more digitally interconnected and actions to decarbonize economic activity intensify. Companies will be the primary vehicles of these economic changes, which means they will face important decisions with regard to the timeline and nature of the corresponding restructuring and redeployment of their workforces and making human capital investments in the communities or regions where they operate.

In the absence of an understanding of what constitutes a just transition for people and a strategy to make such a transition as humane and economically orderly as possible in cooperation with workers, governments and other stakeholders, companies may inflict severe yet avoidable damage on the social fabric of the communities and countries in which they operate. This could ultimately affect the political stability and economic viability of that context, limiting the company's own prospects for value creation and growth. Accordingly, a new dimension of business leadership requiring attention from boards and management teams is the need to identify salient just-transition risks related to automation, restructuring, climate change or other plans and to ensure that the company has adequate policies and practices for mitigating them.

In 2015, governments and worker and employer organizations developed a set of consensus guidelines for steps that can be taken by each to manage change and its impact on the world of work, which is to say, on people.[40] These ILO guidelines were written with environmental change and the transition to more sustainable economies specifically in mind; however, many of the suggestions are relevant for managing major transitions and their impact on workers and their communities related to other causes. The trade union movement has taken an active role in advancing the just-transition concept and supporting social dialogue—tripartite government-worker-employer discussion and consensus building—on specific transition risks, opportunities and solutions in this regard.[41] Governments, too, are increasingly active on this topic. For example, the European Union has created a Just Transition Mechanism to provide concrete support to the transition to a climate-neutral economy. It provides "targeted support to help mobilise at least €65–75 billion over the period 2021–2027 in the most affected regions, to alleviate the socio-economic impact of the transition."[42]

## 3.4.2    Fair Payment of Taxes to Support Public Goods and Services

Government tax bases have come under pressure, as digitization, deregulation, trade liberalization and global value chains have increased the economies of scale and geographical fragmentation of production as well as the capital share of national income in many countries. This situation has been further exacerbated by the COVID-19 pandemic and the heavy and urgent demands it has placed on public finances. Long-term economic value creation requires functioning public institutions in a wide variety of domains, and these depend on adequate public finances.

Thus, companies have not only a legal obligation to pay taxes, but also a broader fiduciary responsibility stemming from their sustainable enterprise value creation mandate to ensure that they pay their fair share, which may not always be the same amount as that resulting from aggressive, multi-jurisdictional corporate tax planning. Directors and executives have a responsibility to ensure that their firms are acting not only legally but also in keeping with the trust that society has placed in them to contribute fairly and responsibly to the long-term viability of the economy in which they operate.

The OECD's Inclusive Framework on Base Erosion and Profit Shifting brings together over 115 countries and jurisdictions to collaborate on the implementation of the OECD/G20 Base Erosion and Profit Shifting (BEPS) Package. BEPS refers to corporate tax-planning strategies that exploit gaps and mismatches in tax rules to artificially shift profits to low- or no-tax locations where there is little or no economic activity. Although some of the schemes used are illegal, most are not. The BEPS Package provides 15 actions that equip governments with the domestic and international instruments needed to ensure that profits are taxed where the economic activities generating the profits are performed and where value is created. These tools also give businesses greater certainty by reducing disputes over the application of international tax rules and standardizing compliance requirements.

This initiative took a major step forward in 2021 when the G7 and G20 endorsed the approach outlined the "Statement on a Two-Pillar Solution to Address the Challenges Arising from the Digitalisation of the Economy" which the OECD released in July of that year.[43] As of mid-August 2021, 133 jurisdictions had signed the Statement; however, support for it is not yet unanimous.

In 2020, the Global Reporting Initiative issued a new global standard for public reporting on tax payments by corporations. The standard contains three management approach disclosures and one topic-specific disclosure on country-by-country reporting. The combination of management approach disclosures and country-by-country reporting gives insight into an organization's tax practices in different jurisdictions. Boards should have oversight of these practices, including transparency and reporting. In addition, the World Economic Forum's International Business Council as part of its *Measuring Stakeholder Capitalism* project has recommended that firms disclose the total global tax borne by the company, including corporate income taxes, property taxes, non-creditable VAT and other sales taxes, employer-paid payroll taxes and other taxes that constitute costs to the company, by category of taxes. It further recommends as a best practice a breakdown of total tax paid and, if reported, additional tax remitted, by country for significant locations.

### 3.4.3   Tackling Structural Inequality and Injustice

In many countries, deep-seated inequality and injustice persist, even after changes in regulation, government policies, business practices and social norms. Although capitalism, globalization and market-based economic growth have helped lift several billion people out of extreme poverty over the past few decades, in too many cases inequality has increased in terms of asset accumulation and wealth creation, access to jobs and essential services, such as education, health and housing, and access to criminal and social justice and political voice. The COVID-19 crisis has highlighted and exacerbated many of these existing structural inequalities and hundreds of millions of people risk falling back into poverty due to the pandemic's devastating impact on their health and food security, their livelihoods, jobs and income and their education and learning. Governments must take the lead in addressing these issues. At the same time, there is a growing expectation among employees, consumers, activists, the public and even investors and governments themselves that businesses, especially large companies, should play a more proactive role in tackling inequality and injustice.

There is the growing expectation that companies should be responsible and held accountable for: the impact of their own operations and business relationships when it comes to respecting human rights, workers' rights and civil rights; promoting diversity, equity and inclusion in their own workplaces and global value chains; as outlined in previous pages, paying their fair share of taxes; and making investments in skills development and a just workforce transition for relevant employees and communities where they operate.

At the same time, pressure is growing for companies to pay adequate entry-level wages to become advocates for higher minimum wage legislation in many countries and to commit to paying a living wage for their immediate employees and workers along their global supply chains if this is higher than the legally mandated minimum wage in the locations where the company operates. The Global Living Wage Coalition has drawn on the ideas found in over 60 living wage descriptions and definitions to define a living wage as "[t]he remuneration received for a standard workweek by a worker in a particular place sufficient to afford a decent standard of living for the worker and her or his family. Elements of a decent standard of living include food, water, housing, education, health care, transportation, clothing, and other essential needs including provision for unexpected events."[44]

Millions of workers around the world earn less than a minimum wage, let alone a living wage, and in many cases, it is women and racial or ethnic minorities who are the most vulnerable to the combination of low wages and insecure jobs. Take the US, for example, where efforts to raise the federal minimum wage from US $7.25 to $15 per hour failed in 2021. It is estimated that "[a]bout 39 million people earned less than $15 in 2019. That is a substantial decline from more than 61 million in 2014, and it fell further—to around 30 million—after the covid-19 crisis as the closures of countless low-wage employers erased millions of jobs. Black and Hispanic women are more than twice as likely as White men to fall into this low-wage category, and their share of the low-wage workforce has increased even as the U.S. economy enjoyed its longest expansion in history."[45] Tackling this systemic issue, and focusing on the most vulnerable workers, will be a key driver in achieving more inclusive growth.

Improving access to paid sick leave, health insurance and other benefits for low-income, low-skilled and/or temporary, contractual and gig economy workers are other systemic challenges that underpin inequality and must be addressed to achieve more inclusive business models and economies.

Beyond their own business operations, there are growing demands for business leaders to step up, both individually and collectively, to help address systemic and structural obstacles to overcoming inequality and injustice. For example, a vanguard of companies is establishing and creating coalitions to advocate for higher minimum wages and to make commitments to implementing living wages in their own operations and supply chains. One example is Business for Inclusive Growth, which was launched by the French G7 Presidency in August 2019. It is a global CEO-led coalition working in partnership with the OECD to coordinate with governments in tackling inequalities of income and opportunity. Collective business efforts are also needed to support specific government or community-based programmes focused on improving access to education, healthcare, housing and economic opportunities. In addition, companies can become more engaged in advocacy for public policy reforms and institutional changes such as implementing better social safety nets, access to universal health, direct cash transfer mechanisms and criminal justice reform.

There are of course limits to what companies can influence on deep-seated social challenges. But there are also limits to how much a company can remain insulated from such problems. If severe and long-standing enough, and the firm has a track record of being passive and insensitive to them, they can evolve into threats to its brand and even business continuity in the event of social upheaval. Companies need to have a serious internal discussion about their role as stakeholders in the basic health of their operating context and their agency to affect it positively. This should take place not only at the corporate level, but it should also be encouraged in areas in which the firm has significant operations.

### 3.4.4 Advancing Implementation of the Sustainable Development Goals and Paris Climate Agreement

In September 2015, 193 UN member states signed up to support the 2030 Agenda and its 17 Sustainable Development Goals (SDGs). They were followed in December 2015 by 196 countries committing to support the Paris Climate Agreement, and its core goal to limit global warming to well below 2, preferably to 1.5 °C, compared to pre-industrial levels. Most governments are now translating these commitments into national plans and policy priorities, described as National SDG Plans or Voluntary National Reviews in the case of the SDGs and Nationally Determined Contributions (NDCs) in the case of the Paris Agreement. In both cases, the private sector has a place at the table and a major responsibility and opportunity to work with other companies, civil society organizations, the UN system and national, state and local governments to help achieve these ambitious and urgent goals.

The corporate responsibility to be part of the systems-level changes that are required is clear. There can be little doubt about the urgency and scale of the climate crisis and the inadequate progress that has been made on achieving the SDGs, further challenged by the devastating effects that the COVID-19 pandemic has had on the lives, livelihoods and learning of millions of people. The business risks and costs of inaction are increasingly well understood. They are operational and physical, they are financial, they are reputational, they are transitional in terms of companies having to adapt to changing policies and regulations, disruptive technologies and new markets, and in some cases, they are existential to corporate survival. Furthermore, they are rising for almost all companies that fail to act.

The corporate opportunity to be part of the solution to tackling the climate crisis and achieving the SDGs is also high, especially for companies that can operate at scale, work with industry peers and competitors on system-level solutions and engage with governments on driving policy reforms and market incentives. Setting goals for cutting carbon emissions and achieving net zero by 2050 can spur companies and entire industries to greater resource efficiencies, lower emissions energy sources, innovative products, services and technologies, new markets and greater resilience and ability to prepare for or recover from shocks and crises. Likewise, the SDGs represent an enormous growth opportunity for businesses, including through strengthening their operating context. The Business and Sustainable Development Commission, for example, has concluded that achieving the SDGs has the potential to generate up to $12 trillion of opportunities in 60 different market segments within four economic systems: food and agriculture, cities, energy and materials, and health and well-being.[46]

Accordingly, companies focused on sustainable enterprise value creation should make commitments to support the Paris Climate Agreement and the SDGs that are relevant to their firm's core competencies and markets and integrate these into their company strategy and operations. This includes appointing senior executives and identifying board and executive champions to prioritize and drive execution as well as working with peer companies, financial institutions, governments and other stakeholders to drive the enabling environment improvements and investments that can affect the necessary transformation of economic systems. As outlined in more detail in Chap. 7, there are a growing number of multi-stakeholder coalitions that are being established to achieve the system-level changes that are needed. In line with the theme of its 50th Annual Meeting in 2020, *Stakeholders for a Cohesive and Sustainable World*, the World Economic Forum and its International Business Council prepared a report that presented over 150 concrete examples of such multi-stakeholder and corporate "lighthouse" projects.[47]

## 3.5   Integrate Financial and Material Non-financial Information in Mainstream Reporting

Integrated reporting follows naturally from the integrated thinking that the simultaneous pursuit of long-term shareholder, other stakeholder and societal value—that is, sustainable enterprise value—requires. In practical terms, this means integrating material ESG&D considerations into the company's core communications with its investors and in particular its annual report, including as appropriate in the statement of accounts and management discussion and analysis and proxy statements. In some cases, companies are aligning their annual financial reports and annual sustainability reports to providing investors and other stakeholders with clear and consistent performance metrics and analysis of risks and future goals. However, best practice and to a growing extent regulatory requirement is to combine and connect these elements in an integrated report which serves as the firm's mainstream communication with its providers of capital and securities regulators. A further best practice is to have the ESG&D elements in the report independently assured by an external third party along the same lines that financial accounts are externally audited.

The integrated reporting of ESG&D risk, strategy and performance in mainstream corporate communications with investors and regulators remains at a formative stage, but it is evolving rapidly. A number of collaborative efforts over the past 20 years among non-governmental organizations, accountants, industrial firms and investors have laid the foundation for this approach. They include:

* The International Integrated Reporting Council has developed a principles-based framework to help companies think about their reporting strategy in an integrated fashion and develop their own approach spanning various reporting formats, mainstream and otherwise.
* The Global Reporting Initiative issued the first global standards for sustainability reporting, which are designed to be used by any organization that wants to report on its impacts and how it contributes towards sustainable

development. They encourage and enable credible non-financial reporting by companies and also provide sector-specific guidance.

- The Sustainability Accounting Standards Board has created a set of key performance indicators that serve as a standard for particularly quantitative reporting of material aspects of a company's environmental and social sustainability. It provides materiality maps for companies in 77 different industry sectors.
- The Climate Disclosure Standards Board has issued a framework to guide the reporting of material natural capital-related aspects of corporate performance, strategy and risk—both qualitative and quantitative material information—in mainstream reports.
- CDP is the foremost global platform for the disclosure of climate and other environmental data by companies, investors and other stakeholders and, as such, serves as a de facto standard.
- In an effort to accelerate progress towards a more harmonized and globally comparable system for disclosure of material ESG&D information, the WEF's International Business Council of approximately 120 large multinational firms has developed a two-tier core-and-expanded set of ESG&D metrics and reporting requirements in collaboration with the four largest accounting firms, drawing wherever possible from existing standards such as those referenced above.
- The Human Rights Reporting and Assurance Frameworks Initiative (RAFI) and the UN Guiding Principles Reporting Framework provide guidance for companies to report on salient human rights issues.
- The Corporate Reporting Dialogue has been facilitating a dialogue among sustainability and financial standard setters to advance progress towards a system that better captures and integrates financial and non-financial performance and strategy.
- The Impact Management Project (IMP) is a forum for organizations to build consensus on how to measure, compare and report impacts on environmental and social issues. It convenes a Practitioner Community of over 2000 organizations to debate and find consensus (norms) on impact management techniques and it facilitates a collaboration of organizations that are coordinating efforts to provide complete standards for impact measurement, management and reporting.

Notwithstanding the considerable progress achieved by the voluntary initiatives described above, the absence of a generally accepted international framework for the reporting of material aspects of ESG and other relevant considerations for long-term value creation contrasts with the well-established standards that exist for reporting and verifying financial performance. The existence of multiple ESG measurement and reporting frameworks and lack of consistency and comparability of metrics hinder the ability of companies to credibly demonstrate the progress they are making on sustainability, including their contribution to the SDGs.

As outlined in greater detail in Chap. 6, there are two things business can do to accelerate the adaptation of corporate reporting to stakeholder capitalism. First, individual firms should implement their own integrated reporting in the form of a combined, best-practice application of existing standards in their annual report. This will ensure that their reporting is fit for the purpose of sustainable value creation in today's new business context and can be benchmarked against comparable information from other firms for use in decision-making in both their boardroom and financial markets. There is no need to wait for further action by regulators; better returns and more satisfied investors and other stakeholders await those companies that act to integrate and improve their disclosure now. Second, business leaders, including colleagues from the investor and accounting communities, should work to accelerate the birth of an international standard or system of standards for non-financial information reporting, similar to how the private sector played a critical leadership role in the early stages of financial reporting standard setting. The International Organization of Securities Commissioners (IOSCO) and International Financial Reporting Standards (IFRS) Foundation have announced plans to create such a global standard. They will need strong engagement from the private sector in order to succeed.

\*  \*  \*

This chapter has provided a thematic overview of the key priorities business leaders should embrace and guidance tools they can access to embed sustainable enterprise value creation more deeply within their firm and to help translate the principles of stakeholder capitalism into more rigorous and widespread practice. But while these *principles* may be universally applicable, their *practice* is context specific. There is no single ideal approach to addressing these issues and applying good practice because ESG&D issues vary in relevance and emphasis across industrial sectors and societies. The practical implementation of stakeholder capitalism is fundamentally about institutionalizing *integrated thinking and decision-making* in board governance, corporate strategy and resource allocation, reporting and partnerships with other stakeholders in ways that enable the full integration of ESG&D considerations. Chapters 4, 5, 6 and 7 provide more specific, functional guidance in each of these respects, with concrete illustrations of good practice drawn from leading companies.

# Notes

1. Parts of this chapter have been drawn from an earlier white paper, Richard Samans and Jane Nelson, *Integrated Corporate Governance: A Practical Guide to Stakeholder Capitalism for Boards of Directors*, World Economic Forum, June 2020.
2. Russell Reynolds Associates and FCLTGlobal Focusing Capital on the Long Term. *Tone at the Top: The Board's Impact on Long-Term Value*. April 2020. https://www.russellreynolds.com/insights/thought-leadership/tone-at-the-top-the-boards-impact-on-long-term-value
3. World Economic Forum. *The Compact for Responsive and Responsible Leadership*, 2017, http://www3.weforum.org/docs/Media/AM17/The_Compact_for_Responsive_and_Responsible_Leadership_09.01.2017.pdf
4. See World Economic Forum. Shaping the Future of Investing. https://www.weforum.org/platforms/shaping-the-future-of-investing/articles
5. Dominic Barton, James Manyika and Sarah Keohane Williamson, "Finally, Evidence that Managing for the Long Terms Pays Off," *Harvard Business Review*, February 9, 2017. https://hbr.org/2017/02/finally-proof-that-managing-for-the-long-term-pays-off
   See also: Dominic Barton et al. *Measuring the Economic Impact of Short-Termism*. McKinsey & Company, McKinsey Global Institute, Discussion Paper. February 2017.
   Dominic Barton, Jonathan Bailey and Joshua Zoffer. *Rising to the Challenge of Short-Termism*. FCLTGlobal, Focusing Capital on the Long Term. 2016.
6. Dominic Barton, James Manyika and Sarah Keohane Williamson, "Finally, Evidence that Managing for the Long Terms Pays Off," *Harvard Business Review*, February 9, 2017. https://hbr.org/2017/02/finally-proof-that-managing-for-the-long-term-pays-off
7. Ibid.
8. See, for example, Lev, Baruch Itamar, Intangibles (July 23, 2018). Available at SSRN: https://ssrn.com/abstract=3218586 or https://doi.org/10.2139/ssrn.3218586
9. FCLTGlobal. *Predicting Long-term Success for Corporations and Investors Worldwide*. September 29, 2019, https://www.fcltglobal.org/resource/predicting-long-term-success-for-corporations-and-investors-worldwide/
10. Ibid.
11. UN Global Compact. *Who Cares Wins: Connecting Financial Markets to a Changing World*. Recommendations of the financial industry to better integrate environmental, social and governance issues in analysis, asset management and securities brokerage. December 2004.

12. Committee of Sponsoring Organizations of the Treadway Commission and World Business Council for Sustainable Development. *Enterprise Risk Management: Applying enterprise risk management to environmental, social and governance-related risks*. October 2018.

13. For details on the Task-Force on Climate-Related Financial Risk (TCFD) and its recommendations and progress updates, see: https://www.fsb-tcfd.org/

14. Climate Disclosure Standards Board and Sustainability Accounting Standards Board. *TCFD Implementation Guide*. 2019. https://www.cdsb.net/tcfd-implementation-guide

15. Climate Disclosure Standards Board and Sustainability Accounting Standards Board. *TCFD Good Practice Handbook*. 2019. https://www.cdsb.net/tcfd-good-practice-handbook

16. World Economic Forum in collaboration with PwC. *How to Set Up Effective Climate Governance on Corporate Boards: Guiding principles and questions*. 2019.

17. See Richard Samans, "How to Make Global Climate Action Go Viral", Forbes, 6 November 2018.

18. See Science-Based Targets Initiative, https://sciencebasedtargets.org/

19. Callie Stinson and Jane Nelson, "3 actions business leaders can take to solve our water crisis." World Economic Forum Agenda, 20 January 2020. https://www.weforum.org/agenda/2020/01/3-actions-business-leaders-can-take-to-tackle-the-worlds-water-crisis/

    See also: Elsa Galarza Contreras and Jane Nelson, "Why the answer to water insecurity is working together." World Economic Forum Agenda, 25 January 2018. https://www.weforum.org/agenda/2018/01/why-the-answer-to-water-insecurity-is-working-together/

20. World Resources Institute. *Creating a sustainable food future: A menu of solutions to feed nearly 10 billion people by 2050*. World Resources Institute with The World Bank Group, United Nations Environment Programme, UNDP, cirad, and INRA. July 2019. Page 1. https://research.wri.org/sites/default/files/2019-07/WRR_Food_Full_Report_0.pdf

    See also: Juergen Voegele and Jane Nelson. "4 priorities in the race to build a sustainable food system." World Economic Forum Agenda, 18 January 2019. https://www.weforum.org/agenda/2019/01/four-priorities-to-help-fix-the-global-food-system/

21. World Economic Forum in collaboration with AlphaBeta. *The Future of Nature and Business. New Nature Economy Report II*. 2020. https://www.weforum.org/reports/new-nature-economy-report-ii-the-future-of-nature-and-business

22. For a good overview on the definition and priorities of the circular economy and the role of companies, see the work of the Ellen Macarthur Foundation: https://ellenmacarthurfoundation.org/

23. For further information on international labour standards and their application in national regulation, see ILO, *Rules of the Game: An Introduction to the Standards-related Work of the International Labour Organization*, 2019. https://www.ilo.org/wcmsp5/groups/public/%2D%2D-ed_norm/%2D%2D-normes/documents/publication/wcms_672549.pdf

24. United Nations Human Rights Office of the High Commissioner. *Guiding Principles on Business and Human Rights: Implementing the United Nations "Protect, Respect, and Remedy" Framework*. OHCHR. 2011 https://www.ohchr.org/documents/publications/guidingprinciplesbusinesshr_en.pdf

25. Shift, *UN Guiding Principles on Business and Human Rights*, https://www.shiftproject.org/un-guiding-principles

26. John Sherman. *Beyond CSR: The Story of the UN Guiding Principles on Business and Human Rights* (March 25, 2020). Chapter 22, Rae Lindsay and Roger Martella (eds), "Corporate Responsibility, Sustainable Business: Environmental, Social and Governance Frameworks for the 21st Century" (Kluwer Law International), June 2020. Available at: https://papers.ssrn.com/sol3/papers.cfm?abstract_id=3561206

27. UK Equality and Human Rights Commission, *Business and Human Rights: A Five-Step Guide for Company Boards*, 2016, https://www.equalityhumanrights.com/sites/default/files/business_and_human_rights_web.pdf

28. Ashleigh Owens. *Using Leverage to Drive Better Outcomes for People.* The Shift Project, July 2021. https://shiftproject.org/resource/using-leverage-to-drive-better-outcomes-for-people/

29. Zahid Torres-Rahman, Jane Nelson and Tara Shine. *Business and Climate Justice: Putting people at the heart of climate action.* Business Fights Poverty with the Corporate Responsibility Initiative, Harvard Kennedy School, March 2021. https://businessfightspoverty.org/business-and-climate-justice-putting-people-at-the-centre-of-climate-action/

    See also: John Gerard Ruggie, Caroline Rees and Rachel Davis, "Ten Years After: From UN Guiding Principles to Multi-Fiduciary Obligations," Business and Human Rights Journal. Volume 6. Issue 2, June 2021, pp. 179–197. Published online by Cambridge University Press.

    Caroline Rees. *Building Bridges for Impact.* A podcast series on the role that business should play in building a sustainable and equitable future, based on respect for people's dignity and fundamental rights. The Shift Project, 2021 https://shiftproject.org/bridges/

30. World Economic Forum. Partnering Against Corruption Initiative. https://www.weforum.org/communities/partnering-against-corruption-initiative

31. World Economic Forum. *Agenda for Business Integrity.* WEF Global Future Council on Transparency and Anti-Corruption, 2020–2021. http://www3.weforum.org/docs/WEF_GFC_Overview_Agenda_for_Business_Integrity.pdf

32. World Economic Forum in collaboration with Boston Consulting Group and Hewlett Packard Enterprise, *Advancing Cyber Resilience: Principles and Tools for Boards*, 2017, http://www3.weforum.org/docs/IP/2017/Adv_Cyber_Resilience_Principles-Tools.pdf

33. World Economic Forum, *The Cybersecurity Guide for Leaders in Today's World*, October 2019, http://www3.weforum.org/docs/IP/2017/Adv_Cyber_Resilience_Principles-Tools.pdf

34. World Economic Forum Centre for the Fourth Industrial Revolution, Empowering AI Leadership: An Oversight Toolkit for Boards of Directors, 2020, https://spark.adobe.com/page/RsXNkZANwMLEf/

35. Mastercard, The Global Data Responsibility Imperative, 2019.

36. See Bank of England's work on operational and climate-related resilience in the financial sector Bank of England and Financial Conduct Authority (December 2019) Building operational resilience: Impact tolerances for important business services. Bank of England News Release (December 18, 2019). Bank of England consults on its proposals for stress testing the financial stability implications of climate change.

37. The World Economic Forum (2020) Stakeholder Principles in the COVID Era. https://www.weforum.org/press/2020/04/world-economic-forum-steps-up-coordinating-efforts-on-corporate-covid-response

38. The World Economic Forum in collaboration with Willis Towers Watson (2020) Workforce Principles for the COVID-19 Pandemic: Stakeholder Capitalism in a Time of Crisis. https://www.weforum.org/whitepapers/workforce-principles-forthe-covid-19-pandemic

39. Business Fights Poverty with the Corporate Responsibility Initiative, Harvard Kennedy School (2020) Business and COVID-19: Supporting the most vulnerable. https://businessfightspoverty.org/articles/protecting-the-most-vulnerablea-business-response-framework

40. ILO, *Guidelines for a just transition towards environmentally sustainable economies and societies for all*, 2015 https://www.ilo.org/wcmsp5/groups/public/%2D%2D-ed_emp/%2D%2D-emp_ent/documents/publication/wcms_432859.pdf

41. See International Trade Union Confederation (ITUC) Just Transition Centre, https://www.ituc-csi.org/just-transition-centre

42. European Union Just Transition Mechanism, https://ec.europa.eu/info/strategy/priorities-2019-2024/european-green-deal/finance-and-green-deal/just-transition-mechanism_en

43. OECD/G20 Base Erosion and Profit Shifting Project, "Statement on a Two-Pillar Solution to the Challenges Arising from the Digitalisation of the Economy" July 1, 2021, https://www.oecd.org/tax/beps/statement-on-a-two-pillar-solution-to-address-the-tax-challenges-arising-from-the-digitalisation-of-the-economy-july-2021.pdf; for a brief summary, see https://www.oecd.org/newsroom/130-countries-and-jurisdictions-join-bold-new-framework-for-international-tax-reform.htm

44. The Global Living Wage Coalition. "What is a Living Wage?" https://www.globallivingwage.org/about/what-is-a-living-wage/ Accessed on August 24, 2021

45. Andrew Van Dam. "Fewer Americans are earning less than $15 an hour, but Black and Hispanic women make up a bigger share of them," The Washington Post, March 3, 2021. https://www.washingtonpost.com/business/2021/03/03/15-minimum-wage-black-hispanic-women/

46. Business and Sustainable Development Commission. *Better Business Better World.* January 2017. http://businesscommission.org/

47. World Economic Forum, Stakeholders for a Cohesive and Sustainable World: The Role of Lighthouse Projects, January 2020, http://www3.weforum.org/docs/WEF_Lighthouse_Project_Report.pdf

# Part II

A Practical Guide to Creating
Sustainable Enterprise Value through
Full ESG Integration

# 4

# Corporate Governance and Oversight

Good corporate governance matters more than ever. The integrity and effectiveness of the structures, systems and norms that determine how a company's priorities are set and how performance is monitored and accounted for are essential. They will determine whether the company succeeds in managing shared risks and creating sustainable enterprise value for as many of its stakeholders as possible, or not.

In 2015, working with the G20 in the aftermath of the global financial crisis, the Organisation for Economic Co-operation and Development (OECD) revised its *Principles of Corporate Governance*, first published in 1999. The revised principles explicitly included stakeholders beyond shareholders. They stated:

> Corporate governance involves a set of relationships between a company's management, its board, its shareholders and other stakeholders. Corporate governance also provides the structure through which the objectives of the company are set, and the means of attaining those objectives and monitoring performance are determined.[1]

In June 2021, the Secretary-General of the OECD, Mathias Corman, re-emphasized the importance of a stakeholder-oriented approach. He commented:

> In the context of rebuilding our economies in the wake of the COVID-19 crisis and promoting stronger, cleaner and fairer economic growth, good corporate governance plays an essential role. It fosters an environment of market confidence

© The Author(s) 2022
R. Samans, J. Nelson, *Sustainable Enterprise Value Creation*,
https://doi.org/10.1007/978-3-030-93560-3_4

and business integrity that supports capital market development. The quality of a country's corporate governance framework is decisive for the dynamism and the competitiveness of its business sector and the economy at large. It will also support the corporate sector to manage environmental, social and governance (ESG) risks and better harness the contributions of different stakeholders, be it shareholders, employees, creditors, customers, suppliers, or adjacent communities, to the long-term success of corporations.[2]

As outlined in Part I, the shift towards a more stakeholder-oriented and integrated corporate governance model that fully embeds ESG&D issues is being driven by a combination of the following:

- *The growing materiality of ESG&D risks and opportunities* to financial and operational performance, as a result of transformational technological, environmental, geopolitical and socio-economic shifts in the business context and more recently the impact of the COVID-19 pandemic and the climate change crisis.
- *Changing investor expectations* as both a result of and a driver of these shifts. The dramatic upward trend in assets under management, proxy resolutions, investment products and indices using an ESG&D lens has continued throughout the pandemic, with no signs of abating.
- *Evolving corporate laws and regulations*, both responding to and driving change. These include corporate ESG&D disclosure requirements in many countries, strengthened employee representation in certain European two-tier, supervisory and management corporate governance models, and expansions or re-interpretations of the fiduciary responsibility and duty of board directors in Australian, British, Indian, Canadian, French, South African, Brazilian and American corporate law, among others. Another example is the creation of the benefit corporation as a legal tool that provides "a traditional corporation with modified obligations committing it to higher standards of purpose, accountability and transparency," including its obligation to "commit to create public benefit and sustainable value in addition to generating profit."[3]
- *Increased demands from other stakeholders and shifting public norms* on the role of business in society, including increased social activism and calls for companies to be held more accountable for their impacts on people, prosperity and the planet, and to make more of a measurable contribution to the public good. After some initial pressure following the global financial crisis, stakeholder demands on companies have reached a crescendo in the face of the global COVID-19 pandemic, climate change and worldwide protests about inequality and racial injustice.

Despite progressive changes underway in many boards to address ESG issues and improve board diversity and stakeholder engagement, there is a long way to go in fully integrating these risks and opportunities and making stakeholder capitalism a reality in standard corporate governance "operating procedures." Take PwC's *2020 Annual Corporate Directors* survey for example.[4] It had participation from 693 directors representing a cross-section of US companies from over a dozen industries, 75% of which have annual revenues of more than $1 billion. The findings included:

- About 45% of the directors surveyed said that ESG issues are regularly part of the board's agenda (up from 34% in 2019). Sixty-seven per cent said that climate change should be taken into consideration when developing company strategy, up from 54%. Yet, only about half the directors surveyed (51%) said their board fully understands the ESG issues impacting the company, and even fewer (38%) think those issues have a financial impact on the company (down from 49% in 2019).
- More than four out of five directors surveyed (84%) agreed that companies should be doing more to promote gender and racial diversity in the workplace. Yet, only 39% of the directors said they support including diversity and inclusion goals in company pay plans; only 34% said it is very important to have racial diversity on their board, and less than half of the directors (47%) said gender diversity is very important. Sixty per cent of female directors saw the link between ESG issues and company strategy compared to only 46% of male directors.[5]

US boards are considered to lag behind their European counterparts when it comes to support for and examples of stakeholder-oriented corporate governance and integration of ESG issues in the boardroom. Consider a 2020 survey on stakeholder capitalism undertaken by the Diligent Institute, which included the views of 406 board directors and corporate leaders. In response to the statement, "We are in the midst of a fundamental change in capitalism from a primary focus on shareholder return towards a system in which corporations must have a societal purpose and serve all stakeholders," there was "a 19 percentage-point difference in agreement between non-U.S. and U.S. respondents (92% vs. 73% respectively), and a 30 percentage-point difference in strong agreement (63% vs. 33%). Meanwhile, the level of disagreement among U.S. directors relative to their counterparts around the world was even more significant: In the rest of the world, only 5% of directors disagreed with the statement, but in the United States, 11% disagreed with it."[6]

Even in Europe, substantial work is required to align corporate governance with the goals of stakeholder capitalism. A July 2020 European Commission study on directors' duties and sustainable corporate governance, prepared by EY, concluded, "The focus of corporate decision-makers on short-term shareholder value maximization rather than on the long-term interests of the company, reduces the long-term economic, environmental and social sustainability of European businesses."[7] Shareholder pay-outs, for example, increased fourfold from less than 1% of revenues in 1992 to almost 4% in 2018, and the ratio of CAPEX and R&D investment to revenues has been declining since the beginning of the twenty-first century.[8] The report identifies the following seven "key problem drivers" and proposes options for addressing them:

1. Directors' duties and company's interest are interpreted narrowly and still tend to favour the short-term maximization of shareholder value.
2. Growing pressure from investors with a short-term horizon contribute to the board's ongoing focus on short-term financial returns to shareholders at the expense of long-term value creation.
3. Companies lack a strategic perspective over sustainability and current practices fail to effectively identify and manage relevant sustainability risks and impacts.
4. Board remuneration structures incentivize the focus on short-term shareholder value rather than long-term value creation for the company.
5. The current board composition does not fully support a shift towards sustainability.
6. Current corporate governance frameworks and practices do not sufficiently voice the long-term interests of stakeholders.
7. Enforcement of the directors' duty to act in the long-term interest of company is limited.[9]

Not surprisingly, there are also clear differences between different industry sectors in the integration of ESG and stakeholder concerns in the board room. In 2018, for example, joint research by Ceres and kks advisors analysed the public disclosures of 475 companies from the Forbes 500, the annual ranking of the largest publicly listed companies in the world.[10] The data was compiled by Vigeo Eiris, an independent provider of global ESG research and services, and the research team reviewed three key aspects of board governance systems—formal mandates for sustainability, director expertise in sustainability and executive compensation linked to sustainability. They found substantial sectoral differences. Utilities, consumer staples, energy and materials companies were the most advanced, and real estate and information technology, the least advanced.

While progress is piecemeal and varies between countries and industry sectors, there are clear examples of leading practice in the drive towards a more stakeholder-oriented and integrated model of corporate governance. In the following pages we illustrate some of the practical actions that all boards of directors can take in the following areas of board leadership:

- Revise corporate governance principles or guidelines to explicitly include stakeholders and ESG&D priorities.
- Enhance the board's role in aligning corporate purpose, strategy and capital allocation with creating sustainable enterprise value.
- Expand the board's oversight of risks, risk appetite and resilience to include material and salient ESG&D risks, not only to the company, but also to people and the planet.
- Focus on people, especially on diverse succession planning, talent management and corporate culture as being crucial to company success.
- Integrate ESG&D factors into oversight of and accountability for executive performance and incentives.
- Enhance the board's own operational practices in terms of organization, composition and engagement with internal and external stakeholders.

## 4.1 Revise Governance Principles and Guidelines to Include Stakeholders and ESG&D Priorities

Publicly listed companies publish documents that are variously labelled as their governance principles, governance guidelines, board regulations, rules of procedure or mandates along with a set of board committee charters, based on the corporate law and listing requirements of the jurisdiction in which they are incorporated. These documents cover topics such as the board's role and responsibilities, board operations and communications, board structure and composition, director qualifications and their selection, succession planning, evaluation and remuneration—in short, the purpose of corporate governance.

In his preface to the *Principles of Corporate Governance*, jointly published in 2015 by the G20 and OECD, the OECD's former Secretary-General, Angel Gurría, stated, "The purpose of corporate governance is to help build an environment of trust, transparency and accountability necessary for fostering long-term investment, financial stability and business integrity, thereby supporting stronger growth and more inclusive societies."[11]

Yet, the explicit language of inclusion, responsibility to all stakeholders not only shareholders, corporate purpose, ESG and sustainability, is still rare or piecemeal in most companies' corporate governance guidelines and formal board mandates.

In the joint research carried out by Ceres and kks advisors in 2018, they looked at whether the boards surveyed had a formal board mandate for sustainability. The research team found,

> Sixty-two percent of the companies we analysed state that they have some form of oversight of sustainability at the board level. However, only 13 percent show truly robust oversight practices, meaning there is both a formal board mandate for sustainability (either through a dedicated sustainability committee or through the inclusion of sustainability in another board committee's charter) and the board receives regular reports on sustainability from management. … On the other hand, 38 percent of companies still have no discernible board practices in place for sustainability oversight.[12]

In a similar vein, while researching their paper entitled "The Illusory Promise of Stakeholder Governance," Professors Bebchuk and Tallarita contacted the 181 companies that signed the seminal 2019 US Business Roundtable statement, which restated the purpose of the corporation to be for the benefit of all stakeholders—customers, employees, suppliers, communities and shareholder, rather than shareholders alone.[13] Less than a third of the companies responded. As the researchers noted in an opinion piece for the *Wall Street Journal*,

> We contacted the companies whose CEOs signed the Business Roundtable statement and asked who the highest-level decision maker was to approve the decision. Of the 48 companies that responded, only one said the decision was approved by the board of directors. The other 47 indicated that the decision to sign the statement, supposedly adopting a major change in corporate purpose, was not approved by the board of directors. … The most plausible explanation for the lack of board approval is that CEOs didn't regard the statement as a commitment to make a major change in how their companies treat stakeholders.[14]

In 2021, Bebchuk and Tallarita published the findings of additional research in a paper entitled "Will Corporations Deliver Value to All Stakeholders?" This was based on the review of a variety of publicly available corporate documents for the 136 public US companies whose CEOs signed the statement.[15] Among their six findings the authors concluded that "examining the almost one-hundred BRT Companies that updated their corporate governance guidelines in the sixteen-month period between the release of the BRT Statement and the end of 2020, we find that they generally did not add any language that improves the status of stakeholders and, indeed, most of them chose to retain in their guidelines a commitment to shareholder primacy."[16] Furthermore, they found that "reviewing the corporate governance guidelines of BRT Companies that were in place as of the end of 2020, we find that most of them reflected a shareholder primacy approach, and an even larger majority did not include any mention of stakeholders in their discussion of corporate purpose," and "reviewing all the corporate bylaws of BRT Companies, we find that they generally reflect a shareholder-centered view."[17] As the authors commented in a second opinion piece for the *Wall Street Journal*, their research "casts serious doubt on whether corporations are matching the talk with action."[18]

In short, for many companies in the US and elsewhere, publicly available board principles and guidelines do not appear to be keeping up with statements about sustainability and stakeholder capitalism made by their CEOs and executive teams or with changing stakeholder expectations about the purpose of business and its role in society. It is important to note, however, that in many companies actual practice and discussion on these topics inside the boardroom and in executive teams is likely to be ahead of what is written in their formal governance guidelines or other documents that are publicly disclosed.

As the BRT commented in response to the Bebchuk and Tallarita critique, "We disagree with the conclusion of the paper and find the thesis that the [BRT] Statement required changes in bylaws, governance guidelines, and corporate policies, as well as support for certain shareholder proposals, to be deeply flawed. The CEOs who signed the 2019 Statement believe it better reflects the conviction that businesses can't flourish over the long term or return value to their long-term shareholders without investing in the stakeholders who make success possible. That view is consistent with existing corporate law and does not require any change to companies' bylaws and governance guidelines."[19]

In today's operating environment, even when not legally required to do so, all boards can and should be proactive in reviewing and where relevant revising their published corporate governance guidelines and committee charters to:

- first, explicitly recognize the board's responsibility for oversight of management in determining corporate purpose and strategy for creating sustainable enterprise value for stakeholders, including but not only shareholders; and
- second, provide language on the board's responsibility for oversight of ESG&D risks, opportunities and performance in addition to financial and operational risks, opportunities and performance.

In addition to boards taking voluntary action to integrate stakeholder and ESG&D considerations into formal board documents and mandates, regulatory requirements are also evolving in this direction. The UK's Companies Act offers an example.[20] It uses stakeholder language similar to the Davos Manifesto and the US Business Roundtable Statement on the Purpose of a Corporation and incorporates it into law and public disclosure requirements. In 2018, new corporate governance and reporting guidelines were issued that require companies of a significant size to explain how their directors comply with Section 172 of the UK Companies Act. Section 172 addresses a director's "[d]uty to promote the success of the company." It states: "A director of a company must act in the way he considers, in good faith, would be most likely to promote the success of the company for the benefit of its members as a whole and in doing so have regard (amongst other matters) to -

- the likely consequences of any decision in the long term,
- the interests of the company's employees,
- the need to foster the company's business relationships with suppliers, customers and others,
- the impact of the company's operations on the community and the environment,
- the desirability of the company maintaining a reputation for high standards of business conduct, and
- the need to act fairly as between members of the company."[21]

Another example of evolving regulation is provided by changes made in 2019 to the provisions of the French Civil and Commercial Codes, which have been supplemented by the so-called Pacte Statute on the Development and Transformations of Businesses.[22] Each French company and French Boards of Directors and Management Boards must be managed "in furtherance of its corporate interest," not shareholder interests, and "while taking into consideration the social and environmental issues arising from its activity."[23] In November 2020, a corporate responsibility initiative in Switzerland that would have mandated that multinational companies demonstrate respect for human rights and the environment was narrowly defeated in a nationwide referendum, despite gaining 50.74% to 49.26% of the popular vote.[24]

In summary, to respond to the changing operating context, boards need to be more explicit about the way they incorporate language about stakeholders, corporate purpose and ESG&D risks, opportunities and performance into their corporate governance principles, guidelines and committee charters.

## 4.2 Enhance Board Oversight on Aligning Corporate Purpose, Strategy and Capital Allocation with Creating Sustainable Enterprise Value

Boards should play a more proactive and deliberative role and provide greater disclosure on their oversight and guidance in:

- Approving and stewarding a clear *statement of corporate purpose*, outlining how the company aims to create sustainable enterprise value by addressing ESG&D issues and/or stakeholder needs
- Providing more *robust and regular guidance on corporate strategy* and its alignment with ESG&D issues and stakeholders
- *Reviewing capital allocation and investment decisions* through the lens of ESG&D issues and stakeholders alongside financial, operational and shareholder lenses

### 4.2.1 Support Management as Stewards of Corporate Purpose

As a growing number of governance practitioners, investors, advisers and academics are noting, the full board of directors should have input into approving the company's purpose. Although it is the role of management to lead the work on developing a company's purpose, values, mission and vision, preferably in a way that actively engages with their employees, the board should also be proactively engaged.

In particular, the board has a role in approving the company's purpose statement and then providing oversight on how this aligns with the company's values, strategy, business planning and operations, what its key goals and performance metrics are and how management is incentivized and compensated for achieving them. If a contribution to solving a social or environmental challenge or creating value for stakeholders beyond maximizing shareholder value is an explicit component of the company's publicly stated purpose, this in turn sets the foundation for integrating material ESG&D issues into core business strategy, business models, risk management and operations. It also serves as a basis for stakeholder engagement and internal and external accountability.

In most countries, the development and disclosure of a corporate purpose statement remains voluntary, although stakeholder or ESG-related disclosure requirements in France, the UK and elsewhere in the EU are evolving. The UK's revised Corporate Governance Code 2018, and Board Effectiveness Guidance, for example, states that the board is "responsible for aligning purpose, values and strategy." It highlights three key principles in relation to corporate governance and purpose:

1. Purpose is the reason a company exists.
2. The board is responsible for setting and periodically reconfirming the purpose of the company.
3. A well-defined, concise purpose helps companies articulate their business models and develop their strategy, operating practices and approach to risk, and facilitates engagement with the workforce, customers and the wider public.[25]

In addition to the widely publicized 2019 US Business Roundtable's "Statement on the Purpose of a Corporation," and the World Economic Forum's 2020 refresh of its original stakeholder-oriented 1973 Davos Manifesto, other business leadership groups are starting to call for boards to be more proactive in defining and disclosing their company's purpose. The World Business Council for Sustainable Development stated in a 2020 report that boards should "[e]nsure that the company's purpose is clearly established and aligned with material sustainable development impacts and opportunities. … Clarity of company purpose can provide a direct communication about the future of the organization and deliver long-lasting and broad benefit to the business."[26]

Along similar lines, a 2020 paper by the Enacting Purpose Initiative (EPI), a coalition of leading academics and practitioners, concluded, "When embedded at the most senior levels of decision-making, purpose acts as a 'north star' for Boards of Directors. It is a key driver informing strategic choices, helping directors make the critical trade offs and decisions that are required to fulfil their board responsibilities. This is purpose as strategy, and it differs fundamentally from purpose as culture. Purpose as strategy will facilitate the choices that need to be made as organizations rebuild or adapt after this crisis."[27]

One of the specific proposals made by EPI is for

> boards to start with a statement of purpose signed and issued by all the directors. The board chair and the governance committee should take the lead in drafting it. The statement should define how the company aims to create value by fulfilling unmet needs in society. It should acknowledge the negative impacts the company must mitigate if it is to retain public support and its license to operate. And it should present a distinctive message—not something so generic that the name of any major competitor could be substituted. If those criteria are met, the statement can be a powerful tool for sharing a company's vision for long-term value creation, even in industries with negative externalities.[28]

While a growing number of companies have a corporate purpose statement that meets many of the above criteria, there are few where the statements have been signed by the board directors.

## 4.2.2  Provide Robust and Regular Guidance on Corporate Strategy

As the US Business Roundtable among others has stated, "The board should have meaningful input into the company's long-term strategy from development through execution, should approve the company's strategic plans and should regularly evaluate implementation of the plans that are designed to create long-term value. The board should understand the risks inherent in the company's strategic plans and how those risks are being managed."[29]

In the journey towards stakeholder capitalism, most boards need to focus on the following three strategy-related areas:

- First, spend more time on strategy and sustainable value creation discussions, generally
- Second, ensure clear and continued alignment between corporate purpose and strategy

- Third, integrate other sustainability- and people-related strategies with the corporate strategy (or at a minimum ensure that they are not working at odds with each other)

**Spend more time on strategy**: Boards need to spend more focused and quality time engaging with management on debating options for corporate strategy and long-term, sustainable value creation.

Drawing on research from McKinsey, Focusing Capital on the Long-Term (FCLTGlobal) states: "Boards with a demonstrated, long-term impact spend nearly twice as much time on high-level issues like strategy, business model, risks, and the company's value-creation proposition."[30]

In his 2016 Corporate Governance Letter to CEOs, BlackRock's Larry Fink stated, "We are asking that every CEO lay out for shareholders each year a strategic framework for long-term value creation. Additionally, because boards have a critical role to play in strategic planning, we believe CEOs should explicitly affirm that their boards have reviewed those plans. BlackRock's corporate governance team, in their engagement with companies, will be looking for this framework and board review."[31]

The benefits of such an approach are obvious. If an experienced and diverse board of directors and management team spend more time together focused on understanding key competitive trends, potential market disruptions, changing stakeholder expectations and the company's short- and long-term value creation opportunities—as well as value destruction risks—they are likely to develop a more robust and successful strategy. If these strategy discussions are regular and strategic plans are regularly stress-tested, the company is also likely to be more agile in adapting and course-correcting when needed and more resilient in times of crisis and systemic shocks. Regular strategy discussions can also help to build trust and values alignment between the board and management, while still enabling constructive and challenging debate around options for value creation.

The obstacles to boards getting more proactively and intensely engaged in strategy discussions are well-documented. They include growing regulatory and compliance burdens requiring more director time, inefficient organization of board agendas, certain issues or quarterly performance reviews that could be delegated to committee-level meetings being covered at the full board, too much time spent on management presentations rather than taking board papers as read, and over-boarding and some directors not having the time or commitment to do the necessary preparation work.

Most of these obstacles can be overcome with effective board leadership and adjustments to the way board meetings and management presentations are structured. Creative use of site visits and engagement with external stakeholders can also help to enrich and strengthen board-level strategy discussions and outcomes. As High Meadows Institute notes in its report on Corporate Governance for the Twenty-First Century, "Historically, boards focused on strategy once annually, often at a one- to two-day off-site retreat. Today, in most firms, discussions on strategy take place at each board meeting to ensure that progress is being made and that new competition or technology is taken into consideration. Many directors support frequent evaluation of strategy, deeper engagement, and greater board involvement at an earlier stage."[32]

**Align corporate strategy with corporate purpose**: Boards need to also have an explicit focus on how corporate strategy helps to deliver on the company's purpose, how it takes the creation of shared and sustained value for all stakeholders into account, including but not only shareholders, and how material ESG&D risks and opportunities are being integrated into strategic planning, alongside financial and operational risks and opportunities. At a minimum, boards should be asking how stakeholders and ESG&D issues may create risks for the achievement of the company's strategic goals and how they might offer strategic opportunities for the company.

**Integrate the company's sustainability and other stakeholder-oriented strategies with corporate strategy**: Board's should monitor that there is internal alignment of goals, incentives and accountabilities between the company's corporate strategy (and the strategic priorities that it presents publicly at investor presentations) with other key company strategies, such as the human capital and talent development strategy, the sustainability or corporate responsibility strategy and the government relations and communications strategy. Failure to "walk the talk" in terms of actual performance against a stated corporate purpose is one of the greatest drivers of mistrust in business.

Ideally, boards should encourage their CEOs and management teams to move beyond the goal of preventing misalignment between these different strategies to explicitly integrating them. The most material ESG&D strategic priorities, for example, should form one or more of the strategy pillars of the corporate strategy itself. Since executives and management are usually incentivized and compensated based on their performance against the company's strategy, the greater the integration of ESG&D issues, the more likely they are to influence behaviour and results.

### 4.2.3   Review ESG&D Implications of Capital Allocation and Investment Decisions

The US Business Roundtable states, "The CEO and senior management are responsible for providing recommendations to the board related to capital allocation of the company's resources, including but not limited to organic growth; mergers and acquisitions; divestitures; spin-offs; maintaining and growing its physical and nonphysical resources; and the appropriate return of capital to shareholders in the form of dividends, share repurchases and other capital distribution means."[33] In turn, it is the responsibility of the board to "have meaningful input and decision-making authority over the company's capital allocation process and strategy to find the right balance between short-term and long-term economic returns for its shareholders."[34]

In today's business context, as outlined elsewhere in the book, "finding the right balance" in capital allocation requires not only balancing short-term and long-term economic returns to shareholders, but also returns to other stakeholders and other forms of capital—especially to human capital or employees and natural capital or the environment. One example is the substantial investments in research and implementation that many companies will need to make in new technologies, products, services and business models to achieve net-zero carbon emissions by 2050 or before. Other examples include investment in the well-being, training and development of employees, building the resilience and capabilities of suppliers and allocation to communities and corporate foundations.

When it comes to major investment decisions and business development activities such as mergers and acquisitions and new market entry, ESG&D risks and opportunities should be integral to competitive analysis and to the scoping, feasibility assessments, due diligence and decision-making associated with these investments and activities. In many industry sectors and companies, these risks and opportunities are also increasingly material to the outcomes of a major investment. Likewise in the case of research and development (R&D). ESG&D risks and opportunities can be a key driver of innovation in new science and technologies as well as a consequence of such innovation, both positive and negative. As such, the board needs to understand and debate both specific ESG&D risks and opportunities and broader scenarios or potential ESG&D outcomes associated with major investments, business development and R&D decisions.

## 4.3 Expand Oversight of Risks to Include Material *and* Salient ESG&D Risks

One of the key functions of any board that has become progressively more complex, dynamic and multi-dimensional is risk oversight. In the words of the Business Roundtable, the board is responsible for "[s]etting the company's risk appetite, reviewing and understanding the major risks, and overseeing the risk management processes. The board oversees the process for identifying and managing the significant risks facing the company. The board and senior management should agree on the company's risk appetite, and the board should be comfortable that the strategic plans are consistent with it. The board should establish a structure for overseeing risk, delegating responsibility to committees and overseeing the designation of senior management responsible for risk management."[35]

Traditional types of operational, financial, market, political and regulatory risks have not gone away. Indeed, for most industry sectors and countries, these risks have increased and become more complex and challenging in the face of globalization, complex supply chains and disruptive technologies, as well as threats to globalization, systemic shocks such as financial crises and pandemics and growing political polarization both within nations and geopolitically. Add to these, the following two categories of risk oversight, which in many cases interact with more traditional risks, and it is clear that boards face a growing challenge in today's world to ensure comprehensive and effective risk oversight:

- Oversight of material and salient ESG&D risks and risk appetite
- Preparedness for and resilience to systemic shocks and crises

### 4.3.1 Ensure Oversight of Material and Salient ESG&D Risks

There have been two related shifts in "risk oversight" that are essential to supporting the transition towards a more stakeholder-oriented and integrated form of corporate governance:

First is the *growing materiality of ESG&D risks* to the company and to its financial and operational performance. As outlined in Chap. 2, the costs to the company of "getting it wrong" when it comes to managing the company's ESG&D performance have grown.

Second are the concepts of *salience, double materiality* and *managing shared risk.* Risk oversight needs to expand from identifying, mitigating and managing risks *to the company*—to its operations, financial liquidity, business continuity and reputation—to also being more explicit about and accountable for identifying, mitigating and managing *risks to people and to the planet* that may result directly or indirectly from the company's activities or those of business partners along its supply chain.

The UN Guiding Principles on Business and Human Rights has started to popularize the use of the term *salient risks* to capture this dimension of risk oversight and management. Whereas material ESG&D risks pose a threat to the company, salient ESG&D risks pose a threat to people and the environment. Clearly, there is often an overlap between them—causing serious pollution or high levels of greenhouse gas emissions, for example, or being responsible for or complicit with human rights abuses, not only harm people and the environment, but increasingly also the company due to changing societal expectations, regulations and investor focus. However, in many cases there is not an overlap—or there is a weak one—and responsible boards and management teams should be systematic and consistent in assessing and being accountable for both material and salient risks resulting from the company's activities.

Just as the audit committee is responsible for monitoring financial risks, ethics, integrity and compliance, a vanguard of corporate boards is establishing processes and/or committees with oversight responsibility for monitoring both material and salient ESG&D risks.

At a minimum, every board should engage in a regular review of the company's enterprise risk management system and understand how material ESG&D risks are being integrated, ranked and managed alongside other risks. In addition, ESG&D risks should be one of the topics addressed in board discussions on the company's risk appetite and tolerance.

Clearly, there are some substantial ESG&D risks that have risen to prominence in major companies over the past decade, which were outlined in Chaps. 2 and 3. At the top of most lists are climate change, human rights, inclusion and diversity, and data privacy and data use issues. Box 4.1 provides the example of the Climate Governance Initiative, which is focused on supporting boards to become "climate competent."

## Box 4.1  Building Climate Competent Boards

Changing regulations and more demanding and explicit climate-related disclosure requirements by both governments and investors are making climate competence a central pillar of directors' fiduciary duties. In 2019, the World Economic Forum, in collaboration with PwC, published a set of Guiding Principles for setting up effective climate governance on corporate boards.[36] These principles are relevant for all boards regardless of industry sector or jurisdiction and provide a useful framework for action. The eight principles focus on the following areas:

1. Board accountability for climate
2. Command of the climate subject through diverse board knowledge, skills, experience and background
3. Integration of climate considerations into board structure and committees
4. Material climate risk and opportunity assessment
5. Strategic and organizational integration into investment planning, decision-making and management systems
6. Incentivization of executives
7. Public reporting and disclosure of climate-related risks, opportunities and strategic decisions
8. Exchange with peers, policymakers, investors and other stakeholders on climate issues and good practices

These principles are also aligned with the recommendations of the *Task Force for Climate-Related Financial Disclosure*, which call on companies to publicly disclose their climate-related risks and opportunities under the four pillars of governance, strategy, risk management and metrics and targets.

In 2020, the Centre for Climate Engagement at Cambridge University, together with the World Economic Forum, established the *Climate Governance Initiative*. Its goal is to support chapters around the world focused on mobilizing, educating and equipping non-executive directors with the skills and knowledge to implement these principles and effectively address climate change at the board level. To date, more than a dozen national chapters or existing board leadership organizations have affiliated with the network. In addition, most Institutes of Directors and other director-led professional groups, as well as universities and climate-focused initiatives such as Ceres, are stepping up their skills building activities to help companies build climate competent boards. Every board should be assessing its capabilities and responsibilities against these principles and recommendations and taking action to address gaps.

In 2020, the COVID-19 pandemic and global protests on racial injustice and inequality also highlighted and intensified the "S" in ESG. As outlined in Chap. 3, the UN Guiding Principles on Business and Human Rights have played an important role in placing respect for human rights more clearly on the board agenda. Prior to the pandemic, however, the boards that focused strategically on their company's responsibility to respect human rights or to address social risks defined in other ways were more the exception than the norm. Today, oversight of these topics is becoming central to good corporate governance.

Any company's most salient risks and greatest responsibility are to protect the lives, health and safety of people who work for the company, who purchase its products and services or who live in communities surrounding its operations. Industries such as oil and gas, chemicals, mining, aviation, heavy transportation, construction and infrastructure have learned hard lessons over many years on the human tragedy and business costs of inaction or poor performance on occupational health and safety. As a result, most of the leading companies in these industries have a long-standing focus on health and safety as a priority in their values, risk management systems and board risk oversight. Likewise, road safety has been a long-standing priority for companies with large logistics and distribution networks. Consumer product safety is increasingly well-regulated and a major focus for board oversight in sectors such as healthcare and pharmaceuticals, food and beverages, toys and chemicals. During the pandemic, protecting the health and safety of employees and other relevant stakeholders became more of a priority for all responsible companies.

Moving beyond protecting people's basic health and safety, a vanguard of companies has established employee wellbeing programmes, covering both physical and mental health and wellness, as well as financial health in some cases. Over the past few decades, gender diversity, and to a growing extent racial and ethnic diversity, have also become more of a focus for boards and management in many companies and countries.

As a result of both the pandemic and heightened focus on social injustice and discrimination, boards must address peoples' health, safety and wellness and their inclusion and diversity more systematically and strategically in future. A survey by the Diligent Institute, for example, found that board directors are expecting to "discuss the impact of their decisions on non-shareholder stakeholders with very high frequency in the three years following the COVID-19 outbreak." Forty-two per cent said they expected to discuss these topics at every meeting (compared to 26% in the past three years), and 73% expect to discuss them quarterly, compared to 47% in the past three years.[37]

### 4.3.2 Strengthen Preparedness for and Resilience to Systemic Shocks and Crises

Another core component of effective risk oversight at the board level is monitoring the company's ability to respond to and recover from an acute or systemic crisis. As outlined in Chap. 3, this ability depends on the rigour and scope of the company's risk management systems and its crisis preparedness processes, combined with an adaptive and engaged corporate culture and the quality of leadership at both executive and operational levels of the company. Boards play a vital role in providing oversight and support to management in these areas:

**Improving preparedness**: Boards need to work closely with management to undertake scenario planning, simulations and stress-testing exercises; develop crisis succession plans for key executives and mission critical operators; and review deployment options for emergency response assets and relationships.

**Supporting crisis management and response**: When a crisis happens, boards need to be equipped to immediately respond. Sometimes this will require the board or a senior non-executive director to step directly into an executive role, but more often it will require the board to support its senior management team. The following areas are important for boards to consider in most crisis situations, especially more systemic shocks: putting people first and doing everything possible to protect the lives and livelihoods of employees and other direct stakeholders of the company; supporting critical functions and operations for business continuity; providing oversight of financial risks, liquidity and resilience; and continuing to invest in key stakeholder relationships and partnerships.

**Strengthening recovery and future resilience**: While the duration, intensity and scope of a crisis management situation will obviously vary depending on the nature of the crisis and how systemic it is, as early as possible, the board and management team should be reviewing medium- and longer-term recovery plans and discussing lessons learned to strengthen the company's resilience for the future. In addition to identifying key planning and relationship management priorities, they should be reviewing lessons learned and identifying gaps and opportunities to build future operational, cultural, financial and technological resilience. Once again, the quality of stakeholder engagement and developing or sustaining trusted relationships, both within the company and externally, will be a key factor in this process.

## 4.4    Focus on Diverse Succession Planning, Talent Development and an Inclusive Culture

Over the past decade there has been growing awareness that boards need to "up their game" on the employee and cultural dimension of their responsibilities and expand their oversight from CEO succession and compensation—although these remain as important as ever—to a broader understanding and oversight of talent development and succession planning, employee well-being, diversity and inclusion, and corporate culture. This focus needs to include but go far beyond the more traditional compliance-based approach to governance of employee and labour issues. Board leadership is especially important in the areas of:

- Oversight of CEO and executive performance, compensation and succession
- Guidance on corporate culture
- Championship of diversity, equity and inclusion
- Review and support of talent development

### 4.4.1    Integrate ESG&D into CEO and Executive Performance, Compensation and Succession

Boards play a crucial role in the oversight of CEO performance, compensation and succession planning. In a growing number of cases, this oversight is extending to the senior executive team more broadly, and this is an important shift for ensuring a more stakeholder-oriented approach to governance.

As boards review their CEO and executive team succession plans, in addition to all the traditional leadership capacities and operational, managerial, technical and functional skills that need to be assessed, there is also a growing need to focus on so-called softer skill sets and mindsets. Ensuring that the ability to manage ESG&D risks and opportunities is part of the skills matrix for the CEO and relevant executives, and that targets for ESG&D performance are included in performance reviews, incentive and compensation programmes, is an essential factor in embedding good practice.

### 4.4.2    Provide Guidance on Corporate Culture

There is a growing focus on the role of boards in both contributing to and monitoring corporate culture. All the values and purpose statements, ethical policies and standards in the world will not be effective if the company's culture and, linked to that, its role models, accepted norms and behaviours, incentive systems and rewards are not aligned to these statements and policies. Indeed, failure to "walk the talk" is a key driver of the decline in employee morale and productivity and stakeholder trust more widely. The 2017 National Association of Corporate Directors (NACD) Blue Commission on

"Culture as a Corporate Asset" commented that "organizational cultures and the factors that influence them are complex systems, incorporating elements such as: explicit and implicit rules; norms of behaviour and interaction; compliance and ethics policies; incentives; recruiting and training activities; processes for decision-making and prioritization (including budget setting); communication and information flows; and leadership styles."[38]

Of relevance to the transition towards a more stakeholder-oriented approach, the NACD Commission also concluded, "Culture reaches beyond the company, since it is expressed not only in the treatment of employees, but also in interactions with customers, suppliers, communities and other external stakeholders."[39]

Boards have an increasingly important role to play in "setting the tone from the top" and ensuring the rigorous monitoring of relevant training and awareness programmes, employee engagement surveys, whistleblowing mechanisms and culture reviews, in addition to demonstrating zero tolerance for harassment or harmful and unethical behaviour.

PwC's 2019 Annual Corporate Directors' survey found, "Culture problems are often at the root of corporate crises. Many companies and boards are taking a hard look at their own culture to see where culture problems might originate. Directors are also looking at who's to blame. The tone set by executive management is cited the most often, but more directors are pointing the finger at middle management. Boards themselves are also taking more accountability: 29% of directors strongly agree that a lack of board oversight contributes to problems, up from 18% in 2018."[40]

Research by KPMG highlights four key areas that any board should focus on when assessing their oversight of corporate culture:

- Understand what "culture" is and why it is critical today.
- Establish clarity on the foundational elements of the company's culture: zero-tolerance policies as well as behaviours that will help the company excel.
- Clarify the board's role in overseeing culture—recognizing that visibility is a major hurdle.
- Assess where culture belongs on the board and committee agendas.[41]

### 4.4.3    Serve as a Champion for Diversity, Equity and Inclusion

An increasingly important element of board oversight of corporate purpose, values, value creation, risk management and corporate culture is its role as a champion for diversity, equity and inclusion.

First, this should come from the demonstration effect and role model of the board's own diversity.

Second, it should come from the board working with management to set and monitor clear goals and targets at all levels of the company. This includes making sure that these goals and the accountability for achieving them are owned by the full executive team and operational leaders, with expertise, support and tracking provided by the human resources team.

Third, board leadership on diversity, equity and inclusion should include support for and direct engagement with employee groups, business resource groups and affinity groups. Where relevant, the board should also have access to external subject-matter experts and advisers.

Boards—at the full board or committee level—should ensure that management is allocating sufficient resources to initiatives such as implementing equal pay for equal work throughout the company, supporting unconscious bias training and other types of training and awareness raising, requiring blind resumes and diverse candidate slates for both internal and external hiring, identifying and addressing other discriminatory practices, behaviours and symbols of exclusion, proactively broadening flexible working arrangements and other support systems to facilitate diverse working and family needs, understanding and making commitments to pay living wages, encouraging and facilitating employee dialogues, and creating mechanisms where employees can confidentially address difficult issues.

### 4.4.4    Review and Support Long-Term Talent Development

Linked to all the above is board oversight for the company's overall human capital strategy and the resources that the executive team is allocating to develop the skills, capabilities and management "bench strength" or leadership pipeline in all business units and functional divisions. While much of this can be delegated to the committee level, with regular updates to the full board, it has become an increasingly important board task. As a result, in leading companies the mandate of compensation committees is starting to broaden to include leadership development, talent, human capital, and diversity and inclusion as well as executive compensation and remuneration.

## 4.5   Integrate ESG&D Priorities into Oversight of Executive Performance, Incentives and Accountability

Every quarter the board will be reviewing the performance of the executive team and the company against the strategic priorities and goals that have been established. Clearly, this includes performance against financial, operational, growth and business development targets. In today's world, it should also include quarterly reviews of performance against the company's most material and salient ESG&D risks and opportunities. In particular, the board should:

- Integrate ESG&D into business planning and performance oversight
- Align incentives to corporate purpose and strategy and hold executives accountable
- Commit to integrated reporting of the company's performance and prospects

### 4.5.1   Integrate ESG&D into Business Planning and Performance Oversight

If ESG&D factors are an explicit part of a company's strategy, they will also be integrated into business planning, target setting and performance review processes, and the board's approval and oversight of these. To the extent that this cascades from the corporate level to operating units—be they different lines of business, different brands or different geographies—the more likely it is that the company will be well positioned to understand and manage key ESG&D risks and opportunities.

### 4.5.2   Align Incentives to Corporate Purpose and Hold Executives Accountable

A corollary to the adage "you manage what you measure" is "you implement what you are incentivized for." Incentives for executives and managers are primarily viewed in financial terms, but clearly also include other forms of recognition, ranging from career advancement and promotion to awards and "honourable mentions." Boards—or more specifically compensation committees, have an important role to play in ensuring that compensation and benefits packages are aligned with the company's overall purpose, values and strategy and enable and reward managers for delivering on these. Four key aspects of corporate incentive and recognition programmes need to be reviewed and in many cases changed or refreshed to support a transition towards more stakeholder-oriented approaches.

First is the need to balance rewards for short-term results with long-term value creation and performance. This is an area that has seen considerable progress in recent years, with senior executive compensation packages focused increasingly on longer-term performance metrics and share ownership.

Second is the need to integrate performance on ESG&D issues into executive compensation packages. In certain industries, this has been done in the case of the company's safety performance for several decades, but progress has been slower on other social and environmental issues. Performance on meeting targets for climate change and for diversity and inclusion currently appear to be the most common issues for inclusion in executive packages. Some boards use the company's ranking in ESG indices as a proxy rather than focusing on executive performance in addressing a specific ESG&D issue or set of issues.

Third is the increasingly high-profile topic of fairness. This relates to the question of "equal pay for equal work" and the need for most companies to address gender pay gaps, racial pay gaps and/or nationality pay gaps. It also relates to the question of the gap between CEO and executive compensation and the compensation of employees, which has widened substantially over the past few decades. Over the past decade, regulations such as "Say on Pay" and those limiting so-called golden parachutes or enabling long-term compensation clawbacks for CEOs who have been fired for poor performance have started to address these issues. The first "line of defence," however, should be the board doing a good job on alignment and oversight of executive compensation. Another growing focus in terms of fairness is the extension of share ownership schemes to a larger number of employees and in a few cases even host communities as a way of spreading shareholder wealth, albeit also spreading associated risks, to more of a company's stakeholders.

Fourth is the importance of having clear consequences for non-performance on ESG&D targets as well as financial and operational ones. This can range from decreases in annual bonuses for failure to meet key targets in areas such as safety and the company's other most material and salient ESG&D issues to termination of jobs, including the company's CEO and/or its best performers, in cases where there is a verified breach in ethics and core values. Although still rare, decisions made by boards to fire a CEO or senior executive resulting from such breaches can send a strong internal and external signal that the company's stated purpose, values and ethics really matter.

### 4.5.3 Commit to Integrated Reporting of the Company's Performance and Prospects

In the same way that boards and their audit committees review and approve a company's financial statements, leading boards are also starting to review and approve their company's sustainability or ESG&D materiality assessments, targets, reports and disclosures. Detailed review and oversight are usually most effectively undertaken at a committee level, but the full board should be informed of the company's public disclosures on ESG&D-related policies, commitments and performance and about trends in investor expectations on this topic. This topic is addressed at length in Chap. 6.

## 4.6 Strengthen Board Organization, Composition and Engagement

Finally, there is the important question of the board's own practices and the need to continuously evaluate whether its current organization, composition and stakeholder engagement mechanisms are fit-for-purpose in an increasingly complex operating context. There are obvious differences between ownership structures and corporate governance models in different countries and jurisdictions that have an impact on board organization, composition and engagement, but some important factors and good practices for all boards to consider include the following.

### 4.6.1 Integrate ESG&D into Board Organization and Structure

A core question to consider is the appropriate allocation of discussions and decision-making on ESG&D risks and opportunities between the full board and relevant committees. It is no longer an either/or situation. In every industry sector, ESG&D issues are now sufficiently material and salient that they must be addressed by the full board. At the same time, the range of issues that are likely to be material and salient in any large company—from human rights, ethics and employee safety to climate change, water management and data stewardship—are sufficiently wide-ranging and technically complex and sophisticated that their oversight requires more time than can be allocated in most board meetings. As such, there is a growing need to ensure that relevant board committee charters also include oversight of these issues. This includes regular reviews of the appropriate balance between committee-level work and full board discussions and consideration of which ESG&D-related issues need to be addressed by which committee.

The appropriate balance and committee allocation will vary, depending on the industry sector, corporate law and disclosure requirements in the head-office country and current board structure. The key point is for boards to be intentional and systematic about how they integrate ESG&D issues into their core oversight roles and responsibilities.

## Integrating ESG&D at the Full Board

In many companies, an annual presentation on ESG&D issues is now made to the full board. Growing public disclosure requirements on how companies are addressing climate change risks are resulting in this topic also receiving more systematic and regular attention by the full board. Such presentations are necessary but increasingly insufficient in most large companies that are operating globally. It is important for the full board to have more regular oversight of the ESG&D issues that management considers to be most material to the company and salient to people and the environment, along with changes in stakeholder expectations and the company's policies, standards, strategies and due diligence processes for managing these risks and opportunities and its performance against targets. In addition, as outlined throughout this chapter, it is increasingly necessary for the full board to consider ESG&D issues in the context of and integral to other key board oversight topics and functions. For example:

- Approval of corporate purpose
- Corporate strategy discussions
- Capital allocation and investment decisions
- Enterprise risk management and risk tolerance discussions
- Business planning and target setting
- Oversight of corporate and business unit performance
- CEO and executive succession and incentives

- Public reporting and disclosures
- Corporate culture

### Embedding ESG&D into Board Committee Charters

As emphasized throughout the book, the range of material ESG&D issues that need to be addressed by many companies and the technical complexity of some of these issues, most notably in the areas of digital and other new technologies and climate change, increasingly require additional time and attention of a board committee. There is no one-size-fits-all and no common definitions for the roles of such committees.[42]

Research by Ceres and kks advisors in 2018, for example, focused specifically on how responsibility for sustainability was allocated to different board committees. They found that 25% of the companies reviewed had established a Corporate Responsibility or Corporate Social Responsibility Committee, while 14% had an Environmental, Health and Safety Committee, 13% allocated responsibility for these issues to a Sustainability Committee, and 5% to a Social and Ethics Committee. Other companies had integrated responsibility for sustainability issues into existing board committees—the Nominations and Governance Committee in 18% of cases, a Public Policy Committee in 13% of cases, a Risk, Regulatory or Compliance Committee in 6% of cases, an Audit Committee in 2% of cases, and a Strategy or Compensation Committee in 1% of the companies reviewed.[43]

Committee options include the following:

**A dedicated committee focused on ESG issues**: A growing number of corporate boards have established a committee dedicated to addressing ESG, corporate responsibility, safety and sustainability or public affairs issues. Such committees are able to provide regular oversight of the company's key risks, opportunities and performance with respect to its most material and salient ESG issues; review global strategies for these issues, for example in areas such as employee health and safety, climate and energy, water, and human rights; provide input to materiality and salience analysis and the company's public disclosures related to these issues; and appoint expert advisers or reviews to address specific ESG-related challenges or crises. In some cases, geopolitical risks, government relations and other external stakeholder engagement are also a focus of such committees. Box 4.2 provides some examples.

**A broader risk committee**: In other cases, boards are establishing a dedicated risk committee to provide oversight of a broader range of material risks to the business. These may include ESG-related as well as other material risks such as data stewardship, technology more broadly, geopolitics, and other business continuity and industry disruption risks.

**Box 4.2 Examples of Dedicated Corporate Responsibility and Sustainability Committees**

The following three companies from diverse industry sectors have had dedicated sustainability committees in place for over a decade. Their Charters or Terms of Reference provide useful models for other companies to review.

GSK's *Corporate Responsibility Committee* was established in 2005. Its Terms of Reference were updated in 2021 to reflect the company's refreshed corporate purpose and its three long-term priorities of innovation, performance and trust. The company outlines its trust priority as follows: "We are a responsible company. We commit to use our science and technology to address health needs, make our products affordable and available and be a modern employer."[44] The company has set 13 public Trust commitments in the ESG areas where it can make the greatest difference. These include commitments in the areas of new medical innovations; global health R&D; health security; pricing; product reach; healthcare access; engaged people; inclusion and diversity; employee health, wellbeing and development; reliable supply; ethics and values; data and engagement; and the environment. The Corporate Responsibility Committee oversees progress against these commitments.[45] The board committee's role is defined as follows: "The Committee considers GSK's Trust priority and oversight of progress against the associated Trust commitments which reflect the most important issues for responsible and sustainable business growth. It has oversight of the:

- Views and interests of our internal and external stakeholders and reviews issues that have the potential for serious impact upon GSK's business and reputation; and
- Enterprise Risks determined by the Board to be most relevant to the Committee's area of expertise and responsibility."[46]

Ford Motor Company's *Sustainability and Innovation Committee's* current charter was approved in 2015, building on the experience of previous committees and allocation of responsibilities. It defines the committee's role as follows: "Sustainability and Innovation Committee shall evaluate and advise on the Company's pursuit of innovative practices and technologies, as set forth in Section IV of this Charter, that improve environmental and social sustainability, and that seek to enrich our customers' experiences, increase shareholder value, and lead to a better world."[47] The sustainability topics discussed by the committee include energy consumption, climate change, greenhouse gas and other criteria pollutant emissions, waste disposal, and water use; social well-being, including human rights, working conditions, and responsible sourcing; and trends in global mobility such as mobility infrastructure, vehicle ownership and business models, vehicle connectivity and automation in order to help provide accessible, personal mobility throughout the world. The committee's innovation mandate includes discussing and advising on "the innovation strategies and practices used to develop and commercialize the technologies that contribute to the Company's efforts to: (i) improve the fuel efficiency of our products, (ii) reduce the environmental impact of our facilities, (iii) provide products of the highest quality, (iv) improve the safety performance of our vehicles, and (v) continuously deliver industry-leading technology solutions that enrich customer experiences."[48]

*(continued)*

**(continued)**

Newmont's *Safety and Sustainability Committee* was established in 2004. The committee has the authority "to investigate any activity of the Corporation and its subsidiaries relating to health, safety, loss prevention and operational security, sustainable development, environmental management and affairs, relations with communities and civil society, government relations, human rights and communications matters."[49] In addition, certain safety and sustainability priorities are reviewed and overseen by the full board and by the company's Audit Committee or its Leadership Development and Compensation Committee (LDCC). Underpinning the company's purpose, values and business strategy are five foundational principles that guide continuous improvement and establish the objectives by which performance is measured by management and overseen by the board.[50] They are health and safety; operational excellence; growth; people; and environmental, social and governance. In 2020, the company refreshed its Corporate Governance Guidelines to state:

> The mission of the Board is to oversee the Corporation's efforts to create enduring value for all stakeholders. To deliver on this mission, the Board will adhere to sound governance principles and the Corporation's core values of safety, integrity, sustainability, inclusion and responsibility. In its oversight role, the Board must maintain a sense of responsibility to the Corporation's stockholders, customers, employees, suppliers and the communities in which it operates to enable the Corporation to fulfill its corporate purpose of creating value and improving lives through sustainable and responsible mining.[51]

**A science, technology and innovation committee**: Some companies are establishing science, technology and/or innovation committees to stay on top of key scientific and technology trends and disruptions and to provide better insight and oversight on key science and technology-related risks and opportunities faced by the company. Some of these will be ESG&D related or have substantial implications for the company's performance on ESG&D issues.

**The integration of ESG&D into other committees**: In many cases, even with a dedicated ESG or risk committee, other more traditional committees have started to integrate responsibility for oversight of key ESG&D-related risks and opportunities into their mandates:

- **Governance and nominating committees** can play an essential role in ensuring that ESG&D-related skills, capabilities and experiences are integrated into director recruitment, onboarding, training and succession planning, as well as having oversight of committee charters and board peer reviews and evaluation processes. This tends to be the existing committee most likely to add ESG or sustainability oversight to its committee mandate or charter in cases where a dedicated ESG committee is not established.

- **Audit committees** should be reviewing the company's ethics compliance, anti-corruption and integrity policies, systems and performance and in some cases its data stewardship systems. They should also be discussing and disclosing the financial risks associated with material ESG&D issues. In the case of climate, for example, the Task Force on Climate-Related Financial Disclosure highlights the need for boards to review and report on the financial risks and costs of climate, not only the environmental ones.
- **Compensation committees** in many boards are expanding their mandate and their name to encompass leadership development, talent management and inclusion and diversity, alongside their traditional compensation oversight responsibilities. Such committees can play a crucial role in ensuring the clear alignment of executives' performance incentives and rewards with ESG&D performance, alongside their financial, commercial and operational performance. They can also provide oversight of ESG&D integration into the company's human capital strategies more broadly.

## 4.6.2   Ensure Board Composition Is Fit for the Complex Operating Environment

Board composition or membership is as important as board organization. In today's complex, multi-stakeholder, multicultural and multinational operating environment, there is growing recognition of the need for greater board diversity—diversity not only in terms of gender and race, although both are essential, but also diversity in background, experiences, skills, nationality and age.

The foundations of a strong board are well understood. Every board needs experienced directors who have extensive governance, executive and operating experience, both in the industry in question and in other industries that may offer different, but valuable, insights and lessons. In the wake of various financial scandals and crises, it is clearly essential for every board to have enough directors with financial, accounting and auditing skills.

At the same time, a growing imperative in many boards is to have directors with the technical and/or risk management skills and experiences needed to understand the massive technological disruptions and digital, data stewardship and other technology-related risks that companies are facing. Bringing one or two technically skilled younger directors on board can help in this area, as well as providing insights from a younger generation of leaders. Companies operating globally benefit from directors who live in and/or have worked in some of their most important countries or regions of operation, or a director who has extensive geopolitical and diplomatic experience in relevant areas of operation. And, increasingly, there is a focus on appointing directors who bring operational or academic skills and experiences related directly to understanding the company's evolving ESG risks and opportunities.

There is the obvious need to balance the expanding range of necessary experiences, skills sets and mindsets with ensuring that the board is not too large for effective discussions and decision-making. As such, director recruitment and succession planning need to focus on finding directors who, on an individual basis, can meet a diverse matrix of skills requirements and backgrounds. Certainly, more and more former CEOs and other senior executives are well versed in managing ESG&D-related risks and opportunities, and this should be one of the skills or experience sets to look for in all director recruitment.

In addition, structured and staggered succession planning, alongside term or age limits, can help to ensure that a board balances the need for "institutional memory" with fresh perspectives and generational change in a rapidly evolving and often disruptive operating environment.

One of the topics gaining momentum in light of the growing focus on employees and the "S" in ESG&D, more broadly, is the question of employee representation on corporate boards. Countries with unitary board structures are looking at the experiences of the European two-tier board system, where employees and increasingly other stakeholders are represented on the supervisory tier of the board and engage strategically with the executives who serve on the management board. The question of employee and broader stakeholder representation on boards, including ongoing challenges for board seats from shareholder activists, will continue to grow in volume and significance. At a minimum, as outlined in the next section, boards should be developing more systematic processes for engaging with key internal and external stakeholders.

## 4.6.3 Enhance Board Engagement with Stakeholders

In addition to ongoing rigorous review of board organization and composition, boards need to understand and discuss the evolving boundaries of their engagement with stakeholders, both internally and externally. The growing focus by large institutional investors on stewardship and engagement and increasing calls for stakeholder capitalism suggest that boards need to, at a minimum, have a clear understanding of their company's key stakeholders. Such an understanding needs to be at a much more granular and nuanced level than the broad categories of shareholders, employees, customers, suppliers and communities. At the same time, both shareholders and other stakeholders are demanding more engagement directly with boards. In almost all cases, executive management should take the lead on both internal and external stakeholder engagement, bringing non-executive and independent directors in when there is a specific need or request to do so.

## Board Engagement with Internal Stakeholders

In many companies, non-executive directors are exposed only to the CEO, CFO and her or his executive leadership team. Such engagement is obviously crucial and at the heart of good corporate governance—aiming to achieve a healthy balance of rigorous oversight, questioning and challenging of management with mutual respect and a shared focus on the best long-term interests of the company. There are opportunities, however, for boards to expand their engagement to other managers and employees in the company, ranging from key business unit or site level managers to managers who have functional responsibility for the company's most material and salient ESG&D issues to employee affinity groups and high-potential next generation leaders.

Having the full senior executive team attend all board meetings is an approach some leading companies are taking to ensure more holistic and robust oversight and discussions between the board and all the senior executives who are responsible for delivering on the company's purpose and strategy and managing enterprise risks. From an ESG&D perspective, having the executive who is responsible for these issues attending all board meetings, not only doing an occasional presentation on ESG&D topics, is another way to help integrate these issues in the boardroom. Some companies are also establishing a senior-level ESG or sustainability committee, composed of senior executives in key operational and functional roles, that reports to the CEO and the board as part of the company's governance process.

In addition to regular engagement between the board and the full senior executive team, other approaches that companies are taking to ensure their boards have a better understanding of the company's risks, opportunities and culture include organizing regular site visits to operations and research facilities and inviting directors to participate in either large townhall meetings or smaller group discussions with employees. These approaches can give boards exposure to business unit or country and operational site managers, front-line supervisors, researchers, high-potential young managers, and the leaders of business resource, affinity or diversity groups.

## Board and Executive Engagement with External Stakeholders

In addition to the CEO, CFO and other executives, the number of independent board chairs and committee chairs who meet with shareholders or other external stakeholders is growing.

Some companies are also establishing external ethics, technology, sustainability or country-focused advisory councils that provide regular input to senior management and engage with relevant board directors or board committees on some of the company's most material ESG&D issues. These councils are explored in more detail in Chap. 5.

A growing area of oversight for boards is their company's engagement in lobbying and political funding as well as membership of trade and industry associations. In the case of lobbying, for example, there are growing calls from investors as well as other stakeholders for companies to disclose not only political contributions (in countries such as the US where these are allowed), but also the company's public policy positions and lobbying spending on important social and environmental issues. A 2019 report by the High Meadows Institute concluded, "[T]rade associations are influential, and their actions can either support or hinder adoption of ESG policies and practices by their members. As ESG integration becomes a mainstream investment practice, it will be increasingly important for investors to think critically about the trade association memberships of the companies in which they invest."[52]

## Taking a Holistic and Integrated Approach to Corporate Governance

In summary, a number of changes are underway to integrate oversight of ESG&D risks and opportunities and stakeholder expectations at the board level through changes in board organization, composition and culture, and stakeholder engagement mechanisms. In companies with good corporate governance, this remains a dynamic and ongoing process aimed at ensuring that board directors are well informed and equipped to meet their fiduciary duties and duty of care to the companies they serve.

As should be apparent, there is no one-size-fits-all approach. It is important for every board to consider the most effective way to develop a more integrated and holistic stakeholder-oriented approach. In addition, boards should be considering governance not only in terms of their own role, although this is obviously critical, but also how the board provides oversight of and support to other ESG&D governance structures—such as external advisory councils and panels and internal executive-level committees that have strategic oversight for ESG&D-related issues, as well as the company's participation in trade and industry associations, lobbying and policy advocacy, and voluntary multi-stakeholder initiatives created to set industry-wide rules and standards beyond regulatory requirements. Examples of how some leading companies are addressing governance and stakeholder engagement in a more integrated and holistic manner are explored in Chaps. 5, 6 and 7.

## Notes

1. OECD (2015) *G20/OECD Principles of Corporate Governance.* Page 11.
2. OECD Corporate Governance Factbook 2021. Preface by Mathias Cormann, OECD Secretary-General. https://www.oecd.org/corporate/Corporate-Governance-Factbook.pdf
3. What is a Benefit Corporation? https://benefitcorp.net/what-is-a-benefit-corporation. Accessed on August 19, 2020.
4. PwC's 2020 Annual Corporate Directors Survey. *Turning crisis into opportunity.* PwC, 2020. https://www.pwc.com/us/en/services/governance-insights-center/library/annual-corporate-directors-survey.html
5. Ibid. Page 4.
6. Diligent Institute. *Stakeholder capitalism: Translating Corporate Purpose into Board Practice.* August 2020. https://www.diligentinstitute.com/wp-content/uploads/2020/08/20200713-Diligent-Institute-Report-Stakeholders-and-Boards-R5.pdf
7. European Commission. *Study on directors' duties and sustainable corporate governance.* Final Report. Prepared by EY for the European Commission DG Justice and Consumers. July, 2020. https://op.europa.eu/en/publication-detail/-/publication/e47928a2-d20b-11ea-adf7-01aa75ed71a1/language-en
8. Ibid.
9. Ibid.
10. Ceres and kks advisors. *Systems Rule: How Board Governance Can Drive Sustainability Performance.* 2018. https://www.kksadvisors.com/systems-rule
11. Organisation for Economic Co-operation and Development. *G20/OECD Principles of Corporate Governance.* Preface. OECD, 2015. Page 9.
12. Ceres and kks advisors. *Systems Rule: How Board Governance Can Drive Sustainability Performance.* 2018. https://www.kksadvisors.com/systems-rule
13. Lucian A. Bebchuk & Roberto Tallarita. *The Illusory Promise of Stakeholder Governance.* Working draft, March 2020. https://papers.ssrn.com/sol3/papers.cfm?abstract_id=3544978
14. Lucian A. Bebchuk and Roberto Tallarita. "Stakeholder Capitalism seems mostly for show. If CEOs really intended to amend their companies' purpose,

they'd at least consult their boards first." Opinion/Commentary, *Wall Street Journal.* August 6, 2020. https://www.wsj.com/articles/stakeholder-capitalism-seems-mostly-for-show-11596755220?fbclid=IwAR1yaVWey SKwuR0TMUBewy3lfVsn6YKBPylsJy0JM3o0k_D1dRQ7kbW2q0U

15. Lucian A. Bebchuk and Roberto Tallarita. *Will corporations deliver value to all stakeholders?* Draft of August 4, 2021. https://papers.ssrn.com/sol3/papers.cfm?abstract_id=3899421

16. Ibid.

17. Ibid.

18. Lucian A. Bebchuk and Roberto Tallarita. "'Stakeholder' Talk proves Empty Again." Opinion/Commentary, *Wall Street Journal.* August 18, 2021. https://www.wsj.com/articles/stakeholder-capitalism-esg-business-roundtable-diversity-and-inclusion-green-washing-11629313759

19. Geoff Colvin, "America's top CEOs didn't live up to their promises in Business Roundtable letter, researchers find." Fortune, August 5, 2021. https://fortune.com/2021/08/05/business-roundtable-letter-statement-on-the-purpose-of-a-corporation-stakeholder-capitalism-american-ceos/

20. UK Department for Business, Energy and Industrial Strategy. Corporate governance: new reporting regulations. 12 June 2018. https://www.gov.uk/government/publications/corporate-governance-new-reporting-regulations

21. UK Department for Business, Energy and Industrial Strategy. *Corporate Governance. The Companies (Miscellaneous Reporting) Regulations 2018 Q&A.* November 2018.
    See also: ICSA The Governance Institute and the Investment Association. *The Stakeholder Voice in Board Decision-Making: Strengthening the business. Promoting Long-Term Success.* 2017

22. Pacte, The Action Plan for Business Growth and Transformation. https://www.gouvernement.fr/en/pacte-the-action-plan-for-business-growth-and-transformation

23. Ibid. See also Jean-Philippe Robé, Bertrand Delaunay, and Benoît Fleury. *French Legislation on Corporate Purpose.* Posted on June 8, 2019. Harvard Law School Forum on Corporate Governance. https://corpgov.law.harvard.edu/2019/06/08/french-legislation-on-corporate-purpose/

24. Business and Human Rights Resource Centre, "Switzerland: Responsible Business Initiative Rejected at ballot box despite gaining 50.7% of the popular vote." 30 November 2020. https://www.business-humanrights.org/en/latest-news/swiss-due-diligence-initiative-set-for-public-referendum-as-parliament-only-opts-for-reporting-centred-proposal/

25. Financial Reporting Council. *The UK Corporate Governance Code.* July 2018, https://www.frc.org.uk/getattachment/88bd8c45-50ea-4841-95b0-d2f4f48069a2/2018-UK-Corporate-Governance-Code-FINAL.pdf; and Financial Reporting Council. *Guidance on Board Effectiveness.* July 2018, https://www.frc.org.uk/getattachment/61232f60-a338-471b-ba5a-bfed25219147/2018-Guidance-on-Board-Effectiveness-FINAL.PDF

26. The World Business Council for Sustainable Development. *Modernizing Governance: ESG challenges and recommendations for corporate directors.* 2020. https://docs.wbcsd.org/2020/01/WBCSD-Modernizing_governance-key_ recommendations-for_boards_to_ensure_business_resilience.pdf

27. Enacting Purpose Initiative (EPI). *Enacting Purpose in the Modern Corporation: A framework for Boards of Directors.* University of Oxford, Said Business School, Berkeley Law, Business in Society Institute, Federated Hermes, Wachtell, Lipton, Rosen & Katz, and The British Academy. August 2020. https://www.sbs.ox.ac.uk/sites/default/files/2020-08/enacting-purpose-within-the-modern-corporation.pdf

28. Robert G. Eccles, Mary Johnstone-Louis, Colin Mayer and Judith C. Stroehle. The Board's Role in Sustainability: A new framework for getting directors behind ESG efforts. Harvard Business Review, September-October 2020.

29. Harvard Law School Forum on Corporate Governance, "Principles of Corporate Governance". Article posted by Business Roundtable on Thursday, September 8, 2016. https://corpgov.law.harvard.edu/2016/09/08/principles-of-corporate-governance/

30. FCLTGlobal. *The Long-term Habits of a Highly Effective Corporate Board.* March 2019.

31. BlackRock. Larry Fink's 2016 Letter to CEOs. https://www.blackrock.com/corporate/investor-relations/2016-larry-fink-ceo-letter

32. High Meadows Institute and tapestry Networks. *Corporate Governance for the 21st Century.* Initial report and readings. 2018. https://www.highmeadowsinstitute.org/projects/corporate-governance-for-the-21st-century/
    See also: Margaret Pederson, "Driving Growth and Setting Strategy: the Role of Board of Directors in Strategic Planning," *Financier Worldwide,* June 2015.

33. Harvard Law School Forum on Corporate Governance, "Principles of Corporate Governance". Article posted by Business Roundtable on Thursday, September 8, 2016. https://corpgov.law.harvard.edu/2016/09/08/principles-of-corporate-governance/

34. Ibid.

35. Ibid.

36. World Economic Forum in collaboration with PwC, "How to Set Up Effective Climate Governance on Corporate Boards: Guiding principles and questions." January 2019. http://www3.weforum.org/docs/WEF_Creating_effective_climate_governance_on_corporate_boards.pdf

37. Diligent Institute. Stakeholder capitalism: Translating Corporate Purpose into Board Practice. August, 2020. Page 4 https://www.diligentinstitute.com/wp-content/uploads/2020/08/20200713-Diligent-Institute-Report-Stakeholders-and-Boards-R5.pdf

38. NACD. Report of the NACD Blue Commission on "Culture as a Corporate Asset." 2017. https://www.nacdonline.org/insights/publications.cfm?Item Number=48256
39. Ibid.
40. PwC's 2019 Annual Corporate Directors Survey. https://www.pwc.com/us/en/services/governance-insights-center/library/annual-corporate-directors-survey.html
41. KPMG. *Board oversight of corporate culture.* KPMG Board Leadership Center, 2018
42. See United Nations Environment Programme Finance Initiative, *Integrated Governance—A New Model of Governance for Sustainability*, 2014, for a discussion of ESG implications for board committees and processes, https://www.unepfi.org/publications/investment-publications/integrated-governance-a-new-model-of-governance-for-sustainability-2
43. Ceres and kks advisors. *Systems Rule: How Board Governance Can Drive Sustainability Performance.* 2018. https://www.kksadvisors.com/systems-rule
44. About Us. https://www.gsk.com/en-gb/about-us/#
45. See pages 33–47 of GSK's Annual Report, 2020 for detailed information of Trust Priorities and ESG goals and targets. https://www.gsk.com/media/6662/annual-report-2020.pdf
46. GSK. Corporate Responsibility Committee, Terms of Reference. Approved by the Board on 3 February 2005. Last updated on 6 May 2021. https://www.gsk.com/media/6899/terms-of-reference-corporate-responsibility-committee.pdf
47. Ford Motor Company. Charter of the Sustainability and Innovation Committee of the Board of Directors. March 2015. https://corporate.ford.com/content/dam/corporate/us/en-us/documents/governance-and-policies/company-governance-sustainability-and-innovation-committee-charter.pdf
48. Ibid.
49. Newmont Corporation. Safety and Sustainability Committee Charter. Updated and approved by the Board of Directors, 23 October 2019. https://s24.q4cdn.com/382246808/files/doc_downloads/about_us/board_and_committees/update/SS-Charter-October-2019-FINAL_New-Brand.pdf
50. Newmont, 2020 Sustainability Report. *Focused on Value. Driven by Purpose.* Pages 25–26.
51. Newmont Corporation. Corporate Governance Guidelines. Updated and approved by the Board of Directors effective as of November 12, 2020. https://s24.q4cdn.com/382246808/files/doc_downloads/about_us/board_and_committees/update/Corporate-Governance-Guidelines-FINAL-11-12-20.pdf
52. High Meadows Institute. *The Role of Trade Associations in ESG.* A Research Note, April 2019. https://www.highmeadowsinstitute.org/wp-content/uploads/2019/11/The-Role-of-Trade-Association-in-ESG.pdf

# 5

# Corporate Strategy and Implementation

This chapter focuses on practical actions that business leaders are taking at the firm level to implement a more stakeholder-oriented approach that integrates ESG risks and opportunities into their core business strategy and operations across their value chain.

Business leaders have four over-riding priorities in any company that aims to create sustainable enterprise value and deliver on the principles of stakeholder capitalism:

* Commit to and demonstrate *shared* purpose and values
* Leverage opportunities to create *shared* value
* Manage *shared* risks to protect value
* Evaluate and report on performance for *shared* accountability[1]

This calls for companies to have a clearly articulated corporate purpose beyond profit and a set of values that are embedded in company culture, strategy and decision-making. It requires a rigorous and systematic process to identify the risks and opportunities that are most material to the company and most salient to its stakeholders—its employees, other workers, customers, suppliers, distributors, communities, shareholders, governments and the environment. In turn, this process enables management teams to develop strategies and business plans, to set internal and public goals and targets and to evaluate and report on performance against these to drive business improvement and where needed business transformation.

In today's dynamic and complex operating context, priorities and strategies are likely to change and continuous improvement may not be sufficient.

© The Author(s) 2022
R. Samans, J. Nelson, *Sustainable Enterprise Value Creation*,
https://doi.org/10.1007/978-3-030-93560-3_5

Change is increasingly disruptive, as experienced by rapid technology shifts, the COVID-19 pandemic and other acute and systemic shocks. Even when change occurs more slowly, driven by evolving demographics, environmental conditions, regulations, consumer demands, investor interests, social norms and technologies, there is a growing need for executive teams to be agile, adaptive and resilient.

Comprehensive and consistent stakeholder engagement is essential to achieve all these business leadership goals. Executive leaders and their teams must have systematic plans and processes in place to identify, engage with, listen to, learn from, influence and cooperate with key stakeholders, both internally and externally. They must be able to judge what the company can achieve working within its own business model and value chain and where and when it needs to work with others, including competitors in certain cases, to address systemic market failures and governance gaps. Regardless of whether the company is focused on achieving results through its own business model and value chain or on helping to drive change as a stakeholder itself in the broader system, the ability to navigate a multitude of diverse and dynamic stakeholder relationships—both supportive and adversarial—is crucial to success.

In the book, *Profits with Principles*, one of us made the case with our co-author, Ira Jackson, that to create both shareholder and societal value, business leaders are taking practical action in each of the following areas:

> When managing their wider impacts on society, these companies are moving beyond a mind-set that is bounded by *compliance* with laws and regulations; the *control* of risks, costs, liabilities and negative impacts; and *community investment* or philanthropy. They see compliance, control and community investment as necessary but insufficient building blocks to becoming outstanding corporate citizens. They are also aiming to *create new value* for stakeholders, including but not only shareholders. They are implementing strategies to create new products and services, change operational processes, build new alliances, enter new markets, support new institutional structures, and in some cases even transform business models, so that they meet social and environmental needs as well as customer demands and aspirations. They are looking to create societal value as well as shareholder value.[2]

Figure 5.1 illustrates that these four approaches are not mutually exclusive. Indeed, companies must be implementing them simultaneously if they aim to create sustainable enterprise value and to become more stakeholder oriented:

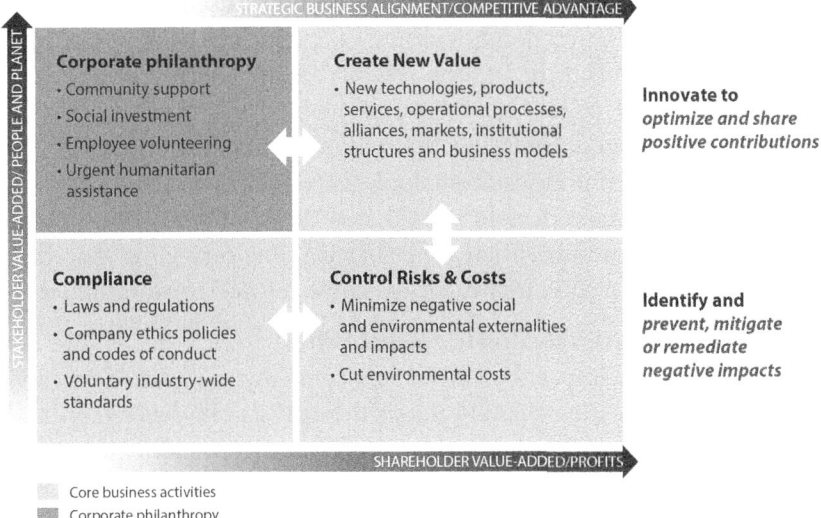

STRATEGIC BUSINESS ALIGNMENT/COMPETITIVE ADVANTAGE

STAKEHOLDER VALUE-ADDED/PEOPLE AND PLANET

**Corporate philanthropy**
- Community support
- Social investment
- Employee volunteering
- Urgent humanitarian assistance

**Create New Value**
- New technologies, products, services, operational processes, alliances, markets, institutional structures and business models

**Innovate to** *optimize and share positive contributions*

**Compliance**
- Laws and regulations
- Company ethics policies and codes of conduct
- Voluntary industry-wide standards

**Control Risks & Costs**
- Minimize negative social and environmental externalities and impacts
- Cut environmental costs

**Identify and** *prevent, mitigate or remediate negative impacts*

SHAREHOLDER VALUE-ADDED/PROFITS

Core business activities
Corporate philanthropy

**Fig. 5.1** Four components of a credible and comprehensive stakeholder-oriented strategy
(Adapted from: Jane Nelson. Chapter 3 *Leveraging the Development Impact of Business in the Fight Against Global Poverty* in Brainard, Lael (ed). *Transforming the Development Landscape: The Role of the Private Sector*. The Brookings Institution Press, Washington DC, 2006. Page 50; and Ira A. Jackson and Jane Nelson, *Profits with Principles*. Currency Doubleday, 2004. Page 54)

- *Compliance* with the law as well as with voluntary corporate and industry-wide codes of conduct.
- *Control* of environmental, social, governance and digital risks, costs and negative externalities (i.e., protecting value or *managing shared risks* to the company, people and the environment).
- *Community investment*, including strategic corporate philanthropy, social venture capital and employee volunteering.
- *Creating new value* that meets societal needs and builds competitive advantage, through new technologies, products and services, processes, alliances, markets and business models.

**Commit to and Demonstrate Shared Purpose and Values**
No company can be effective in implementing and sustaining a stakeholder-oriented approach without having a company-wide sense of shared purpose and commitment to a common set of values. Many major global corporations have a purpose statement. A growing number of these are framed in terms of how the company aims to solve social and environmental challenges and/or address stakeholder needs. Most companies also have a set of values. Yet, there

is cynicism among stakeholders when executive teams do not adhere to these values, especially if the corporate culture, executive behaviours and formal and informal rewards and recognition systems are not aligned with them.

As outlined in the pages that follow, developing a compelling corporate purpose statement and set of values, and ensuring that these are credibly and consistently embedded in decision-making at all levels of the company, is one of the most important leadership roles that a CEO and her or his executive team has. It is foundational to creating shared value, managing shared risks and ensuring shared accountability for the company and its stakeholders.

**Leverage Opportunities to Create *Shared* Value**

The greatest scale and impact by far that any company can have on leveraging opportunities and creating shared value is through its *core business operations and value chains*. These include the company's commercial activities and relationships in the workplace, the marketplace, and along its entire value chain, whether global, regional or local. Later in this chapter, we explore some of the ways that companies are making ambitious commitments and investing in innovation in new technologies, products, services, financing mechanisms and business models to create shared value by explicitly and measurably solving social and environmental challenges. There is a growing consensus that it will be impossible to meet the commitments of the Paris Climate Agreement or achieve the Sustainable Development Goals, without massive private sector investment and innovation of this type. Equally, the companies that undertake these activities in a commercially viable approach have opportunities to tap into the multi-billion-dollar markets that are evolving in systems such as energy, food and agriculture, health, financial products and services, transportation and mobility, and construction and infrastructure.

Over the past few decades, a variety of useful frameworks have emerged to guide companies in creating shared value. The one that has received the greatest traction in corporate boardrooms and executive suites is outlined in Professor Michael Porter and Mark Kramer's 2011 article in *Harvard Business Review*, "Creating Shared Value: How to Reinvent Capitalism—and Unleash a Wave of Innovation and Growth."[3] They identified the following three distinct ways that companies can create economic value by creating societal value:

- Reconceiving products and markets
- Redefining productivity in the value chain
- Building supportive industry clusters at the company's locations[4]

Other terms and frameworks that underpin the same core message of *intentional and measurable management strategies to achieve value creation for both shareholders and other stakeholders* include:

- Impact Investing—an approach developed from an investor perspective and initially framed by the Rockefeller Foundation.[5]
- Corporate Social Opportunity—an idea advanced by Professor David Grayson and Adrian Hodges.[6]
- Reimagining Capitalism—a term and approach framed by Professor Rebecca Henderson and her colleagues at Harvard Business School.[7]
- Conscious Capitalism—a term made popular by the founder and former CEO of Whole Foods, John Mackey.[8]
- Total Societal Impact—a term developed by the Boston Consulting Group.[9]

In addition to core business activities, companies can also create shared value by having a strategic, competence-led approach to their corporate *community investment, philanthropy and employee volunteering* activities. These activities are unlikely to achieve the scale and impact that core business models and value chains can reach. Nor will they have as direct a link to company profit, competitiveness and shareholder value. Yet, they can still provide substantial benefits to a company's stakeholders. If the community investments made by companies or their corporate foundations are aligned with areas of core business competence and capabilities, they are more likely to also benefit the company, achieve scale and impact and be sustainable over the longer term. Examples include:

- banks and other financial institutions leveraging their corporate philanthropy to increase financial inclusion, financial literacy and economic mobility;
- pharmaceutical companies establishing product donation programmes for medicines and diagnostics during a humanitarian crisis or to serve low-income communities in addressing specific disease burdens;
- food and beverage communities supporting smallholder farmers and retailers, community food banks and school feeding programmes in low-income areas; and
- energy, utility and information and communications technology (ICT) companies providing access to essential physical and digital services in times of crisis or to marginalized communities.

In some cases, philanthropic or social investments may also serve as seed capital, incubators, prototypes or catalysts for testing out new technologies, products and services that could over time become commercially viable and profitable, as well as scalable.

**Manage *Shared* Risks to Protect Value**
Effective strategies to create shared value are necessary, but not sufficient. They cannot be implemented in isolation to the corporate responsibility to *manage the shared risks*, costs and negative impacts to the business and to people and the environment that may result from a company's business model and activities.

Whether it is preventing human rights abuses or managing environmental risks, companies are under growing pressure from investors, regulators and other stakeholders to demonstrate they have the necessary capabilities and management systems to identify, mitigate and where necessary remediate risks to people and the environment, as well as risks to the company. Failure to effectively manage such risks can seriously undermine credibility and stakeholder trust in the company, damage corporate reputation, weaken the ability to create sustainable enterprise value and in some cases threaten both the company's social and legal licence to operate.

As detailed further in this chapter, to effectively manage shared risks, companies must have rigorous policies, standards, due diligence processes and internal audit systems in place to be compliant with the law and with industry-wide voluntary standards on ethical, environmental, social and governance issues. They must have their own company-wide corporate codes of conduct and rigorous systems to implement these as well as mechanisms to hold all managers, employees and business partners accountable for doing so. And, they must have enterprise risk management systems in place that embed ESG&D risks, costs and negative externalities. None of this is a "tick-the-box" exercise. Over the past two decades the disciplines of ESG&D compliance and risk management have evolved significantly. The depth and breadth of technical and management expertise that are needed to identify and manage these risks continues to grow in the face of disruptive shifts and longer-term trends.

**Evaluate and Report on Performance for *Shared* Accountability**
Establishing clear and time-bound goals, targets and metrics for creating shared value and managing shared risks, undertaking rigorous data collection, evaluation and analysis of these, and reporting publicly on the company's performance are essential for ensuring transparency and accountability

with stakeholders. They can help to strengthen the quality of business decision-making, reward and hold managers to account, and build and retain the trust of key stakeholders. Goals and targets should be structured in a way that they can be quantitatively measured or qualitatively assessed and comparable from both a longitudinal perspective and relative to the performance of other business peers and competitors. While more companies are making their priority ESG goals and targets public and reporting on their performance against these, increasingly with third-party assurance, there is a long way to go. Chapter 6 outlines the growing importance of integrated corporate reporting and collective efforts to establish a global sustainability reporting framework.

Figure 5.2 summarizes these key business leadership pillars.

The following sections focus on some of the ways that companies are putting a stakeholder-oriented business model into practice through their actions to:

- Embed purpose, values and ESG priorities into corporate strategy and operations
- Strengthen management of material *and* salient ESG&D risks

**Fig. 5.2** Business leadership pillars of values, value creation, value protection and evaluation
(Adapted from: Jane Nelson. *Corporate Citizenship in a Global Context*. Working Paper No. 13. Corporate Social Responsibility Initiative, Harvard Kennedy School. May 2005. Pages 9–10)

- Invest in technology and innovation to drive inclusive and sustainable growth
- Promote employee well-being, talent, diversity and inclusion
- Establish robust and accountable mechanisms for engagement with external stakeholders

## 5.1  Embed Purpose, Values and ESG Priorities into Corporate Strategy and Operations

In today's dynamic, multi-issue and multi-stakeholder operating context, the clarity and credibility of a company's publicly stated purpose, values and ESG priorities, and the way they are communicated and embedded in the company's strategy, operations and culture are more important than ever.

As one of us stated with our co-author in the book *Profits with Principles*:

> Each company has the core purpose of providing goods and services that meet customer needs or aspirations and yield a profit. In great companies, purpose extends beyond short-term profit and the creation of shareholder value. It often encompasses a longer-term vision to contribute to improve people's lives and be a force for progress in the world. Together with principles and values, purpose is what a great company stands for and would stand by even if adhering to them resulted in a competitive disadvantage, missed opportunity or increased costs. Purpose, principles and values are the bedrock of excellence. The way they are articulated and implemented plays a key role in determining the company's strategic direction, its corporate culture, and the policies and incentive systems by which it operates and impacts the world.[10]

As outlined in Chap. 4, strong alignment between corporate purpose, values and ESG priorities with corporate strategy, operational priorities and incentives as well as company culture, norms and behaviours are crucial. A lack of coherence and consistency between these key drivers of business performance is justifiably one of the major drivers of stakeholder cynicism and mistrust in companies and their leaders, both internally among employees as well as among external stakeholders and opinion-formers.

There are too many examples of a company communicating positive social and environmental stories and projects while its government relations teams, trade associations or lobbyists are lobbying governments for policies and regulations that undermine the very same social or environmental goals at a system level. Equally, as ESG becomes a strategic business imperative in most industry sectors, there are more examples of so-called greenwashing where the company's marketing and product promises don't live up to the reality of what the company is in fact delivering. Or examples of CEOs and senior managers who are not held accountable or penalized for actions they have taken that fail to adhere to or undermine the company's stated purpose and values. Regulators as well as journalists, non-governmental organizations, groups of employees and consumer organizations are ramping up efforts to identify such examples where business leaders are failing to "walk the talk."

In short, a corporate purpose and set of values outlining how the company can profitably serve stakeholders should be the lodestar for how executives and managers develop and implement strategy, make major capital allocation, investment and business planning decisions as well as day-to-day operational decisions, lead and motivate their teams, and engage with internal and external stakeholders.

The Enacting Purpose Initiative, a collaborative effort among academic and practitioner organizations, has published several papers providing guidance for boards and executive teams on developing and implementing a credible corporate purpose[11] and on measuring purpose.[12] Business Fights Poverty, one of the world's largest online communities for business and sustainability practitioners, has developed a toolkit on how to embed purpose in business activities, drawing on discussions and written feedback from several hundred business and civil society stakeholders.[13] In her book, *Brands on a Mission*, Dr Myriam Sidibe introduces five key drivers for embedding corporate purpose: behaviour change, partnerships, brand advocacy, measurement and senior executive support.[14]

These guidelines and other research on aligning corporate purpose, values and ESG priorities with strategy and operations highlight three key lessons that are relevant for any company.

### 5.1.1 The Importance of Rigorous Stakeholder Consultation and Engagement

Executives need to support structured and sustained stakeholder consultation, especially with employees, but also with external stakeholders and advisers in defining or revising the company's purpose and values and keeping ahead of key ESG trends, risks and opportunities. Equally important, they need to give employees an active voice and opportunities to "live the company's values, purpose and ESG priorities." This includes empowering employees to integrate them into their daily business responsibilities and activities and into relevant employee engagement and volunteering activities, both internally through business resource groups, employee affinity groups, green teams, social venture networks and other company-supported or self-organizing groups and externally through engagement with customers, suppliers, other business partners, ESG experts and communities. It includes investing in talent development, career progression and incentive programmes that explicitly recognize and value employee leadership in these areas. Equally importantly, it requires robust and credible processes that enable employees to speak up, including in confidence through ethics lines and whistle-blower mechanisms, when they witness misconduct or potential misconduct. Examples of specific mechanisms for engagement with employees and other stakeholders are reviewed later in the chapter.

## 5.1.2  The Importance of Combining Materiality and Salience

It is important that senior business leaders undertake rigorous analysis of external trends and scenarios, internal performance data and stakeholder perspectives to identify those ESG&D risks and opportunities that are most *material* to the company's success and most *salient* to its stakeholders. This includes but goes beyond undertaking a sustainability materiality analysis. They should identify the few key "big bets" where the company has the greatest potential to achieve large-scale and sustained impact through profitably addressing key environmental and social challenges and meeting stakeholder needs. In addition, they should commit to manage, monitor and account for the broader range of ESG&D risks and opportunities that are relevant for the company and its industry sector or areas of operation. Once the ESG&D priorities are identified and there is broad agreement among the executive team, business unit heads and key operational and functional managers, then explicit policies, processes and incentives need to be established or revised to ensure that these ESG&D priorities are aligned with corporate strategy pillars and with the company's core business planning, operational, financial and functional priorities.

### 5.1.3 The Importance of Credible Communication and Accountability

Senior executives, from the CEO, CFO and COO to other functional and business unit leaders, should be proactive champions for the company's values and purpose and sufficiently well-informed and fluent in the company's ESG&D priorities to communicate and demonstrate these clearly and consistently, both internally and externally. In addition to personally "walking the talk," they should ensure that ESG&D priorities are accompanied by specific, time-bound and measurable goals and targets and supported by company policies, standards and incentives. Ideally, these priorities and goals should be included in the full range of company communications and outreach platforms from annual reporting to social media, from presentations to investors to meetings with government officials and community leaders, and from employee townhalls to annual performance reviews and recognition programmes. Underpinning the above, senior business leaders should commit to measuring and accounting for performance on a regular and consistent basis. As outlined in Chap. 6, public reporting of performance data that is independently assured is a crucial foundation for credible communication and accountability.

The examples in Box 5.1 illustrate how four companies from different industry sectors are working to embed a clear purpose and stakeholder orientation into their core business strategy pillars, business planning and operations and their engagement with investors and other stakeholders, not only into the work of their sustainability team. There are a growing number of other examples. They include Mars, Incorporated and its long-standing commitment to the principle of "mutuality" and its *Sustainable in Generation Plan* launched in 2017; PVH's *Forward Fashion* strategy established in 2019; Shell's *Powering Progress* corporate strategy and bp's *Reimagining Energy* strategy, both launched in 2020; IKEA's commitment to becoming *People and Planet Positive*, published in 2018; Marks and Spencer's *Plan A* framework for delivering long-term sustainable business value, which was launched in 2010 and has been refreshed several times; Natura's *2050 Sustainability Vision*; Abbott's *2030 Sustainability Plan*; Solvay's *One Planet Roadmap*; Olam's *Re-imagine Global Agriculture* framework; and A.P. Moller-Maersk's *All the Way* strategy and growth plan to digitize, democratize and decarbonize supply chains; among others.

**Box 5.1 Examples of Companies That Have Integrated ESG and Stakeholder Priorities into Their Corporate Purpose and Strategy**

The following examples illustrate how four diverse companies are working to integrate ESG and stakeholder priorities more fully into their corporate strategies and purpose statements:

*Johnson & Johnson's Credo and Health for Humanity 2025 Goals.* J&J is well known for its pioneering role in explicitly stating its commitment to stakeholders, including but beyond shareholders, through its long-standing *J&J Credo*. Created in 1943, the Credo states, "We believe our first responsibility is to the patients, doctors and nurses, to the mothers and fathers and all others who use our products and services."[15] The Credo then goes on to outline its responsibility to three other groups of key stakeholders, "our employees who work with us throughout the world," and "the communities where we live and work and to the world community as well," and "our stockholders." The company's corporate purpose states: "We blend heart, science and ingenuity to profoundly change the trajectory of health for humanity."[16]

Alongside its corporate strategy focused on innovation and excellence in execution, J&J has established a set of 21 *Health for Humanity 2025 Goals*. These are focused on addressing two of the greatest health challenges facing humanity, namely, pandemics and epidemics and global health equity, as well as raising the bar within and beyond the company's own walls through its focus on employees, planet, and partners and suppliers. These goals are also explicitly aligned with the Sustainable Development Goals. The company's board has oversight of performance against the goals and results are reported annually alongside financial results.

*Bank of America's Responsible Growth Strategy.* The implementation of BofA's Responsible Growth Strategy is one of the foundational shifts that the company has made resulting from lessons learned during the 2008 global financial crisis, alongside its shift from more traditional corporate philanthropy to an enterprise-wide commitment to embedding ESG risks and opportunities into the company's eight lines of business. Today, the bank states its corporate purpose as follows: "We are guided by a common purpose to make financial lives better through the power of every connection." It goes on to state, "We've transformed Bank of America into a simpler, more efficient company that combines two crucial areas: growing the economy while creating tangible value for our business, our clients and the communities we serve. We're helping create jobs, develop communities, foster economic mobility and address society's biggest challenges around the world."[17]

The company's Responsible Growth Strategy consists of four pillars: 1) We must grow and win the market—no excuses. 2) We must grow with our customer-focused strategy, serving three groups of customers: people, companies, and institutional investors. 3) We must grow within our risk framework. Noting that all employees are responsible for proactively managing risk as part of their day-to-day activities through prompt identification, escalation and debate of risks. This includes environmental and social risks. 4) We must grow in a sustainable manner. This requires progress across three dimensions: driving operational excellence, being a great place to work for our teammates and sharing our success with our communities.[18]

(*continued*)

**Box 5.1 (continued)**

The bank has established a Global ESG Committee, composed of the senior executives from the bank's business lines, key functions and geographies of operation. Alongside delivering on its own Responsible Growth Strategy, the bank and its CEO, Brian Moynihan, has also played a leadership role in working with the World Economic Forum's International Business Council and the Big Four accounting firms, Deloitte, EY, KPMG and PwC, to develop a set of common stakeholder capitalism metrics relevant for all companies.[19]

*Danone's One Planet. One Health Vision.* In 2017, building on its 2005 purpose to "bring health through food to as many people as possible," Danone unveiled a new logo and the following vision statement: "One Planet. One Health. These words reflect our vision that the health of people and the health of the planet are interconnected. It is a call to action for all consumers and everyone who has a stake in food to join the food revolution: a movement aimed at nurturing the adoption of healthier, more sustainable eating and drinking habits."[20] In addition to explicitly aligning its corporate strategy and growth model to the concept of "sustainable value creation," the company is also taking ground-breaking action to implement more holistic legal and governance structures and business models. It became the first listed company in France, for example, to adopt the "Entreprise à Mission" model created by the French "Pacte" law in 2019. An "Entreprise à Mission" is defined as a company whose social and environmental objectives are aligned with its purpose and set out in its Articles of Association. The status was officially embedded in Danone's Articles of Association and registered in July 2020.[21]

Danone has also become one of the leading multinational corporate champions of the B Corp certification model. As of mid-2021, it reported, "A total of thirty-seven Danone entities have now earned B Corp™ Certification. As a result, approximately 50% of Danone's global sales are now covered by B Corp™ certification, marking significant progress towards Danone's ambition to become one of the first certified multinationals."[22] Alongside setting nine ambitious goals for sustainable value creation, which are explicitly aligned to the SDGs and verified by a Mission Committee composed of well-respected and mostly independent sustainability experts, Danone has also created three innovative social innovation funds to help it pioneer more inclusive growth models: the Danone Ecosystem Fund, and the Danone Communities and Livelihoods Funds. These funds draw on company resources as well as provide a mechanism for shareholders, employees and other funding partners to participate.

*The Unilever Compass.* Building on the lessons and insights gained from its ten-year Unilever Sustainable Living Plan (USLP), in 2020 the company launched the Unilever Compass, a new corporate strategy with sustainability and a multistakeholder model at its core. As CEO, Alan Jope, outlined, "The Compass sets out our vision to be the leader in sustainable business globally—and we mean sustainable in the broadest sense of the word: socially, environmentally and economically. It is our new, fully integrated corporate strategy which builds on the successes and the lessons learnt over the last ten years of the USLP. It will have nine imperatives and 15 multi-year priorities that cover the full spectrum of our business and our wider ecosystem, with a range of ambitious targets that are more holistic, inclusive and far-reaching than ever before."[23]

*(continued)*

**Box 5.1 (continued)**

The company's corporate purpose to "make sustainable living commonplace" is underpinned by the three beliefs that brands with purpose grow, companies with purpose last and people with purpose thrive. Alongside the company's multi-year financial framework, which is focused on competitive growth, profit growth, cash generation and top one-third TSR performance, it has also set ambitious public sustainability goals and targets in the areas of climate action; protect and regenerate nature; waste-free world; positive nutrition; health and well-being; equity, diversity and inclusion; raise living standards; and future of work. Among these goals are ground-breaking commitments to adopt regenerative approaches to nature and environmental impacts by moving beyond having a net-zero impact to achieving a net-positive contribution. The company has also been one of the first multinationals to make a public commitment to living wages, with the goal of "ensuring that everyone who directly provides goods and services to Unilever will earn at least a living wage or income by 2030."[24]

The company will report on performance against the Unilever Compass and details of its engagement with stakeholders in its annual report. In addition to having a long-standing Sustainability Advisory Council and a Sustainable Sourcing Advisory Board, both composed of independent, external experts, the company has established a Next Gen Sustainability Council, which it describes as "a collective of young advocates, who are independently connected to broader youth bodies. ... [which] aims to capture the voice and expectation of young people across key sustainability issues that are critical to the people and planet ambitions of the Unilever Compass."[25]

In addition to examples of company-wide strategic alignment between sustainability and corporate strategy, there are a growing number of companies that have made substantial commitments and "Big Bets" focused on specific but large-scale and system-level ESG issues. Especially notable are public, time-bound and measurable goals to achieve science-based net-zero or carbon negative climate change solutions, water stewardship and circular economy models and to dramatically scale up people's access and affordability of essential goods and services and pay living wages as pathways to tackle inequality.

In summary, alignment of corporate purpose, values and ESG priorities with corporate strategy, operations and culture matters more than ever in today's complex operating context. Senior executives have a responsibility to "walk the talk." This matters for reasons of individual and institutional ethics, integrity and leadership as well as taking responsibility for the company's social and environmental performance, both positive and negative. It also matters for the quality of the company's stakeholder relations and its operational and financial performance. As Larry Fink the CEO of BlackRock, with US $9.5 trillion in assets under management as of the second quarter of 2021,[26] has commented,

Without a sense of purpose, no company, either public or private, can achieve its full potential. It will ultimately lose the license to operate from key stakeholders. It will succumb to short-term pressures to distribute earnings, and, in the process, sacrifice investments in employee development, innovation, and capital expenditures that are necessary for long-term growth. It will remain exposed to activist campaigns that articulate a clearer goal, even if that goal serves only the shortest and narrowest of objectives. And ultimately, that company will provide subpar returns to the investors who depend on it to finance their retirement, home purchases, or higher education.[27]

## 5.2    Strengthen Management of Material *and* Salient ESG&D Risks

In addition to having a credibly embedded corporate purpose and set of values, responsible business conduct is another core foundation of a company's commitment to implementing stakeholder capitalism and creating sustainable enterprise value.

As the OECD outlines, "Responsible business conduct (RBC) entails above all compliance with laws, such as those on respecting human rights, environmental protection, labour relations and financial accountability, even where these are poorly enforced. It also involves responding to societal expectations communicated by channels other than the law, e.g. inter-governmental organisations, within the workplace, by local communities and trade unions, or via the press, and private voluntary initiatives."[28]

Despite substantial progress made by many companies over the past few decades, there continues to be public mistrust in large corporations in many countries and scepticism about their voluntary commitments to managing and mitigating ESG&D risks. To effectively address these risks and build trust with stakeholders, business leaders must be able to demonstrate that their company has:

- **Policies, standards and due diligence processes** in place to identify, understand, mitigate and manage ESG&D risks that are material to the business and salient to people and the environment. These should include guidance for operational leaders on appropriate escalation pathways to executive management when risks or bad practices are identified at the operational and site level or among suppliers and other business partners.

- **Accountability, grievance and mediation mechanisms** in place that are accessible by relevant stakeholders and that provide access to remedy in situations where it can be demonstrated that people's rights or the environment have been negatively impacted as the result of the company's business model or activities.

In addition to the risk management systems that companies establish within their own operations, they can work with their suppliers and other business partners to spread responsible business practices further along local and global value chains through implementing supplier codes of conduct and working with business partners to agree on shared priorities and implement compliance and auditing, training and capacity building programmes. They can also participate in industry-wide or thematic multi-stakeholder platforms aimed at setting voluntary norms, rules and standards, establishing accountability mechanisms, and harmonizing and spreading common sustainability metrics and reporting standards. Examples of some of these platforms are provided in Chaps. 6 and 7.

Key lessons of effective ESG&D risk management within a company include the following.

### 5.2.1   Invest Time to Engage Stakeholders in Rigorous Materiality Analysis and Due Diligence

Like any type of risk at any level of the company, managers must understand the ESG&D risks that are already or are likely to become *material* to the company's own operational, reputational and financial performance. It is also important for them to be aware which ESG&D risks are *salient*, in terms of having a negative impact on people's rights and livelihoods or on the environment, even if they don't pose a material risk to the company. The concept of *double materiality* is increasingly used, especially in Europe, to include salience. It can be defined as both "financial materiality" and "impact materiality."[29]

Over the past decade, the Sustainability Accounting Standards Board (SASB) and the Global Reporting Initiative (GRI) have been instrumental in making a strong business case for the materiality of ESG risks and in providing companies and investors with useful guidance on how to assess the risks that are likely to be most material in different industry sectors. The Taskforce for Climate-Related Financial Disclosure (TCFD) provides useful guidance for thinking about, assessing and disclosing financial risks associated with climate change.[30] Platforms such as the Greenhouse Gas Protocol, CDP, the Science-Based Targets Initiative and the Science-Based Targets Network are helping companies to think about environmental risks and how to set targets and report on performance. The key role of these and other accountability platforms are covered in Chap. 6. The UN Guiding Principles on Business and Human Rights provide companies with useful guidance on the concept of "salience" and salient human rights risks that all companies should consider when looking at the "S" in ESG&D.[31]

It is important that companies use these and other frameworks as a starting point and not a checklist. One of the most important aspects of undertaking regular and credible materiality and salience analysis is effective engagement with key internal and external stakeholders. Although the "headline risks" such as climate change, human rights, health and safety, water, biodiversity, tax payments, diversity and inclusion, data use and privacy are common across industries and companies, most ESG&D risks are complex, dynamic, nuanced and context specific. They cannot be adequately or credibly addressed through a simple "tick-the-box" exercise. Some have a rigorous scientific base, especially environmental risks, but most of them are relationship-based. Even scientifically measurable environmental risks manifest themselves as stakeholder or relationship risks, with water insecurity, loss of livelihoods due to deforestation and climate injustice being key examples.

As such, structured engagement with stakeholders, ranging from expert advisers and advisory councils to systematic consultation with diverse employees, customers and host communities, and above all establishing mechanisms to hear from affected people, is one of the most valuable ways that companies can widen their risk assessment lens. Listening to and learning from diverse perspectives can help to identify issues that the company's managers may not have considered as material or salient. Stakeholder engagement can also help to identify trends and to mitigate against impediments such as unconscious bias, over-reliance on traditional disciplines and "group think" when it comes to identifying current and future ESG&D risks. Overall, such engagement is important for strengthening the company's due diligence and accountability processes to enable it to better manage and mitigate those risks and to build mutual respect and trust with stakeholders in solving problems when they occur.

## 5.2.2  Integrate ESG&D Risks into Enterprise Risk Management and Risk Appetite Frameworks

As Ceres noted in a 2019 report on ESG risk management, "Historically, ESG issues have been viewed as different from other major categories of risk such as enterprise, business-management and emerging/non-traditional risks. This view is based on an incomplete understanding of how ESG issues have affected companies. Some of the biggest issues facing companies today, such as technological disruption, workforce issues and supply chain concerns, are linked with environmental and social factors."[32]

Just as we've made the case for board-level oversight of ESG risks in Chap. 4, it is essential that such risks, along with new digital and other technology risks, are fully integrated into the company's core risk management systems and not relegated to a "sustainability" or corporate responsibility management silo. This requires ownership of these risks by top executives, business units and operational leaders and their systematic review as part of risk tolerance and appetite discussions, enterprise risk management processes, business planning and budgeting processes and key business development activities, from R&D to mergers and acquisitions. As outlined in Chaps. 4 and 6, the development of public commitments and targets for managing the company's most material and salient ESG&D risks and public disclosure on performance against these, underpinned by rigorous internal audits and independently verified third-party assurance, are essential to creating sustainable enterprise value. Investors are starting to demand it, regulators are starting to mandate it and other stakeholders are starting to expect it.

In terms of mainstreaming ESG&D issues into enterprise risk management, a useful source of guidance for companies comes from a collaboration between COSO and the World Business Council for Sustainable Development (WBCSD). COSO is a voluntary private sector organization dedicated to developing comprehensive frameworks and guidance to companies on internal control, enterprise risk management and fraud deterrence. It is jointly sponsored by the American Accounting Association, the American Institute of Certified Public Accountants, Financial Executives International, the Institute of Management Accountants and the Institute of Internal Auditors. In 2018, COSO and WBCSD published "Enterprise Risk Management: Applying Enterprise Risk Management to Environmental, Social and Governance-Related Risks."[33]

They adapt COSO's well-established Enterprise Risk Management Framework and provide companies guidance on how to integrate ESG risks in the following five areas:

1. Governance and culture for ESG-related risks
2. Strategy and objective-setting for ESG-related risks
3. Performance for ESG-related risks—including identifying risk, assessing and prioritizing risk, and implementing a risk response
4. Review and revision for ESG-related risks
5. Information, communication and reporting for ESG-related risks[34]

In addition to implementing this or a similar process throughout the company, some leading companies are also providing public information on their ESG&D and wider enterprise risk management frameworks, including the executives who have ownership and accountability for managing material risks within the senior leadership team. These frameworks are being published in a variety of channels, for example, through annual reports, proxy statements, sustainability reports and dedicated website pages to cover controversies that the company is facing.

### 5.2.3 Commit to Dynamic Reviews and Stress-Testing of Risks

Linked to the above is the need for ongoing review and stress-testing of ESG&D risks and, where needed, adaptation of priorities. The sheer complexity and dynamism of today's operating environment for companies, especially those with a global footprint, cannot be over-emphasized. This was the case even before the COVID-19 pandemic and the rising impacts of climate change, inequality and injustice that have dominated headlines in countries around the world in recent years. These developments have put risks to people and human rights or the "S" in ESG in the spotlight as rarely before. At the same time, they have reminded us that the "E" risks have not gone away and in many cases have continued to accelerate and intensify, most notably in the context of the climate crisis. And, as corruption and other governance challenges have continued to be a problem in the face of political tensions in many countries, nationalism and public revenue seeking, and the need for massive government recovery and stimulus packages, the "G" remains as important as ever. Not to mention the dramatic acceleration of digital platforms and their influence on business operations, people's lives and politics, all of which have ramped up data stewardship or "D" risk management challenges.

An August 2020 governance newsletter from PwC, drawing on research by Intelligize, captured the dynamism and challenge of the current risk environment for companies. It noted, "In a testament to the COVID-19 pandemic's disruptive influence on business, Intelligize has found that 1,366 companies included risk factors related to 'health epidemics and diseases' on their Form 10-K in 2020. That's up 619% from 190 companies last year. No other risk factor that the firm examined increased by more than 15%. The remainder of the top five fastest-growing risk factors include: international trade restrictions and protectionism (+13.8%); natural disasters, climate change, and extreme weather (+11.4%); anti-corruption law (+10.3%); and employee misconduct (+10.1%)."[35] Almost every one of these increased risk factors is related to ESG&D issues.

Given this level of dynamism and complexity, alongside the long-standing trends outlined in Chap. 2, business leaders must be constantly reviewing and stress-testing their approach to risk management and be agile and adaptive in managing ESG&D risks. A one-off materiality analysis every few years and once a year updates of ESG&D risk registers and risk heat maps are no longer sufficient.

### 5.2.4 Leverage Technology to Improve Risk Management: And Manage the Risks of Technology

Technology is another increasingly valuable tool to improve the identification and management of ESG&D risks. The use of AI and data analytics can be especially valuable in helping companies to:

- Assess and manage their environmental risks, through a variety of surveillance and drone technologies.
- Scrape data from social media and other platforms for patterns and diverse insights on current and emerging issues, trends and views of the company.
- Strengthen integrity and compliance systems within the company.

In the case of integrity and compliance, for example, research by members of the World Economic Forum's Global Future Council on Transparency and Anti-Corruption concludes that tech is one of the most promising drivers of integrity. They state, "Data-driven, tech-based anti-corruption solutions are rapidly expanding in sophistication and potential. The transparency they enable is critical for anchoring confidence in business and restoring trust in government. Tech innovations, powered by data and behavioural insight, are disrupting corruption risks and boosting integrity systems. They are accelerating new forms of accountability based on the smarter exploitation of big data and fostering new public-private partnerships for integrity. In the digital era, data has become a critical asset for integrity actors to detect and deter fraud risks, complex networks and corrupt practices."[36]

There are numerous ways companies can use digital technology to better identify and manage risks. At the same time, this technology—both the analytical capabilities and platforms and the privacy and use of the data that powers them—is obviously in itself a rapidly growing source of ESG&D risk. As we outlined in Chap. 3, it is a material risk to the company, most notably in terms of cybersecurity, and at the same time, it poses a combination of risks to human rights and the environment. Companies increasingly need to look at technology from all these perspectives.

Clearly, the dual impact of technology both as a solution to or mitigator of risk and as a source of or aggregator of risk is not unique to this era. Alongside their benefits, new technologies have always created new risks for people and the planet—and for companies. What is unique to this time is the sheer scale and speed of development and adoption of new technologies—life sciences and materials technologies as well as digital ones—and the convergence between them. This scale and speed have only increased with the COVID-19 pandemic. As such, risk managers need to simultaneously increase their use of technology to better identify and manage ESG&D risks while managing the additional risks caused by using the technology itself.

### 5.2.5  Address Both Acute Risks and Broader Business Model or Systemic Risks

Another challenge that companies need to grapple with is balancing the allocation of resources for risk management between addressing location-specific, short-term or acute risks—such as those that may have a negative impact on a particular business unit or location and negative impacts on people and the environment in the communities or localities surrounding those operations— and addressing and building resilience to more chronic or systemic risks and shocks. As we outlined in Chap. 3, both acute and systemic risks, crises and shocks are on the rise. Large companies particularly, which are exposed in hundreds of locations and contexts, need to be effective at identifying and managing this full range of risks and building resilience at all levels.

A different but related systemic risk challenge is the fact that to date most companies have managed their ESG&D-related risks from the lens of specific operations, projects, products and services. Relatively few have looked at or engaged with external stakeholders on the risks they create for people and the environment through the nature of their *core business model*. Examples include the following:

- Companies paying workers below a living wage in order to deliver cheap and convenient products and services to wealthier consumers, often on the same day they were ordered in the case of e-commerce.
- Companies producing carbon-intensive products and services while setting carbon emissions goals for their own facilities and operations—that is, managing what the Greenhouse Gas Protocol has framed as Scopes 1 and 2 emissions but not Scope 3.
- Private management of water services and other essential public goods.
- Growing data privacy and ownership issues associated with the ubiquitous and increasingly required use of digital online platforms.

Extensive work is being done in the case of climate change, which is widely recognized both as an acute and a systemic business risk and as a major challenge associated with the business models of many companies, including but not only those in the energy sector. The Taskforce on Climate-Related Financial Disclosure, CDP and the Science-Based Targets Initiative are three leading frameworks aimed at helping companies to identify, manage and account for both the climate-related risks that they face and those that they contribute to as a result of their business model and where and how they operate.

Less work has been done on how to identify and manage the risks to people and human rights caused by systemic trends and different types of business models. This is changing, led by initiatives focused on fundamental shifts related to the future of work and just transition, supported by a vanguard of companies and organizations such as the ILO and international trade unions and employer organizations. The *Valuing Respect Project*, led by Shift, challenges business leaders to answer the question, "Is your business wired in ways that put people at risk?"[37] As the Shift team outline, "Companies spend a lot of time thinking about how to increase value for customers in ways that increase profits for the company: in essence, their business model. Yet few of them consider how the ways in which they do so can carry inherent risks for people's rights. Failing to see the big picture, they risk wasting time and valuable resources on efforts to address issues at an operational level when the reality is they are wired for trouble."[38]

### 5.2.6 Combine Quantifiable Metrics and Science-Based Targets with Qualitative Insights and Stakeholder Surveys

Financial and operational risks and performance metrics, while increasingly complex, are quantifiable. So too are most environmental risks. Social and governance risks are far less so. As stated earlier, even quantifiable risks and metrics—that is, financial fraud, large gaps between the pay of CEOs and their workers or environmental pollution—have a strong "people" dimension and often an impact on people's lives and livelihoods as well as the quality and trust of stakeholder relations. As such, effective risk management requires a combination of strong technical expertise with relationship management skills. It requires commonly agreed and auditable targets and metrics as well as context-specific and "open to interpretation" conversations and consultations. Given the range and complexity of ESG&D risk factors in today's world, it requires well-resourced internal functional experts as well as access to external guidance and capabilities.

In summary, for almost all companies, the risk management, auditing, accounting and legal functions are more complex, more dynamic, more multi-dimensional and more important than ever. Developing, recruiting and retaining the best possible functional skills and capabilities are crucial. Making sure they include ESG&D-related risk management skills and capabilities is key. This can also be achieved by increased coordination between these functions and those of human resources, health and safety and sustainability. At the same time, ESG&D risk management, just like financial and operational risk management, must be "owned" by senior executives, business unit heads and operating managers, with board-level oversight. In leading companies, the days of relegating it to a "CSR" silo are long gone.

## 5.3 Invest in Innovation to Drive Inclusive and Sustainable Growth

One of the greatest opportunities for achieving sustainable enterprise value creation lies in investments in competitive market-based solutions to address social and environmental challenges at scale. There is an untapped opportunity for business leaders to identify and invest in "Big Bets" and the highest potential "innovation pathways" for their own company and industry—pathways that can develop and scale a package of new technologies, products, services, business models and financing mechanisms that profitably serve the public good. Every executive team should be asking themselves the set of innovation opportunity questions outlined in Box 5.2.

## Box 5.2 Business Innovations for Inclusive and Sustainable Growth

| | Invest in greater equity and inclusion | Invest in environmental conservation and regeneration |
|---|---|---|
| Research, develop, leverage and scale new technologies, products and services | What are the digital, materials and life science technologies—and the products and services—that offer the highest potential for our own business to be more inclusive or that can enable us to commercially support other companies to be more inclusive? | What are the digital, materials and life science technologies—and the products and services—that offer the highest potential for our own business to be more environmentally sustainable or to sell sustainability solutions to other companies? |
| Implement and scale new business models and innovative financing mechanisms | What financing and inclusive business models can we create to include more low-income producers, consumers, workers and business partners in our value chain; enhance lives and livelihoods through paying living incomes and wages; and improve affordability and access of essential goods and services, such as food, nutrition, energy, water, healthcare, housing, transport and education—or to support other companies to meet these goals? | What financing mechanisms and sustainability business models do we need to decrease natural resource use; cut emissions and waste; and deliver transformative solutions to tackle climate change, water insecurity, biodiversity loss and pollution through investing in net-zero or net-positive solutions and pathways—for example, circular economy; frugal innovation; nature-based solutions; regenerative business models? |
| Build "innovation" and "accelerator" partnerships or system-level platforms with others | Who are the key organizations we could partner with—and who are the individual champions we need to build relationships with to overcome policy constraints or market failures and to drive large-scale impact and systems transformation to tackle inequality and increase inclusion? | Who are the key organizations we could partner with—and who are the individual champions we need to build relationships with to overcome policy constraints or market failures and to drive large-scale impact and systems transformation to drive net-zero carbon and nature positive solutions? |

Source: Adapted from: Jane Nelson. *Expanding Opportunities and Access: Approaches that harness markets and the private sector to create business value and development impact.* Corporate Responsibility Initiative, Harvard Kennedy School, 2010. See also: Raj M. Desai, Hiroshi Kato, Homi Kharas and John W. McArthur (eds). From Summits to Solutions: Innovations in implementing the sustainable development goals. Brookings Institution, 2018

As outlined throughout the book, companies cannot do this alone or on an entirely voluntary basis. Substantial changes are required in public policies, regulations and fiscal incentives. ESG&D priorities and market incentives need to be integrated into capital markets and into the investment guidance and decisions of institutional investors, both asset owners and asset managers. Shifts in consumer attitudes and behaviour will also be necessary. Yet, there is much that pioneering companies can and are achieving on their own or through innovation partnerships and accelerators.

The untapped business opportunities of taking ambitious action are immense. As the Business and Sustainable Development Commission concluded in its 2017 flagship report, *Better Business Better World,*

> 60 sustainable and inclusive market 'hotspots' in just four key economic areas could create at least US $12 trillion, worth over 10% of today's GDP. The breakdown of the four areas and their potential values are: Energy US$ 4.3 trillion; Cities: US$ 3.7 trillion; Food & Agriculture US$ 2.3 trillion; Health & Wellbeing US$ 1.8 trillion. 'Global Goals hot spots' identified in the report have the potential to grow 2–3 times faster than average GDP over the next 10–15 years. Beyond the US$ 12 trillion directly estimated, conservative analysis shows potential for an additional US$ 8 trillion of value creation across the wider economy if companies embed the Global Goals in their strategies. The report also shows that factoring in the cost of externalities (negative impacts from business activities such as carbon emissions or pollution) increases the overall value of opportunities by almost 40%.[39]

The following section focuses on three broad and usually inter-related and mutually reinforcing areas of investment and innovation that offer companies and their stakeholders enormous potential:

* Breakthrough technologies, products and services
* Innovative business models and financing mechanisms
* Innovation partnerships and accelerator platforms

## 5.3.1 Breakthrough Technologies, Products and Services

Every day, there are encouraging new announcements of companies that are developing or scaling innovative technologies, products and services that have the potential to deliver large-scale and/or "leap-frog" solutions to delivering more inclusive and sustainable growth. Solutions include technologies that can help to improve people's access to more affordable and sustainable energy, food, healthcare, financial services, physical infrastructure and digital services as well as technology breakthroughs that can help to scale net-zero carbon solutions, water security and other nature positive outcomes.

Over the past 20 years, the Massachusetts Institute of Technology (MIT) has compiled an annual selection of the technologies that MIT's Technology Review team judges will make a real difference. The review avoids what it describes as "the one-off tricks, the overhyped gadgets," and focuses instead on "those breakthroughs that will truly change how we live and work."[40] Over the past five years, most of the breakthrough technologies selected have high potential relevance for solving social and environmental challenges. To achieve scale and sustained impact, they all require leadership by individual companies, including both large-scale multinational incumbent companies and agile technology-led start-ups, as well as partnerships between these companies, research institutes and governments.

In 2020, WBCSD drew on MIT's research as well as its own dialogues with business leaders and technology and sustainability experts, to identify the following emerging technologies that it considers will have the greatest impact on driving more inclusive and sustainable growth:

> artificial intelligence; biosensors; brain-computer interface; connected infrastructure; digital money; digital twin; distributed ledger; edge computing; electric vehicles; energy harvesting; genetic engineering; healthy architecture; nanomedicines; next-gen robotics; plant-based meat; programmable matter; quantum computing; small modular reactors; unmanned aerial vehicles; and 3D-Printing.[41]

The application and scaling of these technologies are resulting in ESG&D-related opportunities and risks for almost all companies, not only those that have developed or commercialized them. Companies that aspire to create sustainable enterprise value should assess the potential of these and other new technologies either to improve the company's own ESG&D performance or to commercially develop new products, services and business models that can help the company to simultaneously meet customer needs and address social or environmental challenges.

## 5.3.2 Innovative Business Models and Financing Mechanisms

Innovative business models and financing mechanisms are usually essential for developing and scaling new technologies, products and services. A growing number of companies are changing or enhancing their business models to mitigate or decrease certain ESG&D risks and costs or to create new markets and opportunities that are more inclusive and sustainable in terms of their impact on people and on the environment. Examples include:

- **Circular economy and frugal business models** that are aimed at developing more lean or circular, closed-loop production processes and industrial design.
- **Restorative or regenerative business models** that not only aim to minimize resources used in sourcing, creating and developing products and services, but also aim to put more back into the system than they take out, essentially restoring or renewing systems and different types of social, human and natural capital and building long-term resilience.
- **Inclusive business models** that explicitly aim to include low-income producers, workers, business partners and consumers in corporate value chains with the aim of improving supplier, distributor and retailer incomes and livelihoods and/or improving the affordability and accessibility of essential products and services to low-income consumers or to smallholder farmers and small- or micro-enterprises.
- **Sustainable infrastructure and digitally enabled technology platforms** that can drive large-scale environmental or social impact beyond what an individual company or business model can achieve on its own. These can also include approaches that are regenerative or restorative, with the potential to deliver net-positive outcomes rather than only mitigate negative impacts.
- **Shared use, subscription and omni-channel models**, aimed at using less resources to serve more people in more flexible and inclusive ways.

Innovations in financing are also crucial. Companies and financial institutions such as banks, institutional investors and insurance companies can work individually or collectively to develop hybrid or blended financing mechanisms that help to seed or scale sustainability innovations that may not initially meet traditional corporate finance or investment hurdle rates. These mechanisms can range from internal company social and environmental venture capital funds and innovation competitions and award programmes to external partnerships or joint, blended finance mechanisms with other private and public sector financiers. The dramatic growth in ESG investment funds and products is another crucially important financial ecosystem innovation. These range from best-in-class ESG funds and thematic or sector-based funds to green, social and sustainability bonds. Many are being created as products by major banks, insurance companies and asset managers, others by companies, social entrepreneurs and foundations. Depending on the product, they can provide retail and institutional investors opportunities to invest in the upside potential of sustainable enterprise value creation while also providing major companies, social entrepreneurs and innovative start-ups with access to capital that can help to fund their ESG priorities.

There are thousands of company commitments and investments emerging in these different types of business models and financing innovations. The following are just a few examples of commitments made in food and beverage value chains and financial inclusion.

In 2021, PepsiCo launched a new Positive Agriculture ambition. This includes a 2030 goal to spread regenerative farming practices across 7 million acres (approximately equal to the company's entire agricultural footprint). Alongside ambitious climate action and water stewardship goals, another goal is to measurably improve the livelihoods of more than 250,000 people in the company's agricultural supply chain by 2030.[42] AB InBev has launched a 100+ Accelerator to fund and support innovators who can deliver breakthrough advances in farmer productivity, water stewardship, product upcycling, responsible sourcing and green logistics.[43] Cargill has set a public goal to provide training on sustainable agricultural practices and improve access to markets for 10 million farmers by 2030.[44] As one of the goals in its sustainable growth strategy launched in 2020, Unilever aims to help 5 million small and micro-enterprises in the company's retail value chain to grow their business through access to skills, finance and technology by 2025.[45] As part of its broader commitment to connect 1 billion people to the digital economy by 2025, Mastercard is working with Unilever and other companies, governments and non-profit organizations through the Mastercard Farmer Network (MFN), which digitizes marketplaces, payments, workflows and farmer financial histories within the agriculture sector.[46] Also focused on financial inclusion, VISA has made public commitments to digitally enable 50 million small and micro-businesses worldwide by 2023 and provide 500 million unbanked/underserved people access to digital payment accounts by 2020, a goal that was met and continues.[47] And through its 5by20® initiative launched in 2010 to enable the economic empowerment of 5 million women entrepreneurs along its value chain, by 2020, the Coca-Cola Company had reached some 6 million women.[48]

These examples and others like them share common lessons:

- In all cases, senior executives have been strong champions. They have set ambitious, time-bound and public goals, and they have empowered their business unit leaders and employees to take scalable action.

- All the companies are leveraging innovative technologies and other capabilities through their core business operations and value chains. They are also participating in innovative financing and implementation partnerships to achieve these goals.
- In each case, they are doing so in a manner that intentionally aims to create tangible and intangible business benefits and value for the company as well as higher incomes and development impact for identifiable groups of stakeholders in their business ecosystem.
- In the case of all the companies profiled, this is already a second round of ambitious, time-bounded goal setting. They recognize the importance of making a long-term commitment while also setting shorter-term milestones, supported by measurable targets.
- They are constantly learning from mistakes and failures, often relying on independent evaluations, and adapting and raising the bar as they move forward.

### 5.3.3  Innovation Coalitions and Accelerator Platforms

While a vanguard of corporate leaders is proactively moving ahead on an individual basis to harness sustainability innovations as a driver of competitive advantage, there are still insufficient public policies or market incentives for most companies to act. As outlined in more detail in Chap. 7, one way of addressing these gaps is for a group of progressive leadership companies in each industry sector or location to collaborate on setting ambitious shared goals for social and environmental objectives, to advocate for policy reforms and sometimes to partner on R&D and building markets while continuing to compete when it comes to the actual delivery of those goals.

Accelerator platforms can be particularly important in helping to fund and accelerate the research and development of essential medicines, such as vaccines, as well as breakthrough environmental technologies. The urgency and scale of both the climate crisis and the COVID-19 pandemic have been particularly important drivers of rapid innovation partnerships between companies, governments, research institutes and other stakeholders. One example is Breakthrough Energy. This is a coalition of private investors created in 2015 by Bill Gates and working in certain cases with governments to invest in and scale innovations and advocate for policies that will support the transition to net-zero carbon emissions, with a focus on key sectors that produce the most greenhouse gases such as electricity and heat production, transportation, agriculture, manufacturing and buildings. As Gates comments, "More than anything, we will succeed because of the network of partners we bring to this effort. The investors, philanthropists, corporate and policy leaders who are part of the Breakthrough Energy ecosystem—it will take all of us to compel the major market changes we need to create the future we want for the world."[49]

The ground-breaking public-private-academic and philanthropic partnerships that have rapidly leveraged innovative technologies, new financing mechanisms and non-traditional business models to develop, manufacture and distribute COVID-19 vaccines, tests, treatments and personal protection equipment continues to be a remarkable and historic work in progress. Vaccine development particularly has been a triumph of science and technology combined with adaptive regulatory frameworks, public, private and philanthropic funding, and widespread public health messaging and government and business distribution partnerships. While vaccine hesitancy remains an obstacle in some countries and vaccine inequity in many others, due to lack of access and affordability and challenges in financing, supply chains and manufacturing, the speed and scale of progress has been unprecedented in human history. Innovation and collaboration have been multifaceted. It has ranged from major public and private vaccine developers such as AstraZeneca and Oxford University, Johnson & Johnson, Moderna, Pfizer and BioNTech, Sinopharm and Sinovac to emerging vaccine manufacturers in the Global South. It has included major logistics companies and retailers as well as companies establishing vaccine mandates for their employees. Some of the innovative new models and alliances developed and the lessons learned will continue to be crucial, not only in beating the pandemic, but also in addressing other large-scale and complex global challenges.

In summary, today, there are literally thousands of high potential value-creating innovation examples from different companies and industry sectors, and they continue to grow in number and impact. Some are already delivering solutions for more inclusive and sustainable growth at scale reaching millions of people or having a substantial impact on cutting carbon emissions and improving other global and national environmental outcomes. Yet, they only scratch the surface on what is both possible and potentially profitable for business and what is urgently needed to improve people's lives and protect the planet. To move forward at the speed and scale that are required, more business leaders need to set ambitious goals backed by rigorous data and their core business capabilities. They also need to leverage the reach and capabilities of stakeholder partnerships. As illustrated in Chap. 7, large companies and technology leaders will have a particularly important role in driving industry-wide transformation and building an ecosystem of innovation partnerships, ranging from specific, on the ground projects to large-scale collective platforms.

## 5.4   Promote Employee Well-being, Talent, Diversity and Participation

Even in an era of massive growth in automation and digitization, companies succeed or fail based largely on the talent, skills, capabilities, productivity, teamwork, vision and creativity of the people who work in them as managers and employees, and of the people who work with them as joint venture partners, contractors, suppliers, distributors and so on. The ability of executive teams to motivate and orchestrate all these people—numbering thousands in large companies—is a more essential leadership skill than it has ever been.

As outlined in Chaps. 2 and 3, the growing importance of intangible drivers of value creation, most of which derive from the creativity, skills and connectivity of people, together with the emergence of a new generation of more digitally connected and socially aware employees, have markedly increased both the importance and the challenge of attracting, recruiting and retaining the best talent. In today's world, companies need people who are not only technically qualified for the job at hand, but also diverse in background and perspective, emotionally intelligent and able to be flexible and adaptive in what is much less of a "command and control structure" than was traditionally the case.

The urgency and the strategic importance of putting people at the centre have grown dramatically because of the COVID-19 pandemic. The most important focus has justifiably been on the need to put people's health and safety first, addressing both physical and mental well-being while managing the acceleration of new models of online and hybrid working and, in many companies, dealing responsibly and humanely with furloughs and job losses.

At the same time, the pandemic has further highlighted inequality in remuneration between corporate executives and their employees in many countries. This is especially the case with respect to essential workers in health, food production, manufacturing, logistics and retail, many of whom have faced substantial health and safety risks when working during the pandemic and yet struggle to earn a living wage while their senior executives earn multi-million-dollar packages.

Prior to the pandemic, research by the Economic Policy Institute, found that average CEO compensation in the US surged 14% in 2019 to US $21.3 million, with CEOs now earning 320 times as much as a typical worker in their company (compared to a ratio of 60-to-1 in 1989 and 21-to-1 in 1965).[50] Compensation inequality in corporate workplaces has combined with the reckoning around racial and other forms of inequality. There is growing recognition in many C-suites that these are valid concerns among the company's own employees, in addition to being a major concern in society more broadly.

In addition, the acceleration towards digitization and a low-carbon economy means that large numbers of current formal jobs will disappear. Managing this transition at the firm level will require a combination of retraining and restructuring to invest in people who will still have jobs in the company and its value chain while also supporting those who are losing their jobs to make a transition. At a broader system-level, large companies and their leaders will need to consider what roles they should and can play in supporting initiatives and policies to improve education and training and to ensure a just transition.

Some of the emerging priorities and good practices in terms of putting people at the centre include the following[51]:

- **Respect**—first and foremost is the corporate responsibility to respect people's rights and dignity. This includes but goes beyond employees and contractors who work directly for or with the company. Many more companies need to endorse the UN Guiding Principles on Business and Human Rights and implement human rights policies and due diligence processes, effective grievance mechanisms and access to remedy for people whose rights are negatively impacted by the company's activities. This includes respecting the letter and spirit of labour standards and taking concrete steps to improve employee diversity, equity and inclusion.
- **Empower**—second, companies should be proactively supporting employee well-being more broadly—their physical, mental, financial and social well-being, through paying a living wage; providing health, sick leave and other benefits; investing in personal and professional development opportunities; promoting diversity and inclusion; supporting employee affinity and business resource groups; and exploring mechanisms to increase employee engagement and participation in decision-making.
- **Advocate**—third, senior executives should decide when and how to engage in policy dialogue, advocacy and lobbying to address systemic obstacles to employee health, safety, well-being and incomes. At a minimum, they should ensure that their government relations and trade associations are not undermining the foundations of employees' rights and well-being.

The following section looks at some tools and good practice examples in several of these areas.

### 5.4.1  Invest in Integrated Employee Health, Safety and Well-being

There is long-standing experience on the management systems and vital behaviours that companies can implement to safeguard and improve the occupational health and safety of their employees, especially in higher-risk sectors. In the past decade, there has also been increased action around the concept of employee well-being more broadly. In many companies this is still focused mainly on physical health and safety in the workplace. Leading companies are extending the concept of employee health and well-being to also include mental and emotional health and the financial and social well-being of their employees.

In 2020, the World Economic Forum in collaboration with Willis Towers Watson published a set of *Workforce Principles for the Covid-19 Pandemic*. The authors noted, "The four dimensions of employee wellbeing—physical, emotional, financial and social—are at the centre of the employee experience and essential to an engaged and productive workforce in normal times. During a pandemic, wellbeing assumes a new urgency. An employer's actions in supporting wellbeing are critical to building and sustaining workforce resiliency and sending the message that employees matter".[52]

In 2020, the Global Reporting Initiative took a similar holistic and integrated approach and published a set of *Guiding Principles to Establish a Culture of Health for Business*.[53] This explores the links between employee health outcomes and business outcomes and provides a framework for companies to benchmark practices for achieving a culture of health through their strategy, policies and benefits, workforce and operations, and community engagement activities.

### 5.4.2  Make Employee Diversity, Equity and Inclusion a Strategic Priority

Momentum on workplace diversity, equity and inclusion has grown substantially over the past decade from being primarily a compliance-driven issue focused on non-discrimination, although such compliance with laws and standards remains essential, to become a strategic issue of central importance to business competitiveness. In addition to action from employees, the issue has risen up the agenda of regulators and investors in many countries. Competitive benchmarks and business leadership networks have also been established to drive a "race to the top," especially in the areas of corporate performance on gender, LGBTQ+, racial, religious and disability diversity and inclusion.

Yet, few companies reflect the diversity of the customers they serve and the communities where they operate, especially in their senior leadership ranks. Progress made on board-level diversity, with respect to gender, has not been matched in the C-suite. Racial and other forms of diversity lag even further behind. Diverse intakes for starting positions, both professional and vocational, tend to become increasingly less diverse as people move up the career ladder. As has been well documented, the reasons are a mix of workplace and external cultures, structures and incentives as well as individual behaviours and attitudes.

The companies that are making the most progress share some common features[54]:

- *Tone from the top*: The tone, style and depth of individual leadership from the top—not only the CEO or the head of human resources, but the board, full senior leadership team and key operational leaders.
- *Credibility of culture and management systems*: The strength and credibility of the norms, behaviours, policies and programmes in place and the specific targets set for improving diversity and inclusion—including a clear demonstration that managers are held accountable for meeting them.
- *Energy from employees*: Employee-led action, whether through formal representative bodies such as trade unions and works councils or more informal employee affinity networks and business resource groups and increasingly "activism" from younger employees.

There is a growing body of academic research and practitioner guidance on how companies can develop credible policies, management systems and programmes to increase diversity, equity and inclusion. One example is the *5-Point Paradigm for Parity Roadmap*, summarized in Box 5.3. Although focused on gender diversity, its five-point action plan can be applied to driving diversity and inclusion more broadly.[55]

## 5.4.3  Invest in Employees' Skills and Opportunities

A research report by Institute for the Future and Dell Technologies, *The Next Era of Human/Machine Partnerships*, predicted that "85% of the jobs that will exist in 2030 haven't even been invented yet." They identify the following

### Box 5.3  The Paradigm for Parity 5-Point Action Plan

The Paradigm for Parity Coalition was launched in 2016 by a small leadership group of corporate board directors and CEOs, who believe that insufficient progress has been made in achieving gender parity in executive leadership teams and boards of directors. Drawing on their collective experience, they developed a practical and actionable 5-point action plan. Today, Paradigm for Parity is a coalition of CEOs, senior executives, founders, board members and business academics with the vision of "achieving a new norm in the business world: one in which women and men have equal power, status and opportunity. Our ultimate goal is to achieve full gender parity by 2030, with a near-term goal of women holding at least 30% of senior roles."[56] More than 120 companies have made commitments to implementing the 5-Point Action Plan and to reporting on their progress and sharing good practice examples and lessons learned. They include Accenture, Bank of America, Newmont, Walmart, Cargill, Sodexo, the Coca-Cola Company and VF Corporation, to name just a few.

The 5-Point Action Plan is as follows:

**Minimize or Eliminate Unconscious Bias**. Initiate unconscious bias training for everyone. Engage men and women at all levels, starting with the CEO and senior leadership. Ensure that your company leaders comprehend, own and address the conscious and unconscious biases that prevent women from succeeding.

**Significantly Increase the Number of Women in Senior Operating Roles**. Make full gender parity (50/50) your ultimate goal. As an immediate goal, don't allow a single gender to account for more than 70% of any leadership level, from the Executive Management Group downward.

**Measure Targets at Every Level and Communicate Progress and Results Regularly**. Set measurable goals and hold yourself and your senior team accountable. Communicate results to your wider organization and board. Expect meaningful progress each year, with the aim of parity by 2030. Work with investors as they increase the pressure to measure and monitor diversity progress. Share statistics with other CEOs and consider publishing results over time.

**Base Career Progress on Business Results and Performance, Not on Presence**. Give women and men control over where and how they work, whenever possible. Acknowledge the needs and expectations of millennials, an important talent pool. Find ways to work more flexibly to meet the needs of all employees. Create cultural change so that working flexibly is embraced and not an underused and over-talked about benefit.

**Identify Women of Potential and Give Them Sponsors, as well as Mentors**. Bust the myth of meritocracy in your corporation, since it probably does not exist. Women need career sponsors and access to networks of influence. Men, who are still the majority of leadership, have a critical role to play in advocating for women, both internally and in the wider corporate world. Look for the best within your organization and help them.

Source: Paradigm for Parity

individual skills and traits that will be needed for the future, illustrating a challenging combination of both technical skills and interpersonal or social skills and awareness[57]:

- **Contextualized intelligence**: nuanced understanding of culture, society, business and people.
- **Entrepreneurial mindset**: applying creativity, learning agility and an enterprising attitude to find workarounds and circumvent constraints.
- **Personal brand cultivation**: a searchable and favourable digital identity as basic work hygiene.
- **Automation literacy**: the nimble ability to integrate lightweight automation tools into one's own work and home life.
- **Computational sensemaking**: ability to derive meaning from blended machine and human-based outputs.

The transition towards a digital economy, digital workplaces and new types of work and jobs has accelerated and scaled due to the COVID-19 pandemic and these traits and skills are more important than ever. In terms of creating shared value and managing shared risks, there is a growing imperative for companies to invest in skills development and other professional opportunities for their employees. Even in times when training budgets are tight for many companies, there are opportunities to harness online training and professional qualification options to increase productivity, competitiveness and employability. Each company should be reviewing its human resource and talent development strategies and exploring ways to increase the agility and reach of these programmes for as many employees as feasible.

For companies that are having to cut jobs, there is potential to provide online learning and training support as part of the transition that former employees will have to make. This is also an area where companies can leverage online learning platforms to support skills development and job matching programmes beyond their own company through their community investment and corporate citizenship programmes.

## 5.4.4   Enable Employee Engagement and Participation

Effective employee engagement and participation requires an ecosystem of different mechanisms that can provide employees with greater voice, participation and influence in the company's strategy, operations and financial success.

Many companies around the world support a range of employee engagement mechanisms aimed at providing employees with grievance mechanisms and opportunities to provide feedback to management and to engage in personal development and volunteering activities beyond their immediate job. These include:

- Whistle-blowing, ethics solutions tools and other types of grievance mechanisms
- Employee surveys and feedback mechanisms
- Online and in-person training and personal development and well-being options
- Affinity networks or business resource groups
- Matched-giving and employee volunteering programmes

Another area of employee engagement and participation that is gaining increased attention in the context of stakeholder capitalism is employee representation in strategic decision-making, including on corporate boards. This is the norm in certain European countries, which have two-tier supervisory and management board structures. This approach, along with the role of Works Councils, ensures that employees have a legal voice in major company deliberations and decision-making. Several initiatives are underway in the US to promote a similar approach, such as the Aspen Institute's Ideas Lab on Worker Voice in the Boardroom.[58]

Employee share ownership models are also receiving a refreshed impetus as a response to the debate on stakeholder capitalism and to the growing income and asset inequality between owners of capital and labour. As the National Center for Employee Ownership (NCEO) in the US outlines,

> Employee ownership is a broad concept that can take many forms, ranging from simple grants of shares to highly structured plans. The most common form of employee ownership in the U.S. is the employee stock ownership plan (ESOP), a highly tax-advantaged plan in which employees own shares through a trust funded by the company. Other forms of employee ownership include stock options, stock grants, synthetic equity (granting the right to the value of shares but not the shares themselves), worker cooperatives, and employee ownership trusts.[59]

Worker and customer cooperatives are a long-standing model, but small in terms of their size and number. Of greater relevance and potential are opportunities for employees to own shares in the companies where they work, and

NCEO estimates that some 6500 US-based companies have ESOP programmes. All companies should review the options for their employees to have a share in the company's profits beyond their base salary while recognizing some of the risks associated with share ownership, especially if over-reliant on the performance of one company.

The existence of trade unions and collective bargaining remains an important mechanism for employees or their representative bodies to protect workers' rights and employee interests on issues such as human rights, health and safety, compensation and benefits, training and jobs. A few leading companies, mostly from Europe, have signed global framework agreements with relevant trade unions to achieve a more consistent and fair approach in their supply chains around the world. Box 5.4 illustrates the example of IndustriALL Global.

---

**Box 5.4 IndustriALL Global Union and Multinational Company Global Framework Agreements**

Millions of workers around the world who are part of corporate supply chains work excessive hours, face harassment and discrimination and earn less than a living wage, especially women and workers in countries where regulatory frameworks and oversight of labour rights are weak. IndustriALL Global Union is one example of a trade union engaging strategically with individual companies to improve the working conditions of some 50 million workers in the mining, energy and manufacturing sectors in 140 countries.[60] Among other tools that it utilizes to improve working conditions along global supply chains, IndustriALL negotiates Global Framework Agreements (GFAs) with multinational corporations on behalf of local trade unions.

By signing a GFA, a company commits to requiring their operations and suppliers to comply with the International Labour Organization's (ILO's) guidelines and uphold international standards for workers' rights, health, safety, equal treatment and environmental practices. IndustriALL's local union partners are also given access to company operating sites and engagement with local workers. Additionally, the GFA creates mechanisms for dispute resolution and dialogue between unions and the company, providing workers with the opportunity to negotiate directly with their employers. As of mid-2021, IndustriALL has signed nearly 50 GFAs, mostly with European headquartered companies, related to health and safety, wages, freedom of expression, collective bargaining, maternity leave and sexual harassment. There is a need for many more similar agreements. Examples of signatory companies include Siemens, Unilever, H&M, Total, Engie and Ford.

## 5.5 Establish Robust and Accountable Mechanisms for External Stakeholder Engagement

As has been argued throughout the book, systematic and ongoing engagement with external stakeholders is key to creating sustainable enterprise value. Many companies now undertake a structured process to identify and map their key stakeholders and have established mechanisms for engaging with them on a regular basis.

One of the models that is being used by a growing number of leading companies is the creation of external advisory councils that engage on a regular basis with senior management and sometimes board directors. Box 5.5 provides examples of seven of these councils from different industry sectors. In addition to having such councils at a corporate level, some companies are establishing them at a country level or a site-based community level or to address specific sustainability, digital or geopolitical challenges. As expectations continue to grow on how individual firms are delivering on their commitment to stakeholder capitalism, the use of such advisory councils offers one model to making external stakeholder engagement more systematic.

---

**Box 5.5 Examples of External Stakeholder Advisory Councils and Panels**

A growing number of the companies that have implemented sustainable enterprise value creation strategies, which explicitly integrate ESG&D priorities into core business activities, have also established external stakeholder advisory councils. While these councils vary in terms of size and mandate, they are usually composed of a combination of independent practitioners, academics and thought leaders who meet on a regular basis with company leaders, serving as "critical friends" who can challenge and support the company in achieving more ambitious sustainability goals. The following seven examples briefly illustrate different models that have been implemented in diverse companies and industry sectors.

**Abbott's** *Global Citizenship Advisory Council* has engaged with the company for over a decade on a wide range of global health, community and environmental issues. Members meet several times a year with company executives and functional subject matter experts to review key priorities, emerging issues and stakeholder expectations. In 2019 and 2020, the advisory council was part of a comprehensive process of internal consultations and external stakeholder engagement to develop the company's 2030 Sustainability Plan and ensure its strategic alignment with the corporate strategy. Spearheaded by the CEO, business unit leaders and functional experts formed internal working groups to identify aspirational goals and pathways to operationalize them. At different stages in the process, specific goals and initiatives were tested and debated with members of the

*(continued)*

**Box 5.5 (continued)**

advisory council, in addition to other external experts in public health and ESG. The top strategic priority identified through this process was to "Innovate for Access and Affordability," with a focus on making access and affordability core to new product innovation, transforming care for chronic disease, malnutrition and infectious diseases, and advancing health equity through partnership.

**Bank of America** has a long-standing *National Community Advisory Council* (NCAC) consisting of practitioners and scholars in civil rights, consumer rights, consumer finance policy issues, financial inclusion, community development finance, economic development, equity, climate change and strategic corporate responsibility and ESG issues. Established in 2005, the council is convened at semi-annual meetings each year, in addition to selected members participating in *ad hoc* meetings and deeper dives to focus on specific issues. Regular dialogues are scheduled with the bank's chair and CEO, vice-chair, business line leaders, functional executives and relevant board directors, with topics ranging from the bank's business policies, practices and products directly relevant to its employees, clients and host communities to its engagement in public policy dialogue, philanthropy and research. Members also participate in site visits and meetings with local community partners. During and between meetings, they engage proactively with the bank's executives to address material ESG risks and opportunities. As one example of the collaboration, the NCAC is credited with advising the bank on strengthening its engagement with lower-income customers, including the development of products and tools such as Advantage SafeBalance Banking®, Affordable Loan Solution™ and Better Money Habits™.

**BASF's** *Stakeholder Advisory Council* was established in 2013, but it built on lessons from a previous Sustainability Advisory Council that was created in 2001 and chaired by one of the company's board members. The Council meets annually with the company's Board of Executive Directors and is chaired by the Chairman of BASF's Board. The company reports that topics discussed in previous meetings have included "corporate strategy and targets, responsibility in the supply chain, climate change, human rights, the impact of externalities and the challenge of renewable raw materials."[61] In 2020, the company established an additional independent advisory structure, its *Human Rights Council*. This is chaired by the company's Chief Compliance Officer and attended by people from the corporate sustainability and legal teams as well as operations andprocurement managers on an as needed basis. In 2019, the company published a Position on Human Rights, which was developed with an external human rights expert and approved by the company's Board of Executive Directors. Like many other manufacturing and chemical companies, BASF also has a long-standing practice of establishing Community Advisory Panels to strengthen dialogue around its larger production sites.

**Dow's** *Sustainability External Advisory Council (SEAC)* is one of the longest-term examples of a continuously operating council of this nature, having been established in 1992.[62]Among other areas of influence, the council has played a key role in supporting the company in the development of its 2015 and 2025 public Sustainability Goals. As an illustration of the company's growing focus on sustainable value creation, in 2021, Dow reported that 80% of its R&D projects now focus on climate protection, the circular economy and safer materials, and 48% of the company's 2020 sales were from products explicitly addressing world challenges.[63] SEAC is chaired by the company's Chief Sustainability Officer and apart from the chair, composed of external experts with social and environmental experience in non-governmental organizations, academia, government and

*(continued)*

**Box 5.5 (continued)**

the private sector. The council's mandate includes providing advice on integration of ESG issues into overall corporate strategy and portfolio, next-generation sustainability goals, public affairs and stakeholder engagement, and an external perspective on emerging trends and externalities. Dow has also established *Community Advisory Panels* around many of its manufacturing sites in the US and other countries, as part of an ongoing effort to strengthen engagement and trust with local community leaders.

**Griffith Foods** is a private, family-owned company that has made a strategic commitment to sustainability through its corporate purpose, "We Blend Care and Creativity to Nourish the World."[64] The company's external *Sustainability Advisory Council* worked closely with its management team and board of directors to develop an ambitious Sustainability Plan and set of aspirational goals aligned directly with the company's corporate strategy. Targeted working groups consisting of relevant company executives, board directors and advisors, worked together between meetings to identify key risks, opportunities and priorities in the areas of health and nutrition, sustainable sourcing, employee well-being and fulfilment and climate action. These formed the basis of a jointly developed Sustainability Plan and a set of business Big Bets and venturing initiatives focused on putting sustainable value creation at the heart of the company's corporate strategy and a key pillar of its engagement with customers in the food industry, which include some of the world's major food brands and retailers.

**Nestlé** was one of the corporate pioneers in coining the term "Creating Shared Value" (CSV). The company identified priority areas of action that were material to its business, salient to people and the planet, and where it felt it could have the greatest impact and influence in achieving sustained and scalable outcomes. In 2009, it established an external *Creating Shared Value Council*. This body has a mandate to advise the company's executive team and board on "the sound development of long-term sustainability and positive social and economic impacts of the CSV business strategy."[65] The council also serves as the judging panel for the company's annual CSV Award, which recognizes high potential andscalable social entrepreneurs and innovators. The council's members have expertise spanning corporate social responsibility, strategy, sustainability, nutrition, water and rural development. The Chair of the Board of Directors' Sustainability Committee also participates in Council meetings.

**Newmont** has established a number of advisory councils and independent review bodies to help improve its sustainability performance. In 2009, for example, in response to a group of socially responsible investors, the company's Board of Directors created a *Community Relations Review Panel* that undertook a comprehensive assessment of both corporate and site-level approaches to managing community relations and social licence to operate, reporting back directly to the board. More recently, in 2020, the company established an *Advisory Council on Indigenous Community Relations* to advise it on strengthening relationships and building trust with indigenous peoples. The council provides advice to the company's Safety and Sustainability board committee and to the sustainability team. The company has also established *country-level advisory councils* to advise regional and local management teams on location-specific economic, environmental, social and political trends and issues. In key technical areas, it has established external technical review boards to provide an additional layer of review and evaluation on key risks and opportunities.

One of the most important challenges that companies are facing in terms of building more trusted and effective stakeholder relations is how to enhance their external transparency and accountability related to their performance on managing ESG&D risks and opportunities. The greatest pressure for this is coming from regulators and investors, but other stakeholder groups are also focused on this aspect of business responsibility and value creation. Some of the actions that leading companies are taking to improve and standardize their corporate reporting and accountability are reviewed in Chap. 6.

# Notes

1. This framework is adapted from: Jane Nelson. *Corporate Citizenship in a Global Context.* Working Paper No. 13. Corporate Social Responsibility Initiative, Harvard Kennedy School. May 2005. Pages 9–10. https://www.hks.harvard.edu/sites/default/files/centers/mrcbg/programs/cri/files/Workingpaper_13_nelson.pdf
2. Ira A. Jackson and Jane Nelson. *Profits with Principles: Seven Strategies for Delivering Value with Values.* Currency Doubleday. 2004. Page 53. See also: Jane Nelson. *Building competitiveness and communities: How world class companies are creating shareholder value and societal value.* The Prince of Wales Business Leaders Forum in collaboration with the World Bank and United Nations Development Programme, 1998. Jane Nelson. *The Public Role of Private Enterprise: Risks, Opportunities and New Models of Engagement.* CSR Initiative Working Paper No. 1, Harvard Kennedy School, March 2004.
3. Michael E. Porter and Mark R. Kramer, "Creating Shared Value: How to reinvent capitalism—and unleash a wave of innovation and growth," *Harvard Business Review*, January–February 2011.
4. Ibid.
5. For a good overview on Impact Investing, see the Global Impact Investing Network. Accessible at: https://thegiin.org/
6. David Grayson and Adrian Hodges. *Corporate Social Opportunity: Seven Steps to Make Corporate Social Responsibility Work for your Business.* Greenfield Publishing. 2004.
7. Rebecca Henderson. *Reimagining Capitalism in a World on Fire.* Public Affairs Books. 2020.
8. For more details on this term, see: https://www.consciouscapitalism.org/
9. BCG. *Total Societal Impact: A new lens for strategy.* The Boston Consulting Group. October 2017.
10. Ira A. Jackson and Jane Nelson. *Profits with Principles: Seven Strategies for Delivering Value with Values.* Currency Doubleday. 2004. Principle #7: Pursue Purpose Beyond Profit, page 299.
11. Enacting Purpose Initiative (EPI). *Enacting Purpose in the Modern Corporation: A framework for Boards of Directors.* University of Oxford, Said Business

School, Berkeley Law, Business in Society Institute, Federated Hermes, Wachtell, Lipton, Rosen & Katz, and The British Academy. August 2020. https://www.sbs.ox.ac.uk/sites/default/files/2020-08/enacting-purpose-within-the-modern-corporation.pdf

12. Clara Barby et al. *Measuring Purpose—An Integrated Framework.* Enacting Purpose Initiative, 15 January 2021. https://enactingpurpose.org/assets/measuring-purpose%2D%2D-an-integrated-framework.pdf

13. Business Fights Poverty. How can companies and investors collaborate to embed purpose authentically into business? A Discussion Paper. June 2020.

14. Myriam Sidibe. *Brands on a Mission: How to Achieve Social Impact and Business Growth Through Purpose.* Routledge, 2020. For other books focused on corporate purpose and broader social impact, see: Colin Meyer. *Prosperity: Better business makes the greater good.* Oxford University Press, 2019. See also: Akhtar Badshah. *Purpose Mindset: How Microsoft inspires employees and alumni to change the world.* HarperCollins, 2020.

15. Johnson and Johnson. Our Credo. https://www.jnj.com/credo/

16. Johnson & Johnson, Health for Humanity 2025 Goals. https://www.jnj.com/health-for-humanity-goals-2025

17. Bank of America. "Delivering Responsible Growth." https://about.bankofamerica.com/en/our-company/responsible-growth

18. Ibid.

19. World Economic Forum in collaboration with Deloitte, EY, KPMG and PwC. *Measuring Stakeholder Capitalism: Towards Common Metrics and Consistent Reporting of Sustainable Value Creation.* White Paper. September 2020. http://www3.weforum.org/docs/WEF_IBC_Measuring_Stakeholder_Capitalism_Report_2020.pdf

20. Danone. Our Vision. https://www.danone.com/about-danone/sustainable-value-creation/our-vision.html

21. Danone Enterprise a Mission. https://www.danone.com/about-danone/sustainable-value-creation/danone-entreprise-a-mission.html

22. Danone. B Corp. https://www.danone.com/about-danone/sustainable-value-creation/BCorpAmbition.html

23. Unilever. "Making sustainable living commonplace for 8 billion people." https://www.unilever.com/news/news-and-features/Feature-article/2020/making-sustainable-living-commonplace-for-8-billion-people.html

24. The Unilever Compass. https://assets.unilever.com/files/92ui5egz/production/ebc4f41bd9e39901ea4ae5bec7519d1b606adf8b.pdf/Compass-Strategy.pdf

25. Unilever. "Our Sustainability Governance". https://www.unilever.com/planet-and-society/sustainability-reporting-centre/our-sustainability-governance/

26. BlackRock. Earnings Release, "BlackRock Reports Second Quarter 2021 Diluted EPS of $8.92, or $10.03 as adjusted". New York, July 14, 2021. https://s24.q4cdn.com/856567660/files/doc_financials/2021/Q2/BLK-2Q21-Earnings-Release.pdf

27. Larry Fink. Letter to CEOs. January 17, 2018. https://www.blackrock.com/hk/en/larry-fink-ceo-letter

28. OECD. Policy Framework for Investment: Responsible Business Conduct. https://www.oecd.org/investment/toolkit/policyareas/responsible businessconduct/

29. European Financial Reporting Advisory Group. *Proposal for a Relevant and Dynamic EU Sustainability Reporting Standard-Setting.* Brussels: European Reporting Lab @ European Financial Reporting Advisory Group, 2021. Page 8. https://ec.europa.eu/info/sites/default/files/business_economy_euro/banking_and_finance/documents/210308-report-efrag-sustainability-reporting-standard-setting_en.pdf

30. Task Force on Climate Related Financial Disclosures (TCFD). https://www.fsb-tcfd.org/

31. UN Guiding Principles Reporting Framework, "Salient Human Rights Issues." https://www.ungpreporting.org/resources/salient-human-rights-issues/

32. Ceres. *Running the Risk: How corporate boards can oversee environmental, social and governance (ESG) issues.* November, 2019.

33. COSO and WBCSD. *Enterprise Risk Management: Applying enterprise risk management to environmental, social and governance-related risks.* 2018.

34. Ibid.

35. PwC. Governance Insights. A biweekly newsletter for directors and investors. August 26, 2020. https://www.pwc.com/us/en/services/governance-insights-center.html

36. World Economic Forum. *Hacking Corruption in the digital era: How tech is shaping the future of integrity in times of crisis.* Global Future Council on Transparency and Anti-Corruption. Agenda for Business Integrity. May 2020. http://www3.weforum.org/docs/WEF_GFC_on_Transparency_and_AC_Agenda_for_Business_Integrity_pillar_3_2020.pdf

37. Shift. *Business Model Red Flags. Is your business wired in ways that put people at risk?* Beta model publication of the Valuing Respect Project. 2020. https://shiftproject.org/val-respect-focus-area/business-model-red-flags/

38. Shift. "Business Model Red Flags: Starting with the Big Picture," online. https://shiftproject.org/val-respect-focus-area/business-model-red-flags/

39. Business and Sustainable Development Commission. *Better Business Better World. The report of the Business and Sustainable Development Commission.* January 2017. Quotes taken from press release for the report accessed at: http://businesscommission.org/news/release-sustainable-business-can-unlock-at-least-us-12-trillion-in-new-market-value-and-repair-economic-system

40. MIT Technology Review, "Ten Breakthrough Technologies 2020". https://www.technologyreview.com/10-breakthrough-technologies/2020/

41. World Business Council for Sustainable Development. Innovations that could shape and transform 2020–2030. Vision 2050 issue brief. WBCSD, August 2020. https://docs.wbcsd.org/2020/08/WBCSD_Vision_2050_Innovations_2020_2030_Issue_Brief

42. PepsiCo, "2020 Sustainability Report: Focus Areas. Agriculture". Accessed August 20, 2021. https://www.pepsico.com/sustainability-report/agriculture

43. AB InBev, "100+ Sustainability Accelerator". Accessed August 19, 2021. https://www.ab-inbev.com/sustainability/100-accelerator/

44. Cargill, "Farmer Livelihoods: Partnering with farmers around the world". Accessed August 20, 2021. https://www.cargill.com/sustainability/priorities/farmer-prosperity

45. Unilever, "Raise Living Standards: Helping SME retailers grow". Accessed August 19, 2021. https://www.unilever.com/planet-and-society/raise-living-standards/helping-sme-retailers-grow/

46. Mastercard, "Mastercard Lab for Financial Inclusion". Accessed August 20, 2021. https://www.mastercard.com/global/en/vision/corp-responsibility/the-mastercard-labs-for-financial-inclusion.html

47. VISA, "Social Impact". Accessed August 19, 2021. https://usa.visa.com/about-visa/social-impact.html

48. The Coca-Cola Company. *2020 Business & Environmental, Social and Governance Report*. Page 46.

49. Breakthrough Energy, "Our Story." https://www.breakthroughenergy.org/our-story/our-story (Accessed October 8, 2021).

50. Lawrence Mishel and Jori Kandra. *CEO compensation surged 14% in 2019 to $21.3 million*. Economic Policy Institute. August 18, 2020. https://files.epi.org/pdf/204513.pdf

51. Drawn from comments by Jane Nelson to the Global Reporting Initiative panel, "Elevating Oversight of Health and Wellbeing to Boards," June 23, 2020. See also: Jane Nelson, Marli Porth, Kara Valikai and Honor McGee. *A Path to Empowerment: The role of corporations in supporting women's economic progress*. Corporate Responsibility Initiative, Harvard Kennedy School with U.S. Chamber of Commerce Foundation. 2015. https://www.uschamberfoundation.org/sites/default/files/Path%20to%20Empowerment%20Report%20Final.pdf and Jane Nelson. "Giving Women a Seat at the Table," in GE Perspectives. July 1, 2014. https://www.ge.com/news/reports/giving-women-a-seat-at-the-economic-table

52. World Economic Forum in collaboration with Willis Towers Watson. *Workforce Principles for the Covid-19 Pandemic; Stakeholder Capitalism in a Time of Crisis*. March 2020. http://www3.weforum.org/docs/WEF_NES_COVID_19_Pandemic_Workforce_Principles_2020.pdf

53. Global Reporting Initiative. *Culture of Health for Business: Guiding Principles to Establish a Culture of Health for Business*. 2020. https://www.globalreporting.org/cultureofhealthforbusiness/Pages/default.aspx

54. Jane Nelson. *Delivering results on diversity: What the leaders are getting right*. Corporate Responsibility Initiative, Harvard Kennedy School (Forthcoming: 2022). See also: Jane Nelson, Marli Porth, Kara Valikai and Honor McGee. *A Path to Empowerment: The role of corporations in supporting women's economic progress*. Corporate Responsibility Initiative, Harvard Kennedy School with U.S. Chamber of Commerce Foundation. 2015.

55. Paradigm for Parity. *The 5-Point Plan for Action*. 2017. https://www.para-digm4parity.com/
56. About Paradigm for Parity. https://www.paradigm4parity.com/about#who-we-are
57. Institute for the Future and Dell Technologies. *The Next Era of Human/Machine Partnerships*. 2017 https://www.delltechnologies.com/content/dam/delltechnologies/assets/perspectives/2030/pdf/SR1940_IFTFforDell Technologies_Human-Machine_070517_readerhigh-res.pdf
58. The Aspen Institute, Business and Society program. "A Seat at the Table: Worker Voice and the New Corporate Boardroom". 2021. https://www.aspeninstitute.org/wp-content/uploads/2021/08/Worker-Voice-and-the-Corporate-Boardroom.pdf
59. National Center for Employee Ownership, "What is Employee Ownership?" https://www.nceo.org/what-is-employee-ownership
60. Affiliates. "IndustriALL." Accessed July 11, 2021. http://www.industriall-union.org/affiliates
61. BASF, "Stakeholder Dialog." https://www.basf.com/global/en/who-we-are/sustainability/management-goals-and-dialog/stakeholder-dialog.html
62. Dow. Sustainability External Advisory Council. https://corporate.dow.com/en-us/science-and-sustainability/working-together/external-advisory-council.html
63. Dow. 2025 Sustainability Goals. https://corporate.dow.com/en-us/science-and-sustainability/2025-goals.html
64. Griffith Foods. https://griffithfoods.com/
65. Nestlé. Creating Shared Value Council. https://www.nestle.com/csv/what-is-csv/governance

# 6

# Corporate Reporting and Accountability

The two previous chapters have argued that in order to faithfully implement the principles of stakeholder capitalism a board and its executive team must rigorously integrate non-financial and intangible aspects of corporate performance into their firm's strategy and management practices. There is a strong business case for doing so; these factors are increasingly material to enterprise value creation and resilience in today's more technologically disruptive, environmentally constrained, socially fragile and geopolitically uncertain business context.

Integrated reporting goes hand in hand with such integrated corporate governance. Integrated information and communication, which is to say routine data collection and reporting of material non-financial and intangible aspects of corporate performance for internal as well as external consumption, is both the starting point and concrete expression of a firm's practice of stakeholder capitalism.

But while there has been great progress over the past decade in the development and implementation of sustainability and other non-financial corporate performance metrics and reporting, the field remains underdeveloped and unfit for purpose in certain critical respects, particularly with regard to the comparability, completeness, consistency and relevance to providers of capital of such information.

In this chapter, we provide a practical guide for individual companies wishing to navigate this complexity and apply best practice in their own reporting. We also suggest how the business community as a whole could play a stronger leadership role in helping to improve the overall quality and comparability of non-financial reporting and its connection to financial reporting through the creation of an international standard or set of standards for this purpose. A

© The Author(s) 2022
R. Samans, J. Nelson, *Sustainable Enterprise Value Creation*,
https://doi.org/10.1007/978-3-030-93560-3_6

global sustainability reporting standard adopted by regulators that guides full ESG&D integration into mainstream corporate reporting on a comparable basis is ultimately what is needed to bring the resource allocation of companies, capital markets and entire economies into better alignment with the fundamental objective of stakeholder capitalism: sustainable enterprise value creation.

## 6.1    Assessing the Current State of Integrated Corporate Information and Reporting

Non-financial and particularly sustainability-related corporate reporting has expanded dramatically in the past two decades. However, it remains far short of what is needed to enable stakeholder capitalism to become the dominant mode of behaviour among companies, investors and market economies. This is in large part because material ESG&D factors have yet to be widely and comparably integrated into companies' core strategies, governance processes and corresponding communications with investors and lenders. Only when material social and environmental externalities are systematically internalized in capital and other resource allocation decisions, both within and across firms, can the win-win, stronger-economy-and-society promise of stakeholder capitalism be fully realized.

The conceptual argument for integrated reporting has been well made[1] and largely won.[2] However, three preconditions necessary for its scaled application remain largely unfulfilled. First, the new reality of the heightened financial materiality of ESG&D factors has yet to be fully assimilated into the thinking and behaviour of most directors, managers and investors. Second, even the converted—those companies and investors that do accept the strong relevance of these factors for business value creation—do not yet have the information at their disposal to act on this conviction in a systematic and efficient fashion because of serious weaknesses in the comparability and relevance of such information in core communications with investors, especially the annual report. Third, in the absence of these two other preconditions, neither the magnetic pull of customary peer practice (to which managers and investors are very susceptible) nor the brute force of *specific* regulatory requirements has materialized at scale.

As a result, integrated reporting remains the exception rather than the rule—best rather than customary practice. Surveys confirm that systematic internalization of ESG&D considerations remains far from the dominant paradigm in board rooms, management suites and investment committees.

To be certain, non-financial information reporting in the form of corporate responsibility or sustainability reports has risen remarkably in the past two decades and has become customary practice now among large and mid-cap firms. KPMG research in 2017[3] concluded that about three-quarters of the leading 100 firms in each of 49 countries issue corporate responsibility or sustainability reports, up from about one-fifth in 2001–2002. The global average reporting rate is now at least 60% in each industrial sector, and nearly half of such companies seek third-party assurance of at least some of this data.

However, integrated reports—those systematically combining financial and so-called non-financial (sustainability, governance and certain intangible asset) information in firms' annual reports to investors and regulators with all of the added CFO and board scrutiny this entails—remain at a formative stage. Only about 22% of firms in KPMG's most recent sample labelled their reports as integrated reports, and the methodology used in preparing them remains a long way from the comparability needed for effective benchmarking.

Stock exchanges have played an important role in driving reporting trends in a positive direction. In a global survey[4] of 63 stock and derivatives exchanges around the world, 84% reported encouraging or requiring ESG disclosure. One-third encouraged or required firms to do so in an integrated fashion within their annual report. But most exchanges that reported investor interest in ESG disclosure said that such investor demand was limited; only 18% perceived investor interest to be "extensive." Regarding climate change, only six exchanges (19%) included the recommendations of the Task Force on Climate-Related Financial Disclosures in their reporting guidance; however, 56% said they planned to include it.

The trend is unmistakably in the right direction. Over the past decade, sustainability reporting has become the norm for larger firms, and many are beginning to contemplate the next step in this journey, namely integrating these considerations into their core strategy, governance and reporting processes. Indeed, a recent survey of 400 CEOs, CFOs and other C-suite executives and senior accounting professionals at large firms in over 50 countries found that an overwhelming majority believe their companies and investors need to shift their focus to a wider conception of value creation and that financial and non-financial information need to be brought together to support enhanced risk management, decision-making and trust in this regard. [5] But only 24% of this group have confidence that current reporting satisfactorily meets the information needs of investors, and 84% of surveyed investors said that the reason they often do not use non-financial information in their decisions is lack of availability of comparable information among firms and lack of consistency and assurance of the information that is available. Thus, for all of its movement in the right direction, the non-financial reporting landscape remains fragmented and is producing information of limited value to providers of capital.[6]

But here, too, the winds of change are blowing with increasing force. The sharp and sudden economic contraction triggered by the COVID-19 virus may be a turning point. It has been characterized as the mother of all ESG&D shocks to value creation, leaving few companies and communities unscathed. The national health system weaknesses it exposed—coming in many countries on top of #MeToo sexual harassment and discrimination scandals; air pollution- and water scarcity-related production losses; employee health and safety disasters; trade war-related supply chain disruptions; cybersecurity breaches; consumer and regulatory backlashes about personal data privacy and ownership; skilled-worker shortages and related immigration restrictions; and social protests for faster progress on inequality, racial injustice and climate change—should eliminate any doubt in boardrooms that ESG&D factors have the potential to destroy substantial value in short order or even threaten the viability of a business.

Indeed, recognition is growing rapidly among companies, investors, accountants and governments that in this new context integrated reporting of sustainable enterprise value creation is a hallmark of a well-governed firm. Companies therefore need to get on with the job of adapting their annual reports and primary communications with investors and regulators accordingly, notwithstanding the complexity and still-evolving nature of practice and regulation. In particular, material ESG&D factors need to be more fully integrated into such mainstream reporting rather than segmented and de facto subordinated as matters of corporate social responsibility in stand-alone corporate responsibility or sustainability reports that are not subject to the same level of scrutiny by CFOs, boards and external assurers as financial information in annual reports.

Signs of this growing consensus include:

*Businesses*. The World Economic Forum's International Business Council (IBC), approximately 120 of the world's largest firms, agreed in 2019 to develop a core set of common metrics and disclosures[7] of sustainable value creation that they could report against on a consistent basis in their mainstream reports. Impatient to demonstrate the shared value they create on a more credible and comparable basis and convinced that they could provide catalytic leadership to encourage regulators and private standard setters to improve the coherence and quality of corporate reporting in this respect, they worked in 2020 with the four largest accounting firms to refine 21 metrics and disclosures of relevance to all industries drawn from existing standards.[8] Most IBC firms have indicated that they plan to begin implementing these. In a similar sign of progress, the number of companies using the SASB standards in their reporting rose from less than 200 in 2018 to over 800 in 2021.[9]

*Investors.* In 2006, when the UN-backed Principles for Responsible Investment was launched, 63 investment companies (asset owners, asset managers and service providers) with $6.5 trillion assets under management (AUM) signed a commitment to incorporate ESG issues into their investment decisions. Today, the number of signatories has grown to over 3000, including 500 asset owners, representing $90 trillion in AUM.[10] A recent study of institutional asset owners found that 95% are integrating or considering integrating sustainable investing in all or part of their portfolios, and 57% envision a time when they will only allocate to third-party investment managers with a formal ESG approach.[11] As for individual investors, 81% of people in a global survey[12] said they wish to align their consumer spending behaviour with their values and 39% already have sustainable investments in their portfolios. Investors across all ages, wealth levels and regions said sustainable investing was growing in importance, and a majority (58%) expected it to become the new normal in a decade.

*Accountants.* The International Federation of Accountants (IFAC), representing nearly 3 million accountants in 130 countries and jurisdictions, sees "a significant opportunity to enhance trust in companies and confidence in markets by including information in corporate reporting … derived from the financial statements (i.e., 'non-GAAP' or 'non-IFRS' measures), other 'Key Performance Indicators' connected to financial performance, and broader information related to value creation, sustainability or environmental, social, and governance factors." [13] It believes that "integrated reporting, bringing together the relevant information about a company, provides a holistic picture of performance and provides insights on an organization's ability to create sustainable value over time. Integrated reporting supports 'integrated management thinking'—which fosters organizational decision-making and change focused on broader, longer term value creation." Similarly, Accountancy Europe, representing about 1 million accountants from 35 countries, states that "inclusion of a core set of global metrics for non-financial information in mainstream reports and in a connected way with financial information would respond to stakeholders' concerns that these issues that are often material to business resilience are not reported with the same discipline and rigour as financial information. An approach to interconnected standards setting for corporate reporting is therefore needed that will standardise the qualitative characteristics of information and disclosure principles for mainstream reports, connecting non-financial information will financial reporting."[14]

*Regulators.* Governmental and regulatory authority interest in mainstream ESG disclosure is also increasing rapidly. As of 2016,[15] there were 248 mandatory ESG and sustainability reporting requirements around the world, up from 35 in 2006. The number of reporting instruments that require such disclosure in the annual or integrated report grew from 67 to 127 between 2013 and 2016. As of 2020, the total number of mandatory provisions had risen further to about 350.[16] While many of these instruments are narrowly sector- or issue-specific, some are broader such as the EU's 2014 Non-financial Reporting Directive and related 2016 UK regulations as well as Japan's 2014 Stewardship and Corporate Governance Codes. Intergovernmental institutions have also become more active. The 2017 recommendations of the Financial Stability Board's Industry-Led Task Force on Climate-Related Financial Disclosures have prompted the 95 governments and financial regulators that are members of the Network for Greening Financial Systems to encourage "all companies issuing public debt or equity as well as financial sector institutions to disclose in line with the TCFD recommendations."[17] Many are preparing to make such disclosure mandatory. More recently, the Board of the International Organization of Securities Commissions (IOSCO), whose member agencies regulate more than 95% of the world's securities markets in some 130 jurisdictions, agreed in February 2020 to establish a Task Force on Sustainable Finance aimed at enabling it to play a driving role in improving sustainability-related disclosures made by issuers and asset managers and in avoiding duplicative efforts among regulators and other organizations.[18] Pursuant to the work of that Task Force, the organization announced in February and June 2021 its priorities and vision for the establishment of an International Sustainability Standards Board (ISSB) under the IFRS Foundation.[19] And in the US, following a December 2020 recommendation of the ESG Subcommittee of its Asset Management Advisory Committee, the Securities and Exchange Commission in March 2021 launched a public consultation process on how it could facilitate the disclosure of consistent, comparable and reliable information on climate change.[20]

*International Accounting Authorities.* Reflecting the growing interest in more consistent reporting of material sustainability-related information, the Board of Trustees of the IFRS Foundation, which oversees International Accounting Standards Board (IASB) financial reporting standards required in more than 140 countries and jurisdictions, launched a formal consultation process in late 2020 to determine whether and how it should enter this field.[21] Based on the feedback received, the Foundation in April 2021 published a draft set of amendments to its constitution that would authorize it to establish an International Sustainability Standards Board (ISSB) as a sister body to the IASB. It also formed an informal working group of voluntary standard setters to help it undertake technical preparations for such a board.[22] In parallel, the IASB has been reviewing its guidance regarding the Management Commentary,[23] which is a potential vehicle for narrative and other qualitative information about a firm's strategy in advancing long-term value creation, including with respect to ESG&D matters.

Thus, there is a growing consensus behind mainstreaming ESG&D and sustainability reporting in the sense of formally integrating it into the annual report and other core communications to providers of capital and connecting it to financial reporting. However, this practice remains nascent, with the complexity and lack of comparability of such reporting continuing to frustrate progress. International accounting authorities and national securities regulators are at long last mobilizing to solve this problem by creating a baseline global reporting standard that individual national jurisdictions could apply in a coherent, interoperable fashion. However, the challenges they face in this regard are not to be underestimated.

Among these challenges are first the ESG corporate reporting ecosystem consists of multiple types of actors serving different purposes (e.g., rating agencies, disclosure frameworks, sustainability stock and bond indices, advocacy initiatives and proprietary service providers) and multiple tools and frameworks within each of these functionally different layers of the ecosystem.[24] Second, it includes different audiences often interested in different information (e.g., investors, NGOs, governments and the public). Indeed, investors themselves are a heterogeneous group, encompassing active, passive, quantitative, value, engagement and other styles of asset management, each with slightly different information preferences. Third, there are considerable differences in the relevance or materiality of information according to industrial sector; for example, some sustainability issues are inherently more important for B2C businesses than B2B businesses, and others are more relevant to extractive industries having extensive dealings with governments and poor, remote communities and so on.

This complexity drives the lack of comparability in current reporting. In the absence of a central international authority prescribing a common system of metrics and disclosures, multiple frameworks and mandates have emerged over time spanning these different scopes and primary audiences, contributing to confusion and costly inefficiencies. This patchwork quilt of reporting requirements and tools has been mapped by The Reporting Exchange, a free online platform developed by the World Business Council for Sustainable Development that collates comprehensive and reliable information on ESG reporting mandates and resources across more than 70 countries.[25]

The primary *international* standards, each of which is voluntary and serves a slightly different and fundamentally complementary purpose, have been under rising pressure from companies, investors, accountants and governments to align or merge, or at least to become more explicitly modular and interoperable. However, they have been slow to heed this call until recently, and companies, investors and governments have grown impatient. The International Business Council's recent project to identify and collectively implement a common set of material metrics and disclosures drawn from existing voluntary frameworks is a case in point. Some governments have also begun to move forward on their own.

In particular, the European Commission launched an initiative in early 2020 to provide more specific guidance regarding how listed companies with more than 500 employees should report on an annual basis with regard to the environment, social and employee issues, human rights and bribery and corruption. It explained its rationale as follows:

1) There is inadequate publicly available information about how non-financial issues, and sustainability issues in particular, impact companies, and about how companies themselves impact society and the environment. In particular:

   a) Reported non-financial information is not sufficiently comparable or reliable.
   b) Companies do not report all non-financial information that users think is necessary, and many companies report information that users do not think is relevant.
   c) Some companies from which investors and other users want non-financial information do not report such information.
   d) It is hard for investors and other users to find non-financial information even when it is reported; and

2) Companies incur unnecessary and avoidable costs related to reporting non-financial information. Companies face uncertainty and complexity when deciding what non-financial information to report, and how and where to report such information. [...]

The underlying drivers of these problems arise from regulatory and market failures. The reporting requirements in the NFRD (Non-Financial Reporting Directive) are not detailed, are difficult to enforce, leave a lot of discretion to reporting companies, and do not apply to some companies from which users say they need information. Market pressures on their own have not proven to be sufficient to ensure that companies report the non-financial information that users say they need. The market is characterised by a number of overlapping and sometimes inconsistent private non-financial reporting frameworks and standards, and companies face significant challenges in deciding whether and to what extent they should use these different frameworks and standards.[26]

The EU initiative, which is being extended to cover a larger universe of companies including those not listed,[27] has created a sense of urgency within the business community and among other actors in the sustainability reporting world. Large businesses and investors have a natural interest in the emergence of a coherent international system of ESG&D reporting because they tend to operate in complex supply chains across many jurisdictions. The IBC firms undertook their project for the express purpose of accelerating the creation of such a system. They thought that leading by doing—taking a shared view about what constitutes best practice based on the respective strengths of the main existing voluntary private standards and implementing this composite best-practice framework at scale—might spur both these private standard setters and regulators to act more rapidly and coherently to form a generally accepted international standard and thereby help to avoid the emergence of a new patchwork quilt of national or regional regulatory standards.

This is similar to how financial accounting standards developed over the past century—through the iterative cooperation of companies, investors, accounting authorities and governments. In the US, financial accounting standards evolved over many decades through the interplay of private sector practice, independent public-private standard-setting bodies and regulators who adopted the standards set by such multi-stakeholder processes. In response to the advent of railroads needing to raise large amounts of capital in public markets, big industrial firms seeking better information to manage complex and far-flung operations, institutional investors requiring better and more transparent metrics to permit more efficient portfolio allocation, and individual investors wishing to guard against the risks of asymmetric information (e.g., misrepresentation or self-dealing by managers and institutional investors), financial accounting and disclosure practices evolved out of the practical experience of companies and their professional accountants.

Innovations evolved into best practices, with many eventually codified first as private standards set by the accounting community (the American Institute of Certified Public Accountants Accounting Principles Board) and later as official standards under the auspices of the quasi-public independent authority of the Financial Accounting Foundation and its two similarly independent and public-private standards boards, the FASB and GASB, whose decisions have been formally recognized as authoritative by the US securities regulator, the Securities and Exchange Commission, since 1973.

The past 20 years can be thought of as a period of "market discovery" for sustainability reporting not unlike the innovation of more structured forms of financial reporting by the private sector during the late nineteenth and much of the twentieth centuries. Several essentially complementary sustainability reporting frameworks have been created and tested in the market during this period. These constitute the natural building blocks of the systemic solution which all stakeholders now desire.

However, the complexity of the sustainability reporting ecosystem (the different layers, audiences and substantive disciplines) has meant that no existing international authority has had sufficiently broad technical competence and stakeholder legitimacy to create it. There is an international financial accounting standard-setting body whose standards have been adopted in 144 jurisdictions with a governance structure that is analogous to that of the quasi-public independent public-private authority described above in the US: the IFRS Foundation and its International Accounting Standards Board. These are overseen by a Monitoring Board of public authorities, specifically financial market regulators. In principle, this three-tier structure could serve as a vehicle for the desired global integration and rationalization of existing ESG/sustainability standards under the auspices of public authorities. But as recognized by the IFRS Foundation in the recent changes to its constitution, this structure needs to be adapted to incorporate certain additional technical capabilities and broader oversight features important for the credibility and ultimate success of such a societally and politically sensitive endeavour. In addition, care must be taken to engage the primary intended producers and consumers of such reporting, the industrial and investment communities, which are far from monolithic in their information and disclosure preferences, as well as the world's regulators, including particularly those of the largest markets. The US, for example, has never engaged fully in the IFRS, preferring to maintain its own GAAP accounting standards.

Thus, conditions are ripe for rationalization of material ESG/sustainability disclosure over the next few years, with the history of financial accounting standards development providing a template for the way forward, namely an initial reliance upon the private sector to develop and market test practices, followed by the translation of these into standards by a quasi-public, independent and multi-stakeholder technical body overseen by public authorities representing relevant regulatory domains and jurisdictions. This is the model that IFRS and IOSCO are now following for their entry into this field, closely tracking the vision originally articulated by the private sector and voluntary standard setters in the Accountancy Europe Cogito paper published in late 2019[28] and Joint Statement of the so-called Group of 5 leading voluntary standard setters in the fall of 2020, respectively.[29] To add the necessary additional technical competence and multi-stakeholder character to this endeavour, IOSCO and IFRS have been consulting closely with these five private standard setters and the TCFD on the design and resourcing of the International Sustainability Standards Board, including with respect to its governance and initial substantive agenda. It is also negotiating with some of them the potential integration of their teams and intellectual property, building on the merger of SASB and IIRC into the Value Reporting Foundation in the spring of 2021.[30] These preparations culminated in the Foundation's announcement at the United Nations COP26 climate conference in Glasgow, Scotland, in November 2021 that it will form the new standards board in 2022. Two prototype standards were published for the board's initial consideration, including one on climate change reporting that is included in Appendix A.[31]

The shared goal of all of these parties is to enable the new board to hit the ground running while ensuring that its standards build on rather than reinvent the important elements the market has developed over the past 15 years. At the same time, by making the process ultimately accountable to *public* authorities—overseen but not (micro-)managed by them—the intention is to increase the chances that the standards it produces will be widely adopted by such regulators while keeping politics at a distance during the board's deliberations. Finally, there is a shared understanding that the process will focus on the nexus of ESG factors and sustainable enterprise value creation, that is, it will consider social, environmental and economic governance factors only to the extent that these are material to such value creation and therefore belong in annual reports and other core communications to investors.

In sum, mirroring the arrangements by which leading financial accounting practices have been standardized would appear to offer the right formula for balancing the need for speed, quality, legitimacy and independence in an international process having the task of delivering generally accepted standards for the reporting of material non-financial information. However, success is not a given, and the process will take time. Having been launched as a sister board to the IASB at the United Nations Framework Convention on Climate Change (UNFCCC) Conference of Parties (COP26) meeting in Glasgow, UK, the ISSB plans first to issue a climate standard exposure draft based on the prototype developed through informal consultations with its Technical Readiness Working Group of voluntary standard setters cited above. The full process, beginning with the formal consideration and issuance of a climate standard in 2022 and continuing through the development of a fuller set of ESG standards, is likely to take a number of years.

The private sector—the business, investor and accounting communities—has a key role to play in helping to ensure the continued momentum and ultimate success of this process, which depends upon the relevance of the standards to corporate decision-making. These communities have a powerful influence when they move together, and they are the natural constituency for the efficiencies that international standardization would bring given the cross-jurisdictional nature of their activities. They are also closest to the state of play in the market and best positioned to frame best practices and ensure the strong engagement of relevant NGOs and experts, who for reasons of both representation and expertise will need to participate in and support the process. Finally, CEOs have considerable convening power, particularly when they work together. They could help with the convening of leaders of the most relevant international organizations, governments, firms and civil society organizations in order to sustain the necessary political support for the process.

However, business leaders intent upon translating the principles of stakeholder capitalism into action in order to strengthen the sustainable value creation performance of their firms should not merely support and then await the outcome of this international standard-setting process. They should move rapidly to implement their own approach to integrated reporting in the form of a composite, best-practice application of existing standards in their annual report. This will ensure that their disclosures are fit for purpose in today's new business context and can be benchmarked against comparable information from other firms for use in decision-making in their own boardroom as well as in financial markets. There is no need to wait for the international standards landscape to shake out over the next few years. Better returns and more satisfied investors and other stakeholders await those companies that act to improve their communications with investors and other stakeholders now.

The following section of this chapter provides a practical implementation guide for both of these business leadership action items: implementing integrated reporting in one's own firm; and engaging collectively with other business leaders to expedite the creation of an international standard for non-financial information reporting, reprising the critical role that the private sector played decades ago in helping to establish generally accepted standards for financial reporting.

## 6.2 Implementing Integrated Reporting in the Firm

As discussed in Chap. 2, any firm that commits to align itself with the principles of stakeholder capitalism, such as those articulated by the World Economic Forum, the US Business Roundtable or any one of a number of conceptually related legal frameworks around the world, is by definition committing to "hardwire" or rigorously integrate material ESG&D considerations into its core governance, strategy and reporting. This is the practical essence of stakeholder capitalism—the bottom-line determinant of whether a company is "walking the talk."

Most firms—even those that have done a good job of articulating to stakeholders their wider social purpose—are still at an early stage of the journey towards the systematic integration of material ESG&D considerations in their reporting on strategy and performance. The following is a practical guide that can be used by any business wishing to progress on this journey based on the experience of industry leaders in this regard.

### 6.2.1 Lay the Foundation: Embrace ESG&D Materiality and Design It into the Annual Report

- Recognize within the board and management team the inherent implications of the growing materiality of ESG&D considerations for the structure and content of the company's mainstream reporting and commit to adapt the annual report for this purpose.
- Map ESG&D materiality through engagement of internal business units and functions as well as external stakeholders, and cross-check this against current strategy, performance and information and reporting systems.
- Mobilize a thought process within the company and in consultation with key stakeholders around purpose, and cross-check this against current strategy, performance and information and reporting systems.

As documented above, more and more firms are embracing a wider concept of value creation and reflecting this in their governance, strategic thinking and disclosure by integrating material ESG&D considerations within them. The trend is unmistakable and inexorable. Companies need to get ahead of or at least on this curve rather than end up behind it and falling short of the expectations of their investors, employees, communities and, sooner or later, regulators.

The International Integrated Reporting Council (IIRC) has been tracking this trend. It reports that there are now over 2000 businesses using principles of the <IR> Framework in more than 70 markets.[32] This includes:

- Over 500 businesses (including 75% of the Nikkei 225) in Japan where the government has encouraged integrated reporting as a means of enhancing investor/company dialogue and building long-termism. The government backed this approach as part of the governance reforms undertaken by former Prime Minister Abe.[33]
- Over 500 businesses in South Africa, where integrated reporting is core to the corporate governance code.
- Around 400 companies in the UK, according to Deloitte's annual report insights 2019, where 38% of their sample of FTSE companies use the IIRC's concept of the capitals, in a country where integrated reporting is substantially equivalent to the local strategic report requirements.[34]
- Hundred in Malaysia according to the local regulator, where integrated reporting has been adopted as part of corporate governance reform.
- Ninety-six (74% of the ASX200) in Australia according to KPMG, again linked to corporate governance reform.
- Fifty-eight per cent of the CAC40 in France—according to PWC.[35] In France it has been a case of some of the big businesses providing leadership which has led others to follow suit.

The quality of practice is inconsistent and for the most part at a basic level. However, two best practices have emerged: ESG&D materiality mapping and corporate purpose articulation and alignment.

A recent quality review of 50 integrated reports identified Nedbank's approach to materiality mapping as a best practice and helpfully excerpted a graphical representation of its key elements.[36] A World Business Council for Sustainable Development (WBCSD) analysis[37] of 159 of its members' company reports found that the clear majority (97%) of reports (of which 39% were integrated reports of some sort, up from 26% in 2015) included a materiality assessment that considered stakeholder inputs. Most of these (86%) disclosed an overview of the process and often published a matrix of results within the report, continuing an upward trend (2015: 82%). Nearly half

(46%) of members reviewed demonstrated strong alignment between report content and materiality assessment outcomes, representing a significant upward trend (2015: 24%). Based on its review, WBCSD defined the 30 top material ESG&D considerations and 10 further relevant topics; this list can serve as a useful starting point for company materiality mapping exercises.[38] It also provided a case-study graphical illustration of a company best practice, that of Stora Enso, a Finnish wood and biomass products company.[39]

As for articulating the larger purpose of a company and connecting it to strategy and resource allocation, there are a wide range of resources and best practices available for consideration. One review identified ten companies with a perfect score regarding this aspect of their integrated report: ABN AMRO, KPN, Kumba Iron Ore, Nedbank, Philips, Redefine Properties, Suez, United Utilities, Valéo and Vodacom.[40] The British Academy has issued two influential reports on corporate purpose stating that "profit should be a product of a corporation's purpose, but not the purpose of the corporation. (…) Corporate purposes should profitably solve problems for people and planet and avoid profiting from creating problems for people and planet." It further argues that defining corporate purpose requires identifying and creating accountability to a firm's stakeholders, and thus the process of identifying and articulating a company's purpose should involve consultations with its stakeholders. It cites the reports of three companies—Novo Nordisk, Danone North America and Anglian Water—as illustrations of good practice and defines eight principles for organizing businesses around their purpose.[41] WBCSD cites the reports of two companies—Rabobank and SCG—as illustrating good practice with respect to stakeholder engagement, which is essential for both framing core purpose and mapping material considerations.[42]

**Box 6.1 Materiality Disclosure Best Practice**

A materiality process identifies and prioritizes the most significant ESG risks and opportunities from the perspective of the organization and its key stakeholders. It looks at the relative importance of issues to stakeholders and their impact on the business to help determine priority issues. Materiality forms the foundation for effective strategic decision-making, such as setting strategy, goals and KPIs. Key recommendations include:

- Describe specific steps taken to identify, prioritize and validate material issues, including how you took the perspective of your organization and key stakeholders into account.

(continued)

**Box 6.1 (continued)**

- Include a range of factors when identifying and prioritizing issues, such as external trends, magnitude and likelihood of impacts, changes in materiality and alignment with enterprise risk management.
- Disclose a prioritized list of outcomes through a matrix or concise list of highly material issues.
- Where appropriate, acknowledge divisional and geographical differences.
- Align the content of your report with outcomes of the materiality assessment, including strategy, targets, performance indicators, evidence of activities and details on implementation and control mechanisms.
- Demonstrate internal validation of the results of the materiality assessment.
- Explain how third parties contributed to the assessment process or validation of outcomes.

In assessing the quality of company reporting, WBCSD looks for this information in the body of the report or through clear links to additional information such as PDFs or webpages. We emphasize clear disclosure around internal validation and outside organizations that assisted in or validated the process; and we factor disclosures on the materiality assessment and outcomes into the Content analysis and they form an important part of our evaluation.

Source: World Business Council for Sustainable Development. *Reporting Matters: Navigating the landscape—a path forward for sustainability reporting.* 2019. Page 27

## 6.2.2  Assemble the Building Blocks of the Integrated Annual Report by Constructing Your Firm's Disclosure "Stack"

- Use the principles of integrated reporting in the <IR> Framework to set the conceptual foundation and guiding logic of the annual report, ensuring that it reflects the extent of integrated thinking within the firm about its purpose, financial/ESG&D interdependencies and their implications for sustainable value creation.
- Identify salient financial and ESG&D performance themes to address in the report, including their interconnection and the corresponding implications for risk and strategy going forward, and assess the extent of their materiality.
- Apply the most relevant combination of best-practice standards and frameworks (e.g., TCFD, CDSB, SASB and GRI) to report specific qualitative and quantitative aspects of performance and the implications for the firm's governance, strategy, risk management, and metrics and targets, on an internationally comparable basis (construct your IR disclosure "stack").

By articulating its core purpose and mapping the economic and ESG&D factors that have a material bearing on the firm's ability to create value in line with this purpose, a management team lays the foundation for communicating the highlights of recent performance and forward strategy in shared and sustainable value creation terms. To ensure that it does so in a structured and rigorous manner, the team should familiarize itself with the fundamental concepts and guiding principles for integrated reporting enumerated in the Integrated Reporting Framework.[43] Following these will ensure that the report conveys the full extent of the firm's integrated thinking, that is, its assimilation of the principles of stakeholder capitalism through concrete practices and decisions like those described in Chaps. 4 and 5.

The <IR> guiding principles provide the key design criteria for a good integrated report:

- Strategic focus and future orientation
- Connectivity of information
- Stakeholder relationships
- Materiality
- Conciseness
- Reliability and completeness
- Consistency and comparability

With these principles as a foundation, the team should then structure the firm's material disclosures across the relevant parts of the annual report or other core communication with investors. This includes not only the financial statements but also the formal management commentary as well as other narrative elements of the report.

There is no one-size-fits-all approach to organizing an integrated annual report; however, there are a handful of well-established, best-practice standards and frameworks to guide disclosure of material quantitative and qualitative aspects of recent performance related to sustainable value creation and attendant risks and strategies. Just as utilizing the <IR> Framework as the conceptual foundation for the report will ensure the quality and comparability of its underlying logic and overall approach, so applying the methodologies prescribed by leading disclosure standards and frameworks like TCFD, CDSB, SASB and GRI will ensure that the specific metrics and narrative discussions used to convey historical performance and forward-looking strategies and targets are robust and comparable in the market.

Given their different primary emphases, these standards can be used in a complementary manner on top of the <IR> framework to construct the firm's ESG&D disclosure "stack," with the mainstream integrated annual report as the vehicle for communication particularly but not only to providers of capital. Figure 6.1 is a graphical depiction of the different substantive layers of the ESG&D corporate reporting stack and how the primary existing voluntary standards map onto these in an essentially complementary fashion by virtue of their respective primary areas of emphasis and use in the market.

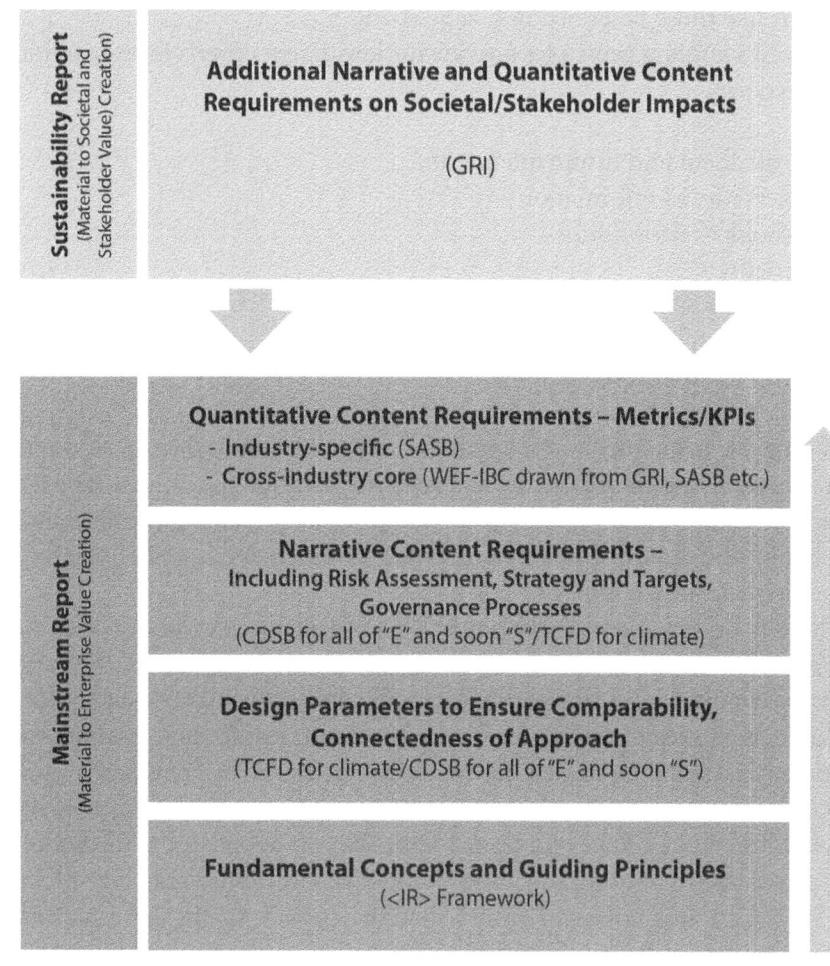

**Fig. 6.1** ESG&D disclosure stack (principal elements and corresponding standards/frameworks)

Starting from the bottom, or foundation, of the stack:

- <IR> Framework: The conceptual framework and set of guiding principles for use in constructing an integrated report (as described above).[44]
- TCFD Recommendations: For climate change only, an industry task force convened by financial regulators that are members of the Financial Stability Board has issued recommendations regarding corporate climate change disclosure. These recommendations are not a standard in the sense of pre-scribing a specific set of disclosure requirements following formal external consultations on preliminary drafts. Rather, this influential guidance from a balanced and respected group of private sector institutions has done something more fundamental. It has established a new behavioural norm of good corporate governance in respect of climate change by asserting that all organizations with public debt or equity, as well as other types of organizations, should provide climate-related financial disclosures in their mainstream (i.e., public) annual financial filings. To this end, it provided a standardized categorization of climate risks and opportunities and recommended that these disclosures be made in four functional areas: governance; strategy (with reference to scenarios); risk management; and metrics and targets. It provided further guidance regarding what should be disclosed in these four areas. But as a set of industry recommendations rather than a formal standard, it did not prescribe a detailed set of requirements in this regard. The three relevant global voluntary standards described below have since aligned their specific reporting requirements with the TCFD recommendations to facilitate their practical implementation by companies within their existing disclosures. In the case of CDSB and SASB, they have done this jointly in the form of a co-branded TCFD implementation guide[45] and good practice handbook.[46]
- CDSB Framework: For environmental and natural capital (the "E" in ESG&D), the CDSB framework is a prescriptive standard resulting from a structured consultation process developed with the technical support of all of the largest accounting firms and key professional accounting associations. It prescribes 12 specific reporting requirements and multiple specific sub-requirements, addressing particularly the "how" of translating material environmental information into a mainstream report. While largely leaving it up to each company to determine its choice of quantitative metrics, it defines the specific nature, format and boundary conditions of qualitative reporting, the firm's narrative communication of its targets, strategies,

risks, performance, outlook, policies, governance processes, assurance procedures and so on. This is crucial context for the quantitative metrics the firm reports, as it provides insight into the firm's interpretation of its historical performance and what it plans to do going forward as a result. The CDSB, whose secretariat is hosted by CDP, has recently expanded its framework to cover the "S" of ESG&D issues. It is used by nearly 400 firms across 10 industry sectors worldwide.

- SASB Standards. SASB prescribes <u>industry-specific and largely quantitative metrics</u> (KPIs) for 77 different industries across 11 sectors of the economy. It provides a materiality map to guide preparers in determining which thematic disclosures are likely to be <u>financially material</u> for their firm. The SASB standards were developed through a structured consultation process and are the most specific and comprehensive industry sector metrics available to use in disclosing material information in mainstream reports and core communications to investors. Thus, the qualitative reporting primary focus of CDSB and quantitative reporting primary emphasis of SASB are quite complementary and can be "stacked" together for environmental and soon social topics insofar as both standards are designed for mainstream reporting of financially material matters (those relevant to business value creation).

- GRI Standards. The GRI standards are by far the most widely applied sustainability reporting framework; however, they have traditionally been applied primarily in stand-alone sustainability reports rather than mainstream or integrated reports. This reflects GRI's <u>different definition of materiality, which focuses on stakeholder and societal impacts rather than the intersection of business value creation and stakeholder/societal value creation</u>, which is the focus of integrated reporting. Nevertheless, as represented by the downward arrows in the graphic, many individual GRI metrics and required disclosures are relevant for both enterprise and wider societal value creation, and companies may wish to include these in their mainstream and integrated reports subject to an assessment of their materiality, including those selected by the World Economic Forum's International Business Council for inclusion in its recommended core set of cross-industry metrics and disclosures (see below). In addition, companies may wish to issue both an integrated annual report having investors as the primary audience and a stand-alone sustainability report having additional stakeholders and the public as the primary audience. These two reports and their content can be highly complementary and overlapping, particularly in the form of these "dual-purpose" GRI metrics.

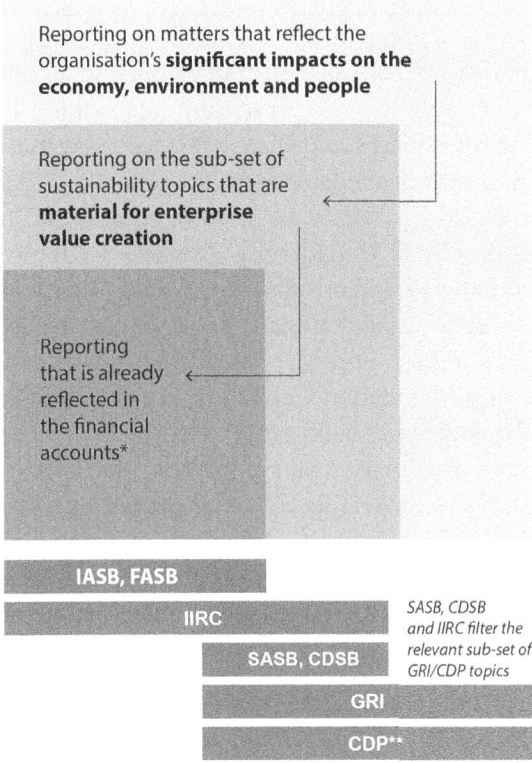

Reporting on matters that reflect the organisation's **significant impacts on the economy, environment and people**

Reporting on the sub-set of sustainability topics that are **material for enterprise value creation**

Reporting that is already reflected in the financial accounts*

IASB, FASB

IIRC

SASB, CDSB

GRI

CDP**

SASB, CDSB and IIRC filter the relevant sub-set of GRI/CDP topics

\* Including assumptions and cash flow projections

\*\* Reflects the scope of the CDP survey, insofar as it functions de facto as a disclosure standard for climate, water and forests, as well as the scope of CDP's data platform

**Fig. 6.2** Main voluntary standards address different materiality concepts in a complementary manner[47]

Thus, as illustrated in Fig. 6.2, these five key frameworks and standards, all of which are global in scope and have been applied across multiple industry sectors for many years, are fundamentally complementary. Each primarily addresses a distinct part of the ESG&D corporate disclosure stack illustrated in the diagram above, and each has an important role to play in the integrated annual report portion of that stack.

There is one additional, more recent initiative that prescribes a subset of metrics and disclosures, drawn from all of those listed above, which it deemed to be relevant for all industries to include in their mainstream reports:

- **WEF International Business Council Core Metrics and Disclosures**: Concerned that most companies have not been applying these five essentially complementary standards and frameworks on a consistent, comparable basis, and that this is preventing companies from effectively communicating their shared and sustainable value creation and contribution to progress on the Sustainable Development Goals, the member companies of the World Economic Forum's International Business Council undertook a project in 2020 to identify a baseline set of metrics and disclosures drawn from these standards that are relevant to virtually all industries. These 21 core and 34 expanded metrics and disclosures were issued in its September 2020 report entitled "Measuring Stakeholder Capitalism: Towards Common Metrics and Consistent Reporting of Sustainable Value Creation."[48] The companies will begin reporting on these common metrics and disclosures in their mainstream reports or other core communications to investors in 2021–2022. This collective action initiative, supported by the world's four largest accounting firms, aims to create a common cross-industry foundation of sustainability disclosures drawn from particularly GRI, SASB, CDSB and TCFD that could be supplemented by more detailed industry-specific metrics, such as those prescribed by the SASB standards. This would provide the market with a core set of comparable information to enable better benchmarking and investment decision-making even as international accounting authorities and governments develop fuller official standards and legal requirements over the next several years.

Even with a good understanding of the individual elements of this disclosure stack, the task individual firms and their report preparers face in pulling these pieces together into a coherent whole may seem daunting. While the IFRS/IOSCO process has great potential to simplify matters by prescribing a baseline global standard, this is likely to take a few years potentially in a number of stages, and its early, widespread adoption by regulators is not guaranteed.

Under such fluid circumstances, taking a wait-and-see posture and maintaining current disclosure practices may seem like the most logical course of action. However, there is a stronger case for firms to act without delay to construct their own integrated report based on their particular considerations and context. First, investor expectations of their portfolio firms are evolving rapidly and well ahead of regulators' actions, as initiatives such as the Net-Zero Asset Owner Alliance,[49] recent BlackRock letters[50] and ambitious Glasgow Financial Alliance for Net Zero[51] illustrate. Second, employee, consumer and general public attitudes are shifting as well, and this is turning up the heat, so to speak, on governments and stock exchanges around the world. Third, the evidence from <IR>, TCFD and other such initiatives is that companies do not achieve the high quality of reporting they aim for in one reporting cycle. Enhancing governance, controls and measurement of ESG information are all essential parts of the implementation process, and it takes time to refine them. An early start is thus certainly better than a late start.

The writing would appear to be on the wall: mandatory mainstream ESG/sustainability reporting is coming sooner or later to some or all of the jurisdictions in which your firm operates. It would be far better to anticipate these changes than be compelled to completely overhaul the firm's disclosure practices in a few years' time. Moreover, the outline of a global baseline standard for material ESG/sustainability-related disclosure to investors and financial regulators is already coming into focus by virtue of the work of the private standard setters' collective input into the IFRS/IOSCO process.[52] This preparatory technical guidance suggests the following four-part approach to applying this stack in an integrated annual report during the next few transitional years until the formal promulgation of a global standard by international accounting authorities and its adoption or adaptation by national regulatory authorities:

1. Report against the most recent version of the IFRS **climate change** standard (see Appendix A for the prototype standard on which the new International Sustainability Standards Board will base its exposure draft in 2022).
2. Report against the 21 World Economic Forum IBC *Measuring Stakeholder Capitalism* **cross-industry** "core" metrics and recommended disclosures and consider reporting against the most relevant of its "expanded" metrics and disclosures (see Appendix B).
3. Report against the SASB **industry-specific** metrics that pertain to the firm's main business lines as per its "materiality map" (see Appendix C).
4. Report any **other information** that careful consideration of the IFRS General Requirements for Disclosure of Sustainability-Related Financial Information Prototype Standard[53] leads the firm to believe would be of important relevance to its value creation over the medium term (e.g., three to five years).

As the ISSB moves beyond climate change in the coming years to establish standards on additional ESG/sustainability topics, firms should plan to refine those elements of their reporting accordingly, progressively replacing reporting based on one or more of the voluntary frameworks listed above with a revised treatment of the topic based on these new standards as they become available. In taking this approach, firms will place themselves on the best-practice frontier of ESG/sustainability reporting, anticipating the likely path of regulatory requirements and reducing the transaction costs of having to catch up to these through a more radical, one-time reinvention of information systems and reporting practices.

### 6.2.3    Review, Assure and Approve for Issuance

- Obtain comments on draft report from relevant internal governance and advisory committees.
- Assure key elements, including key material ESG&D disclosures.
- Secure approval of the CFO for presentation to and approval by the CEO and board.

As the firm's main disclosure to investors, the integrated annual report will require the CFO's review and comments, and it should also seek the same from relevant internal and external advisory committees. As much of the report as practicable should be assured, whether in terms of the verification of specific data or strength of related management systems. Finally, as the custodian of the firm's purpose and its accountability to investors and other stakeholders in terms of its risk management, value creation and licence to operate, the board and its Audit Committee, as well as the CEO, should review and approve the report before issuance. Some firms have a specific committee on sustainability and ESG matters. The views of this group will be particularly relevant.

## 6.3    Accelerating the Creation of an International Standard Through Collective Business Leadership

As the foregoing discussion illustrates, although there is considerable complexity in the current ESG reporting landscape, the main existing voluntary standards exhibit a certain complementary logic. They can be applied in a stacked manner by companies wishing to tell a story that is at once coherent and based on market-tested best practice. But while this potential exists and reflects best practice, it is a long way from customary and consistent practice, which is what is needed to more fully align capital allocation decisions within boardrooms and financial markets behind the sustainable value creation strategies that would accelerate the implementation of the SDGs.

This systemic internalization of ESG&D factors in corporate and investor governance awaits a deliberate push, which clearer and more consistent disclosure norms can help provide. But efforts by individual companies, as recommended above, can only go so far. They are unlikely to produce the scale of behavioural change that social and economic conditions demand and the principles of stakeholder capitalism promise. As with the evolution of financial standards in decades past, the time has come for the top-down force of governmental action to accelerate convergence around a global solution, albeit by leveraging rather than substituting for the bottom-up momentum that has already been built within the business community and voluntary standard-setting community.

Given the highly interdisciplinary, public-private nature of ESG&D disclosure, the global business community has a crucial role to play in catalysing and shaping the process of international standards harmonization. In the first instance, it should wholeheartedly support the IOSCO and IFRS initiatives and strongly encourage national policymakers to do so as well rather than pursue their own national or regional solutions. It should encourage regulators around the world to adopt this common, baseline standard outright recognizing that it can be supplemented where required with additional national building blocks while maintaining the global interoperability of the ISSB cornerstone intact.

IOSCO and IFRS are keen to have this corporate engagement and support, as they are acutely aware of the threat disparate national approaches pose to the entire endeavour of improving capital allocation through more complete, consistent and comparable information. And they are mindful of the important role of civil society in shaping the decisions taken by political authorities, including the NGOs which have set the voluntary standards that have been widely adopted thus far. These have all been multi-stakeholder partnerships in which the industrial, investment and accounting communities have been deeply involved. Accordingly, the private sector and IFRS and IOSCO have a mutual interest in anchoring global standards for mainstream reporting of material ESG&D factors in a clear understanding of how these leading voluntary standards and frameworks, as well as the recent WEF IBC cross-industry metrics which are a composite of them, fit together based on the primary role each plays in the ESG&D disclosure stack outlined above (see Fig. 6.1).

As the primary producers and consumers of such information, business, accounting and investor leaders have a crucial role to play in helping to establish and sustain a broad political mandate for the kind of international and public-private-civil society cooperation that will be needed for IFRS and IOSCO to succeed. Today's business leaders should take inspiration from the history of financial accounting standards—the Financial Accounting Foundation and Financial Accounting Standards Board in the US, and IFRS and IASB at the global level, as discussed in the preceding section. Other multi-stakeholder international governance efforts may also be instructive, such as the birth of Internet Corporation for Assigned Numbers and Names (ICANN) for which a global consultative process to consider governance options was overseen by the US Department of Commerce[54]; the Global Fund to Fight AIDS, Tuberculosis and Malaria for which a preliminary public-private Transitional Working Group was formed to develop governance options[55]; or indeed the Financial Stability Board's experience in organizing the Task Force on Climate-Related Financial Disclosures.

Each of these was a purpose-built, public-private process to solve an interdisciplinary policy challenge for which much of the relevant expertise and capabilities resided in non-state actors. Each was also a response to a policy challenge that all stakeholders believed required a rapid solution. This is certainly the case for sustainability/ESG disclosure today, as evidenced by recent pronouncements by the EU and other key actors and by the limited time remaining for the world to generate the progress necessary to achieve the 2030 Sustainable Development Goals and targets of the Paris Climate Agreement.

IOSCO, IFRS and the global accounting community[56] are forthrightly, if belatedly, rising to this challenge, and the main voluntary standard setters are showing signs of being ready to come together behind such an integrated solution rather than retain their pieces of the incumbent architecture. In September 2020, facilitated by the Impact Management Project, World Economic Forum and Deloitte, the five leading such organizations issued a joint *Statement of Intent to Work Together Towards Comprehensive Corporate Reporting*[57] in which they provided a clear vision of such a solution, which helped to shape the initial thinking and planning of IOSCO and IFRS in this regard.

Against this backdrop of converging institutional agendas but still significant political uncertainty, strong engagement by the global business community could be decisive; it could make the difference between comprehensive and legitimate global standards emerging within a couple of years and a jumble of NGO and official global and regional frameworks persisting for another decade or more. With ten years remaining in the quest to attain the Sustainable

Development Goals, including the interim progress scientists advise must be achieved by 2030 in order to avert a dangerous accumulation of greenhouse gases in the atmosphere by mid-century, the world cannot afford continued delay in aligning the information supplied to capital markets with these crucial aspects of sustainable enterprise value creation.

The five voluntary standards organizations that issued the Joint Statement of Intent charted a clear and compelling path forward. The IFRS Foundation's International Sustainability Standards Board they foreshadowed would be a global public good. It should not be viewed as a substitute for national regulation, such as that being actively considered by the European Union, but rather as a complement to and enabler of such national action. Only national regulatory authorities can legally require disclosure—their role is thus crucial. But because capital and commerce flow across national boundaries, national disclosure requirements need to be consistent or interoperable at their core if they are to achieve the objective of effecting a more sustainable allocation of capital, and only an international reporting standard or set of standards can provide this.

National jurisdictions can supplement a global standard for reporting of sustainability factors material to enterprise value creation with requirements for reporting of societal impacts and other considerations, such as many of those pioneered by the Global Reporting Initiative. However, they would be ill advised to replicate an underlying global standard for reporting to investors for the same reasons they decided years ago to develop the IFRS regime for financial reporting. The business community has an intrinsic interest in seeing material ESG (& someday D) reporting take a globally coherent form. For this reason, the champions of stakeholder capitalism and sustainable enterprise value creation should play an active role in encouraging the accounting, investor, governmental and NGO communities to rally around the new ISSB without delay.

## Notes

1. See *International Integrated Reporting Framework*, International Integrated Reporting Council, 2013; and *Creating Value: The Cyclical Power of Integrated Thinking and Reporting*, International Integrated Reporting Council, 2016.
2. See, for example, *How Does European Sustainable Funds' Performance Measure Up?*, Morningstar Manager Research, Morningstar, June 2020; *Creating Value: Benefits to Investors*, The International Integrated Reporting Council, 2017; and *Realizing the Benefits: The Impact of Integrated Reporting*, The International Integrated Reporting Council and Black Sun PLC, 2015.

3. *The Road Ahead*, The KPMG Survey of Corporate Responsibility Reporting 2017, KPMG 2017.
4. *WFE Sustainability Survey April 2019: Exchanges Advancing Sustainable Finance*, World Federation of Exchanges, 2019, pp. 13—15.
5. *Purpose Beyond Profit: The Value of Value—Board Level Insights,* Association of International Certified Professional Accountants (AICPA), International Integrated Reporting Council (IIRC) and Black Sun PLC, 2018.
6. For an in-depth discussion of this mixture of recent progress and persisting fragmentation, see *Mapping the Sustainability Reporting Landscape: Lost in the Right Direction*, Association of Chartered Certified Accountants (ACCA) and Climate Disclosure Standards Board (CDSB), 2016.
7. *Toward Common Metrics and Consistent Reporting of Sustainable Value Creation*, World Economic Forum International Business Council, 2020.
8. World Economic Forum International Business Council, *Measuring Stakeholder Capitalism: Towards Common Metrics and Consistent Reporting of Sustainable Value Creation*, September 2020.
9. Global Use of SASB Standards, https://www.sasb.org/about/global-use/
10. *CEO Quarterly Update*, UN Principles for Responsible Investment, March 2020.
11. *Sustainable Signals: Asset Owners See Sustainability as Core to the Future of Investing,* Morgan Stanley Institute for Sustainable Investing, 2020. https://www.morganstanley.com/content/dam/msdotcom/sustainability/20-05-22_3094389%20Sustainable%20Signals%20Asset%20Owners_FINAL.pdf
12. *Return on Values: Most investors expect better performance, bigger impact*, UBS Investor Watch, September 2018.
13. *Point of View on Enhancing Corporate Reporting*, International Federation of Accountants, 2019; see https://www.ifac.org/what-we-do/speak-out-global-voice/points-view/enhancing-corporate-reporting
14. *Interconnected Standard Setting for Corporate Reporting*, Accountancy Europe Cogito Paper, December 2019, p. 9.
15. These statistics are drawn from *Carrots and Sticks: Global Trends in Sustainability Reporting Regulation*, KPMG International, GRI, United Nations Environment Programme (UNEP) and The Centre for Corporate Governance in Africa, 2016.
16. *Carrots and Sticks: Sustainability Reporting Policy—Global Trends in Disclosure as the ESG Agenda Goes Mainstream,* GRI and University of Stellenbosch Business School, July 2020, p. 17.
17. *A Call for Action: Climate Change as a Source of Financial Risk*, Network for Greening the Financial System, April 2019, p. 3.
18. *IOSCO steps up its efforts to address issues around sustainability and climate change,* International Organization of Securities Commissions (IOSCO), April 14, 2020.

19. See "IOSCO sees an urgent need for globally consistent, comparable, and reliable sustainability disclosure standards and announces its priorities and vision for a Sustainability Standards Board under the IFRS Foundation," February 24, 2021 https://www.iosco.org/news/pdf/IOSCONEWS594.pdf, and "IOSCO elaborates on its vision and expectations for the IFRS Foundation's work towards a global baseline of investor-focussed sustainability standards to improve the global consistency, comparability and reliability of sustainability reporting," June 28, 2021, https://www.iosco.org/news/pdf/IOSCONEWS608.pdf

20. Public Statement of SEC Acting Chair Allison Herren Lee, "Public Input Welcomed on Climate Change Disclosures," March 15, 2021. https://www.sec.gov/news/public-statement/lee-climate-change-disclosures

21. "IFRS Foundation Trustees' Feedback Statement on the Consultation Paper on Sustainability Reporting," April 2021 https://www.ifrs.org/content/dam/ifrs/project/sustainability-reporting/sustainability-consultation-paper-feedback-statement.pdf

22. "IFRS Trustees announce working group to accelerate convergence in global sustainability reporting standards focused on enterprise value."

23. See IFRS: https://www.ifrs.org/projects/work-plan/management-commentary/

24. See, for example, Association of Chartered Certified Accountants (ACCA) and Climate Disclosure Standards Board (CDSB), *Mapping the sustainability reporting landscape: Lost in the right direction*, May 2016, https://www.cdsb.net/harmonization/581/sustainability-reporting-lost-right-direction; and this interactive map: https://widgets.weforum.org/esgecosystemmap/#/

25. https://www.reportingexchange.com/

26. *Revision of the Non-Financial Reporting Directive: Inception Impact Assessment*, European Commission Directorate-General for Financial Stability, Financial Services and Capital Markets Union (DG FISMA), February 2020. https://ec.europa.eu/info/law/better-regulation/have-your-say/initiatives/12129-Revision-of-Non-Financial-Reporting-Directive

27. European Commission, "Questions and Answers: Corporate Sustainability Reporting Directive proposal," April 21, 2021 https://ec.europa.eu/commission/presscorner/detail/en/QANDA_21_1806

28. *Interconnected Standard Setting for Corporate Reporting*, Accountancy Europe, December 2019.

29. CDP, CDSB, GRI, IIRC and SASB, Statement of Intent to Work Together Towards Comprehensive Corporate Reporting, Summary of alignment discussions facilitated by the Impact Management Project, World Economic Forum and Deloitte, September 2020, https://29kjwb3armds2g3gi4lq2sx1-wpengine.netdna-ssl.com/wp-content/uploads/Statement-of-Intent-to-Work-Together-Towards-Comprehensive-Corporate-Reporting.pdf

30. Value Reporting Foundation, "IIRC and SASB Form the Value Reporting Foundation," Press Release, June 9, 2021. https://www.valuereportingfoundation.org/news/iirc-and-sasb-form-the-value-reportingfoundation-providing-comprehensive-suite-oftools-to-assess-manage-and-communicate-value/

31. See IFRS Foundation: https://www.ifrs.org/news-and-events/news/2021/11/ifrs-foundation-announces-issb-consolidation-with-cdsb-vrf-publication-of-prototypes/

32. Information compiled and provided for the authors by IIRC staff, June 2020.

33. METI Ministry of Economy, Trade and Industry. "Ito Review of Competitiveness and Incentives for Sustainable Growth—Building Favorable Relationships between Companies and Investors". Final Report, August 2014. https://www.meti.go.jp/english/press/2014/pdf/0806_04b.pdf

34. Deloitte. *Annual report insights 2019: Surveying FTSE reporting.* https://www2.deloitte.com/uk/en/pages/audit/articles/annual-report-insights.html

35. PWC. *Rapport intégré: Les pratiques des sociétiés cotées en 2020.* https://www.pwc.fr/fr/publications/communication-financiere/les-pratiques-des-societes-cotees.html

36. *A Comparative Analysis of Integrated Reporting in Ten Countries*, Robert G. Eccles, Michael P. Krzus, and Carlos Solano, SSRN: https://ssrn.com/abstract=3345590 or https://doi.org/10.2139/ssrn.3345590 March 2, 2019, pp. 15–18.

37. *Navigating the landscape: A path forward for sustainability reporting,* Reporting Matters 2019, WBCSD and Climate Disclosure Standards Board (CDSB), pp. 12–14.

38. *Op. cit.,* p. 5.

39. *Op. cit.,* pp. 24—25.

40. Eccles et al., op. cit., p. 24.

41. *Principles for a Purposeful Business: How to deliver the framework for the Future of the Corporation*, British Academy, 2019, pp. 16–17. See also, *Reforming Business for the 21st Century: A Framework for the Future of the Corporation*, British Academy, 2018.

42. WBCSD, op. cit., p. 28.

43. *The International <IR> Framework*, International Integrated Reporting Council, 2013, pp. 10—22.

44. The IIRC and SASB merged into the Value Reporting Foundation in 2021, albeit retaining the branding of their respective framework and standards.

45. *TCFD Implementation Guide: Using SASB Standards and the CDSB Framework to Enhance Climate-Related Financial Disclosures in Mainstream Reporting*, CDSB and SASB, 2019.

46. *TCFD Good Practice Handbook*, CDSB and SASB, 2019.

47. CDP, CDSB, GRI, IIRC and SASB, *Statement of Intent to Work Together toward Comprehensive Corporate Reporting*, September 2020 https://29kjwb3a rmds2g3gi4lq2sx1-wpengine.netdna-ssl.com/wp-content/uploads/ Statement-of-Intent-to-Work-Together-Towards-Comprehensive-Corporate-Reporting.pdf. All rights reserved.

48. World Economic Forum International Business Council, Measuring Stakeholder Capitalism: Towards Common Metrics and Consistent Reporting of Sustainable Value Creation, World Economic Forum, September 2020, https://www.weforum.org/reports/measuring-stakeholder-capitalism-towards-common-metrics-and-consistent-reporting-of-sustainable-value-creation

49. https://www.unepfi.org/net-zero-alliance/

50. https://www.blackrock.com/corporate/investor-relations/larry-fink-ceo-letter

51. See Glasgow Financial Alliance for Net Zero Progress Report, November 2021: https://www.gfanzero.com/progress-report/

52. *Reporting on enterprise value illustrated with a prototype climate-related financial disclosure standard: progress towards a comprehensive corporate reporting system from leading sustainability and integrated reporting organisations CDP, CDSB, GRI, IIRC and SASB,* Impact Management Project, World Economic Forum and Deloitte, December 2020, https://29kjwb3armds2g3gi4lq2sx1-wpengine.netdna-ssl.com/wp-content/uploads/Reporting-on-enterprise-value_climate-prototype_Dec20.pdf

53. IFRS Foundation Technical Readiness Working Group, "General Requirements for Disclosure of Sustainability-related Financial Information," November 2021: https://www.ifrs.org/content/dam/ifrs/groups/trwg/trwg-general-requirements-prototype.pdf

54. *Technical Management of Internet Names and Addresses*, Federal Register, US Department of Commerce, February 20, 1998. https://www.ntia.doc.gov/legacy/ntiahome/domainname/dnsdrft.htm

55. *Transitional Working Group Archive*, Global Fund to Fight AIDS, Tuberculosis and Malaria https://www.theglobalfund.org/en/archive/transitional-working-group/

56. See, for example, *Enhancing Corporate Reporting,* IFAC Points of View, International Federation of Accountants, 2019. https://www.ifac.org/what-we-do/speak-out-global-voice/points-view/enhancing-corporate-reporting

57. CDP, CDSB, GRI, IIRC and SASB, Statement of Intent to Work Together Towards Comprehensive Corporate Reporting, Summary of alignment discussions facilitated by the Impact Management Project, World Economic Forum and Deloitte, September 2020, https://29kjwb3armds2g3gi4lq2sx1-wpengine.netdna-ssl.com/wp-content/uploads/Statement-of-Intent-to-Work-Together-Towards-Comprehensive-Corporate-Reporting.pdf

**Open Access** This chapter is licensed under the terms of the Creative Commons Attribution-NonCommercial 4.0 International License (http://creativecommons. org/licenses/by-nc/4.0/), which permits any noncommercial use, sharing, adaptation, distribution and reproduction in any medium or format, as long as you give appropriate credit to the original author(s) and the source, provide a link to the Creative Commons licence and indicate if changes were made.

The images or other third party material in this chapter are included in the chapter's Creative Commons licence, unless indicated otherwise in a credit line to the material. If material is not included in the chapter's Creative Commons licence and your intended use is not permitted by statutory regulation or exceeds the permitted use, you will need to obtain permission directly from the copyright holder.

# 7

# Corporate Partnerships and Systemic Change

As outlined in the previous chapters, improvements made by business leaders and board directors to their own company's governance, strategy and reporting are all essential. Individual actions taken by companies, especially the largest, can have a meaningful impact on the lives and livelihoods of millions of people and on the environment. At the same time, they can help the company better manage its risks and protect value, harness its opportunities and create value, and commit and adhere to its values. In short, individual business action is crucial. However, it is not sufficient.

Even the most responsible and impactful actions by individual companies are not enough on their own to drive the type of transformation that is needed to ensure widespread implementation of the principles and practices of stakeholder capitalism. Nor are these individual company actions sufficient to tackle complex system-level challenges that increasingly shape companies' operating contexts, such as climate change, inequality, food security, economic recovery, energy transition or health crises. Partnerships among companies and between companies and other stakeholders, such as governments, investors and civil society organizations, are essential for achieving scale and systemic impact. Indeed, they have never been more important.[1]

In many situations requiring system-level change, governments should take the lead. There is an urgent need for reforms in government policies, regulations and fiscal incentives if the world has any chance of mitigating and adapting to climate change, recovering from the pandemic, tackling inequality and achieving the Sustainable Development Goals. At the same time, companies can, and in their own interests must, play a key role in working together both to advocate for such reforms and to partner with the public sector to leverage

© The Author(s) 2022
R. Samans, J. Nelson, *Sustainable Enterprise Value Creation*,
https://doi.org/10.1007/978-3-030-93560-3_7

scarce resources and drive market-based solutions. Even in the absence of government leadership, they can form coalitions with other companies and with investors to develop industry-wide, voluntary rules and standards, spread responsible business practices and mobilize blended finance and investments.

As stakeholders themselves in the vitality and resilience of their operating system, companies and their leaders should be both capable partnership practitioners as well as champions and advocates for investing in and sustaining such alliances. To be effective partners in driving systemic change, business leaders need to be effective systems leaders. As outlined in Fig. 7.1, this requires the ability to cultivate a shared vision for change, empower widespread innovation and action and enable mutual accountability for progress.[2]

This chapter looks at some key models and examples of corporate partnerships, with a particular focus on large-scale collective action among

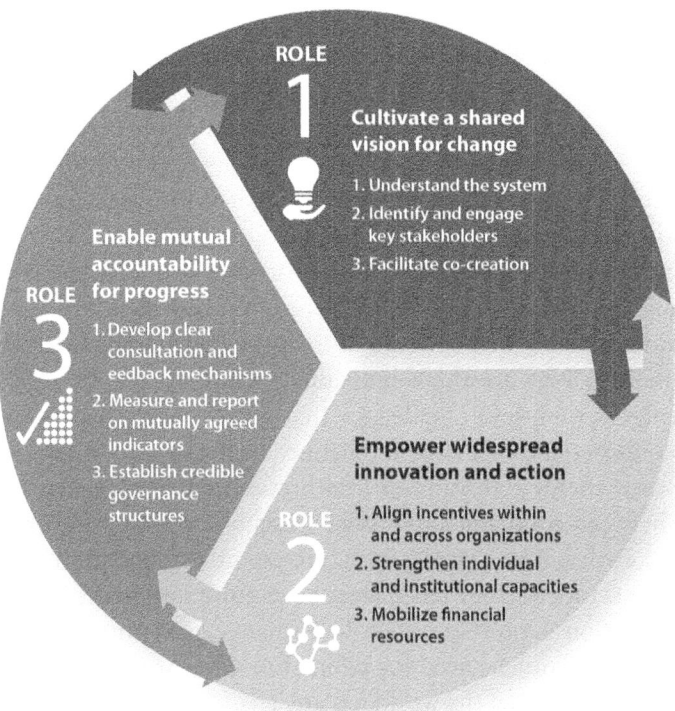

**Fig. 7.1** Three key roles of system leaders
(Adapted from: Jane Nelson and Beth Jenkins. *Tackling Global Challenges: Lessons in System Leadership from the World Economic Forum's New Vision for Agriculture Initiative*. Harvard Kennedy School, Corporate Responsibility Initiative, 2016)

companies across industry sectors and through multi-stakeholder platforms between companies, governments and civil society organizations. It also highlights some key lessons on how to engage in, build and sustain systems change alliances:

- Develop a holistic, multi-level strategy for engaging in partnerships
- Support pre-competitive business alliances to scale industry-wide progress
- Participate in multi-stakeholder platforms to drive system-wide change
- Be a corporate champion for partnerships, even when they are difficult

## 7.1  Develop a Holistic, Multi-level Strategy for Engaging in Partnerships

A typical multinational company will be engaged in hundreds if not thousands of partnerships at any point in time through its core business operations and value chain, its community engagement and philanthropy, and its policy dialogue and advocacy activities. The most robust partnerships share the following core characteristics:

> A collaborative relationship in which all participants agree voluntarily to work together to achieve a common purpose or to undertake a specific task and to share risks, resources, competencies and benefits, with reciprocal obligations and mutual accountability for outcomes.[3]

Given the complexity and uncertainty of most business operating contexts, it should be obvious that there is no over-arching "best practice" partnership model. Most leading companies take a holistic approach, engaging in a wide variety of different levels and types of partnership simultaneously. The following three broad types and levels of partnership are particularly important in achieving scale and impact towards a more stakeholder-oriented way of doing business and effectively managing ESG&D risks and opportunities:[4]

- *Project-level, financing and operational partnerships*: These involve an individual company working with one or a small number of other partners or stakeholders to accomplish a certain objective or set of objectives usually within a set time-frame. Such partnerships typically include a project plan with well-defined roles and responsibilities, and with monitoring and evaluation mechanisms that enable the partners to make "course corrections" as needed over the life of the project. They can be undertaken to improve the performance and impact of the company's own core business activities and value chain or to leverage core business capabilities such as R&D, technology innovation, product development, manufacturing, logistics, marketing and distribution to solve specific social and environmental challenges or to improve the impact of corporate philanthropy and community investment commitments. There are hundreds of thousands of such project-level partnerships between individual companies and external stakeholders around the world, and more are needed.

- *Industry-level, pre-competitive business alliances*: These involve a group of companies working together with their peers and competitors on a pre-competitive basis within or across a specific industry sector to drive sector-wide change. This can include voluntary initiatives to establish and spread responsible industry standards or collaborative efforts to scale and replicate promising innovations and models, respond to a humanitarian crisis or undertake joint research or public policy advocacy. Some of these alliances are part of long-established chambers of commerce or trade and industry associations that have set up new departments to focus on social and environmental issues. Others have been established to have an explicit and dedicated focus on advancing social and environmental goals through industry coordination and cooperation. Such pre-competitive business alliances play a crucial role in scaling the reach and impact of industry-wide changes and commitments to stakeholder capitalism. Some examples are profiled in Sect. 7.2 of this chapter.

- *Multi-stakeholder institutions, platforms and networks*: These involve collaboration among large groups of companies alongside other actors such as governments and civil society organizations aimed at overcoming systemic market failures or governance gaps to achieve transformational change. They include independent institutions with their own governance and accountability structures, such as the Global Reporting Initiative, GAVI The Global Vaccine Alliance, the Global Alliance for Improved Nutrition, the Alliance for a Green Revolution in Africa and the Better Than Cash Alliance, to mention just a few. They also include more informal and dynamic networks and technology-enabled online information and knowledge hubs and open innovation and accelerator platforms. Some examples of this type of large-scale multi-stakeholder platform are provided in Sect. 7.3 of this chapter.

In most cases of successful scaling or systemic impact, there are mutually reinforcing linkages between these different levels and types of partnership. Individual companies will be simultaneously creating or participating in partnerships at each level. At the same time, each company is part of an eco-system of partnerships, some led by business, and others by governments or civil society. Business leaders need to understand and be more actively engaged in shaping this ecosystem and its relationship to their own corporate strate-gies, cultures, performance and material ESG&D priorities.

As outlined above, hundreds of thousands of project-level financing and operational partnerships are being implemented along company values chains and in host communities. They have a valuable role to play and more are needed. Yet, to achieve real scale and system-level transformation, it is pre-competitive business alliances and multi-stakeholder platforms that will make the difference.

## 7.2    Support Pre-competitive Business Alliances to Scale Industry-Wide Progress

One of the most effective ways of accelerating and scaling change is through industry-wide coalitions. If competitors can work together on a pre-competitive basis to establish and spread common goals for sustainable devel-opment, while still competing on their individual ability to execute and innovate, collectively they can have far more substantial and systemic impact than each acting alone. They can achieve this by one or a combination of the following types of collective action:

- Establishing industry-wide standards that all members must meet
- Setting ambitious shared goals or roadmaps for achieving specific social or environmental objectives or the Sustainable Development Goals more broadly
- Reporting and benchmarking members' performance against these stan-dards and goals
- Sharing lessons and good practices
- Supporting pre-competitive research and development consortia
- Undertaking joint policy advocacy

There is untapped potential for business leaders to demand more of their representative industry bodies, especially when it comes to policy advocacy, given the "voice" and influence that many of these business-led groups have with governments. These organizations also influence the activities of millions of companies and could be one of the best multiplier platforms available for scaling business impact beyond the leading companies. At a minimum, as part of good corporate governance outlined in Chap. 4 and integrated reporting outlined in Chap. 6, companies should publicly report on which trade and industry associations they are members of and the financial contributions that they are making to them.

There is also untapped potential for smaller groups of business leaders to work together collectively in business-led organizations or campaigns that are fully dedicated to mobilizing business support for a specific social or environmental issue or set of issues. A vanguard of business-led corporate responsibility coalitions has already demonstrated high potential for achieving impact.[5] In almost all cases, a core group of 20 or so CEOs and their companies have played a crucial "start-up" role as champions, role models and influencers, actively encouraging their business partners, peers and competitors to get engaged.

We look at both of these business-led models in more detail below.

### 7.2.1 Leverage the Sustainability Influence of Representative Business Organizations

Representative business organizations, such as Chambers of Commerce, Organizations of Employers or Trade and Industry Associations, have been established for decades in most sectors and countries as well as at a global level. They focus mainly on advocating for and promoting direct, competitive business interests for their hundreds and sometimes thousands of member companies. As ESG&D issues become material to business success, these associations are starting to take a more proactive stance on these issues, sometimes establishing dedicated units or programmes to address them. In most cases, a small cohort of influential member companies and their CEOs is spearheading this evolving leadership role.

Representative business organizations operating at a national level can provide a valuable collective platform for their members to advocate for policy reforms and engage with government in other ways. Having said that, they can be criticized for playing to the "lowest common denominator" to represent all their diverse members and for defending the *status quo* or undertaking obstructionist or regressive lobbying against policies or regulations that further the goals of sustainability. At the same time, given their influence and reach, these organizations have the potential to play a valuable role in the drive towards stakeholder capitalism and more inclusive and sustainable growth. As a result, growing media, investor and activist attention is being paid to the role of business associations, especially at national levels, and demands for companies to be more transparent about how they are engaging in and funding these organizations.

The following examples illustrate four well-established national business associations that are starting to take a leadership role in advancing the topics and practices of sustainability and stakeholder capitalism at a country level:

**Japan's Keidanren**: Keidanren, the Japan Business Federation, is a comprehensive economic organization representing 1461 Japanese companies, 109 national industrial associations and regional economic organizations from all 47 prefectures. Keidanren's mission is to "support corporate activities which contribute to the sustainable development of the Japanese economy and improvement of the quality of life for the Japanese people."[6]

The federation is particularly focused on promoting sustainable development through digital and economic transformation. In November 2018, Keidanren published *Society 5.0: Co-creating the Future*, a proposal outlining Keidanren's vision for creating a new human-centred society.[7] Keidanren executives assert that today's greatest challenges can be addressed with closer collaboration between industry, academics, government and individuals from diverse backgrounds. This framework was specifically designed to support the achievement of the UN SDGs.[8] Member companies are also involved in addressing climate change. Over 130 members are engaged in 300 projects as part of Challenge Zero, an initiative to develop and deploy new net-zero emissions technologies. Two-hundred and fifty members have also developed long-term plans to mitigate emissions in their operations.[9]

**Confederation of British Industry (CBI)**: Since its founding in 1965, CBI has grown to represent 190,000 businesses and their 7 million employees.[10] It acts as a bridge connecting companies with government stakeholders and other businesses, helping different parties to share best practices, make informed decisions and engage in change-making dialogue.[11] Over the past few decades, in addition to more traditional ongoing priorities such as business regulations, taxes, trade and innovation, CBI has increased its focus on human capital and skills development and on infrastructure, energy and the environment.

CBI is particularly focused on empowering its members to decarbonize their operations. The UK is legally bound to achieving a net-zero economy by 2050. CBI recognizes that business cooperation is essential to achieving these targets, and it has publicly committed to work with its members and local governments to meet this pressing challenge. For example, CBI is encouraging every member to decarbonize their operations and collaborate with sector partners to reduce emissions throughout supply chains. CBI is also advocating for the government to pass specific climate change legislation and invest in a low-carbon economy to help businesses transition.[12]

***US Business Roundtable (BRT)***: The US Business Roundtable is an association of CEOs from America's top 200 largest companies, representing 20 million employees and over $9 trillion in annual revenue. BRT's statement redefining the purpose of the corporation from shareholder primacy to stakeholder responsibility on August 19, 2019, which was signed by 181 member CEOs, illustrates the influence and leverage impact that an industry association can have. Although there have been some critiques of the way member companies have implemented the commitment in practice,[13] there can be no doubt that the BRT's members collectively stating that the purpose of business is to "serve not only their shareholders, but also deliver value to their customers, invest in employees, deal fairly with suppliers and support the communities in which they operate" has influenced many other companies, investors and activist groups to take action.[14] Since 2019, member CEOs and their companies have adopted a number of initiatives related to increasing minimum wage, improving the health and safety of employees, investing in communities, supporting voter rights and prioritizing climate action and environmental protection.[15]

***Confederation of Indian Industry (CII)***: CII partners with industry, government and civil society partners to build an economy that will promote India's development. The Confederation has 900 private and public sector members and an indirect membership of 300,000 enterprises from 294 national and local trade associations.[16] CII promotes several initiatives related to corporate social responsibility, climate change, sustainable development and more by utilizing cross-sector partnerships and providing corporations with consulting services and research findings.[17]

The CII National Committee of Corporate Social Responsibility & Community Development was founded in 2001 to promote the sharing of best practices among members. The Committee partnered with the Bombay Stock Exchange and Indian Institute of Corporate Affairs to create Sammaan, an online platform that connects businesses with NGOs and community projects in need of funding.[18] Additionally, the Confederation hosts trainings and consults companies in areas related to environmental and climate change policy, sustainability reporting, stakeholder engagement,[19] decarbonization[20] and disaster management.[21]

At a global level, four examples of trade and industry associations that have taken specific actions to spread ESG practices among their members and which offer useful lessons for other industry sectors are summarized in Box 7.1.

These are only eight examples from a possible universe of hundreds of representative trade, industry and business associations. If more associations were to take a more strategic and ambitious approach to encouraging or requiring

**Box 7.1** Four Global Trade and Industry Associations Scaling Up Industry-Wide Sustainability Leadership

| | |
|---|---|
| Making <u>industry-wide public commitments</u> for members to achieve social and environmental goals and targets | *The Consumer Goods Forum (CGF)*. CGF can trace its history back to 1953 and today has the vision of "achieving better lives through better business."[22] With over 400 manufacturing and retail member companies[23] and a 50-member CEO-led board,[24] the CGF has established pillars of work on environmental and social sustainability, health and wellness, and food safety, among others. The work of each pillar is guided by public resolutions and commitments, with specific time-bound targets that aim to drive industry-wide focus and performance on relevant challenges. They include commitments on addressing deforestation, the use of HFC refrigerants, food waste, forced labour, and health and wellness.[25] |
| | In 2016, the Global Social Compliance Programme (GSCP) was also integrated into CGF, which is a cross-industry effort to drive convergence in tools and reporting to improve social and environmental performance in consumer goods supply chains. CGF will build upon GSCP's work by promoting the Sustainable Supply Chain Initiative, which will streamline benchmarking of third-party auditing and certification schemes according to the CGF's Global Food Safety Initiative.[26] |
| Establishing <u>industry-wide performance standards</u> for members in health, safety, environment and security and creating a sustainability Technology Roadmap | *The International Council of Chemical Associations (ICCA)*. Alongside some of its regional affiliates, ICCA was one of the first trade associations to publicly address issues of health, safety and the environment. In 1985, in response to the Bhopal Disaster, which was the world's worst industrial disaster with an official death toll of more than 5000 people, the Canadian chemical industry established the Responsible Care® programme to drive continuous improvement in health, safety, environmental and security performance and improve stakeholder engagement and over the years has made it a requirement for membership.[27] A global charter was adopted in 2006 and the programme was implemented by national chemical associations and companies in more than 60 countries. Today, ICCA's members employ 120 million people in 70 economies around the world and account for 90% of all global chemical sales.[28] |
| | In the past few years, ICCA has launched programmes on sustainable development, focusing on the role of chemicals in addressing challenges and stakeholder concerns related to public health, food security, clean water, climate change and plastics. ICCA's programmes include the Technology Roadmap initiative, focused on exploring and promoting technologies that can drive new business value while explicitly tackling global, social and environmental challenges.[29] |

*(continued)*

**Box 7.1** (continued)

| | |
|---|---|
| Producing an <u>industry-wide Code of Conduct</u> for members and partnerships and campaigns to tackle global health challenges | *The International Federation of Pharmaceutical Manufacturers and Associations.* IFPMA represents some of the largest biopharmaceutical companies[30] and regional and national associations[31] in the world. All members are required to sign IFPMA's Code of Practice, the first of its kind for any sector. The Code was first written in 1981 and has undergone five revisions over the past four decades to ensure that members' practices align with evolving ethical standards. A 2012 revision expanded the Code's scope beyond marketing practices to "cover all interactions with healthcare professionals, medical institutions and patient organizations." The most recent 2019 edits set standards even higher, including banning gifts and promotional aids and developing the IFPMA Ethos which shifted the Code from a rules-based to a values-based document.[32]

IFPMA also works with its member companies on initiatives to collectively address a variety of global health challenges and to profile partnership opportunities to strengthen health systems and improve access to affordable medicines, including sharing policy options for Universal Health Coverage. In 2020, more than 20 of its members launched the AMR Action Fund to bring 2–4 new antibiotics to patients by 2030, to address the rapid rise of antimicrobial resistance. IFPMA is also a founding partner of the Access to COVID-19 Tools ACT-Accelerator. This includes the COVID-19 Vaccine Global Access Facility (COVAX), which aims to support public-private partnerships to accelerate the development, production and equitable access to safe, effective and affordable COVID-19 vaccines. In addition, IFPMA has launched a #TeamVaccines campaign to spread trust and confidence in vaccines. Clearly, relevant members stand to benefit from being able to sell more of their products due to these initiatives, but at the same time the industry's R&D, production and distributions capabilities are essential for improving global public health and working together can help to scale impact. |

(continued)

**Box 7.1** (continued)

| | |
|---|---|
| Establishing an <u>industry-wide benchmark</u> to assess contributions to the SDGs and hosting the Mobile for Development platform | *The GSMA Association*: GSMA represents more than 750 operators and nearly 400 other companies in the broader mobile communications ecosystem. This includes handset and device makers, software companies, equipment providers and internet companies, as well as organizations in adjacent industry sectors.[33] Essentially, the companies that produce the products and networks that reach more than 5 billion unique mobile subscribers around the globe. |

GSMA was the first representative industry association to develop a methodology to benchmark the industry's contribution to the Sustainable Development Goals, publishing its first *Mobile Industry Impact Report* in 2016.[34] In its 2020 impact report, GSMA noted that with the use of mobile services accelerating, the industry's impact on the SDGs grew faster than ever, "for example, 1.6 billion mobile subscribers used their phone in 2019 to improve or monitor their health, representing an increase of 330 million since 2018. Moreover, 2.3 billion subscribers used mobile financial services, an increase of 620 million since 2018."[35] At the same time, the report highlighted the increased exclusion and vulnerability of people who do not have access to digital technology, exacerbated by the COVID-19 pandemic, and the growing urgency to address the digital divide.

Additionally, GSMA's Mobile for Development Initiative supports numerous projects that aim to test and spread scalable innovations and partnerships in mobile solutions to address a range of development priorities. These include solutions in mHealth, AgriTech, Digital Identity, Mobile Money, Connected Women and Disaster Response.[36]

Source: Adapted and updated from: Jane Nelson. *Partnerships for Sustainable Development: Collective Action by Business, Governments and Civil Society to Achieve Scale and Transform Markets*. Corporate Responsibility Initiative, Harvard Kennedy School. Report commissioned by the Business and Sustainable Development Commission, 2017

their member companies to support specific social and environmental goals, the multiplier effect would be substantial. Collectively, these associations reach millions of companies in almost every country, with hundreds of millions of employees, substantial influence with governments, and several trillion dollars in revenues and R&D spending.

A 2013 study of five associations (the Consumer Goods Forum, IFPMA, CropLife International, the International Fertilizer Industry Association and the European Chemical Industry Council), for example, found that the annual revenues of their member companies were about US $4.3 trillion. The authors concluded, "As trade associations advance their programming along a business and society trajectory, they will not only increase their ability to be force multipliers on important issues; they will also simultaneously increase their value proposition for their member companies."[37]

The CEOs of leading companies are starting to put pressure on their trade associations to take a more progressive stance on lobbying for social and environmental goals. Given public distrust in the political lobbying activities of many trade and industry associations, there is a danger that such actions could raise additional concerns about "big business" having undue influence, or a critique that business associations are "greenwashing" by making progressive statements, but then continuing to lobby for policies or incentives that benefit companies at the expense of other stakeholders. These concerns must be understood and respected. Trade associations can help to address them by being transparent about their activities, setting public goals and commitments and being open to independent evaluations on progress, as the four associations profiled in Box 7.1 are all doing.

## 7.2.2    Establish Targeted Corporate Responsibility Leadership Coalitions

Although representative business associations at the global, regional, national and industry levels reach the largest number of companies, a second group of business-led, pre-competitive alliances has emerged over the past two decades that engages a smaller number of companies, but which has been more influential in driving the agenda for sustainable development. These are corporate responsibility coalitions—self-selected, voluntary business leadership groups that have a dedicated focus on integrating sustainability or ESG issues into core business practices and playing an active collective role in driving more inclusive and sustainable growth.[38] In almost all cases, they have been established by a relatively small start-up cohort of business champions at the CEO or senior executive level, and the most successful ones retain the active engagement of senior business executives. Box 7.2 illustrates the reach and focus of

**Box 7.2  Examples of Business Leadership Coalitions Focused on Addressing Social and Environmental Challenges**

These examples illustrate how coalitions of investors and business leaders in specific industry sectors can work together to advance industry-wide progress on ESG and sustainable development.

**1. Industry-Focused Corporate Responsibility Coalitions**

*The Principles for Responsible Investment*: Created in 2006, with support from the UN Global Compact and the United Nations Environment Programme, the PRI was one of the first coalitions composed of major asset managers and asset owners with a dedicated focus on sustainability and responsible investment. It established a set of six principles to accelerate the integration of ESG factors into financial investment and ownership decisions and produces research and collective action platforms on a variety of ESG topics and for a variety of asset owners, managers and asset classes. As of mid-2021, it had grown from an initial 100 to some 4000 signatories, collectively managing an estimated US $120 trillion.[44]

*The International Council on Mining and Metals*: This is a coalition of over 20 of the world's leading mining companies and about 30 regional and national mining associations, which together are responsible for a significant proportion of global minerals and metals production. It is dedicated fully to improving safety and sustainable development in the sector. Founded in 2001, membership is at the CEO-level and all members are required to commit to a set of ten Sustainable Development Principles, supporting position statements and transparent and accountable reporting practices against a set of performance expectations.

*The Responsible Business Alliance*: Initially established by eight companies in 2004 as the Electronics Industry Corporate Citizenship Coalition, to develop and implement a code of conduct aimed at driving industry-wide improvement on social, environmental and ethical issues on the electronics supply chain. Today, it has expanded its mandate to more than 100 member companies in the electronics, retail, auto and toy sectors, and a strong focus on workers' rights and well-being alongside environmental performance, with working groups targeted at addressing challenging issues in the value chain.

*The Equator Principles*: In 2006, the IFC co-convened a small group of seven banks to develop a joint risk management framework, modelled on the IFC Performance Standards to identify and manage social and environmental risk in projects. Today, the principles have been officially adopted by about 84 financial institutions around the world, both public and private, and they cover over 70% of international project finance debt in emerging markets.

*2. Country-Level Corporate Responsibility Coalitions*

There are a growing number of coalitions focused on promoting corporate sustainability and responsible business practices at a national or regional level. They include organizations such as Philippine Business for Social Progress; Business in the Community in the UK; the National Business Initiative in South Africa; Swedish Leadership for Sustainable Development; the Dutch Sustainable Growth Coalition and Maal'a in Israel, to name a few. Research by one of the authors with Professor David Grayson, published in 2013, identified national-level, business-led corporate responsibility coalitions in some 70 countries, including more than two-thirds of the world's largest 100 economies.[45]

just a few of these coalitions that are focused on specific industry sectors or within specific countries. All companies should review the corporate responsibility leadership coalitions in their industry and key countries of operation to explore opportunities for engagement.

There are also a number of cross-industry initiatives with a dedicated focus on working collaboratively to achieve sustainable development at global and national levels. Two CEO-led global examples are:

- **The World Business Council for Sustainable Development**: WBCSD was established in January 1995 as a merger between the Business Council for Sustainable Development, which had been created in 1990 to provide business input to the 1992 UN Conference on Environment and Development (the Rio Earth Summit), and the World Industry Council for the Environment, which was created by the International Chamber of Commerce for the same purpose.[39] As such, it is one of the world's most long-standing, global and multi-industry CEO-led organizations that is fully dedicated to "working together to accelerate the transition to a sustainable world."[40] As of mid-2021, WBCSD's over 200 member companies represented a combined revenue of more than US $8.5 trillion and 19 million employees, working together with a network of almost 70 national business councils around the world.[41]
- **The United Nations Global Compact**: In January 1999, the late UN Secretary-General, Kofi Annan, made a keynote speech to leaders attending the World Economic Forum's annual meeting. He issued the following call to action, "I propose that you, the business leaders gathered in Davos, and we, the United Nations, initiate a global compact of shared values and principles, which will give a human face to the global market."[42] Six months later, the UN Global Compact was launched by a small group of CEOs and the heads of several UN agencies and global trade unions. Today it is the world's largest corporate sustainability initiative, with some 12,000+ signatories in over 160 countries, representing a large range of industry sectors and sizes, as of mid-2021.[43] CEOs sign up to the Compact by committing to align their companies' strategies and operations with a set of ten principles based on international agreements in the areas of human rights, labour, environment and anti-corruption, and reporting publicly on their progress. They also engage in coalitions aimed at supporting local or national achievement of the Sustainable Development Goals.

These are only a small sample of sector-specific or country-level corporate responsibility coalitions. They all demonstrate the multiplier effect of large companies working together on a pre-competitive basis to drive sustainable development in their own industry sector and along their own global supply chains. Several of them have undergone independent reviews or evaluations to assess their impact. A review of the most effective business leadership coalitions highlights the following crucial success factors:

- **CEO-led**: Most of them are led by CEOs or senior business executives, with a core group of active CEO champions who galvanize their peers and competitors.
- **Foundational set of principles or code of conduct based on extensive and rigorous consultation**: The vast majority gain credibility through requiring their participants to adhere to and report progress against clear principles, performance standards or codes of practice.
- **Public goals or commitments**: Some of them have also set public goals for specific sustainable development outcomes.
- **Active working groups with clear responsibilities**: In addition to strong CEO support, many have formed practitioner-level working groups to drive industry-wide action on the most material sustainability risks and opportunities faced by their participants.

## 7.3   Participate in Multi-stakeholder Platforms to Drive System-Level Change

The most challenging partnerships of all are multi-stakeholder platforms that involve collaboration among large groups of companies alongside other actors such as governments and civil society organizations and are aimed at overcoming systemic market failures or governance gaps to achieve transformational change. Some of them are established at a global level with national platforms. Others are national or city-wide alliances. Some are set up as independently governed and funded bodies, while others are hosted or incubated within existing multi-stakeholder or "backbone" organizations such as the World Economic Forum or intergovernmental bodies such as the United Nations and the World Bank Group.

The World Economic Forum has described these ambitious platforms as "Lighthouse Projects," which it describes as being "multi-stakeholder; transformative in seeking to correct systemic issues that can trigger a big change on a recognized challenge; future-oriented in seeking to leverage Fourth Industrial Revolution technologies and science; well-championed by industry with support from top level executives and directors; and with potential for growth or replicability."[46] Box 7.3 illustrates some of the ways in which the Forum has either catalysed, convened, incubated or hosted some leading global multi-stakeholder platforms.

## Box 7.3  The World Economic Forum's Role in Catalysing, Incubating and Hosting Multi-stakeholder Platforms

The World Economic Forum (WEF) has been recognized by the Swiss Federal Agency as an International Organization for Public-Private Cooperation. The Forum supports multi-stakeholder platforms (MSPs) at different stages by helping to launch, host or incubate partnerships addressing global, regional and industry challenges in such areas as global health, climate change, sustainable development and trade. The following examples illustrate some of these collaborative initiatives:

### 1. Examples of the Forum Providing a Platform to Help Catalyse or Launch an MSP

*The Sustainable Markets Initiative (SMI)*: This initiative was launched by His Royal Highness The Prince of Wales at the World Economic Forum's Annual Meeting in 2020. Building on his five decades as a champion for sustainability and corporate responsibility, including his role as President of the UK's Business in the Community and the former Prince of Wales International Business Leaders Forum, this new initiative is working with the Forum, a vanguard of CEOs and others to accelerate systems-level change through new business and financing models and engagement with governments. Through industry and issue-specific roundtables and research, a ten-point action plan, TV media content, dialogues with government platforms such as the G7 and Terra Carta innovation and design labs, the SMI aims to accelerate and scale progress towards a sustainable future.

*GAVI, The Vaccine Alliance*: GAVI is an international public-private partnership striving to save lives and protect people's health by increasing immunization rates around the world. The Alliance brings together international institutions such as the WHO and UNICEF, academics, civil society organizations, foundations, vaccine manufacturers and industry.[47] GAVI was launched in 2000 at the Forum's Annual Meeting.[48] Since its founding, as of mid-2021, GAVI and its partners had vaccinated over 822 million children in some of the world's poorest countries, helping to prevent around 14 million predicted deaths.[49] It is playing a central role in efforts to improve COVID-19 vaccines equity by co-leading COVAX with the Coalition for Epidemic Preparedness, the World Health Organization and UNICEF. COVAX is the vaccines pillar of the COVID-19 Tools (ACT) Accelerator, which is itself a global collaboration working to accelerate the development, production and equitable access to COVID-19 tests, treatments and vaccines.[50]

*The Global Fund*: The Global Fund works in partnership with governments, the private sector, civil society and technical agencies to implement innovative models and alliances to end AIDS, tuberculosis and malaria. The Fund invests over US $4 billion each year to support research and treatment programmes in more than 100 countries.[51] As a result of its efforts, 38 million lives have been saved since its founding, including a 50% reduction in deaths caused by AIDS, tuberculosis and malaria in countries where the Global Fund invests.[52] The World Economic Forum has provided the Global Fund a platform to communicate and collaborate with partners since the Fund was launched at the Forum's Annual Meeting in 2002.[53]

### 2. Examples of the Forum Hosting an MSP

*Food Action Alliance (FAA)*: FAA builds on lessons learned over a decade from WEF's New Vision for Agriculture. It is a network of food and agribusiness

*(continued)*

**Box 7.3** (continued)

companies, banks and development finance institutions, UN organizations, non-profits and country-level initiatives hosted by the Forum. Member organizations act collectively to design and invest in country-level "flagship platforms" that aim to produce food "efficiently and sustainably, that is accessible to all, in support of a transition to healthier diets and improved environmental outcomes" aligned with the UN Sustainable Development Goals and Paris Climate Agreement. FAA's network aims to leverage food commodity value chains and multi-stakeholder platforms to transform food systems, through innovation and coordination. To date, the Alliance has catalysed WEF's network of cross-sector partnerships to build over 100 value-chain initiatives in 25 countries, engaging with several hundred private and public organizations.[54]

*Centre for the Fourth Industrial Revolution*: The Fourth Industrial Revolution is a Forum-led programme that facilitates cross-sector partnerships to develop and scale global governance models for responsible use of digital and other technology. The Centre is working with businesses, governments, academic institutions and civil society organizations "to develop, prototype and test pioneering collaborations and governance models to ensure the benefits of technology are maximized, and the risks accounted for."[55] Specifically, the Centre is working with its partners to design policy frameworks and governance protocol areas in the following focus areas: Artificial Intelligence and Machine Learning, Internet of Things and Urban Transformation, Blockchain and Distributed Ledger Technology, Data Policy, and Autonomous, Urban Mobility, and Drones and Tomorrow's Airspace.[56]

*The Global Battery Alliance (GBA)*: A circular and responsible battery value chain is one of the key drivers for achieving the Paris Climate Agreement. In 2017, the Forum convened a public-private collaboration platform of some 70 organizations, with the twofold goal of accelerating the deployment of batteries and developing guidelines and initiatives to ensure that these batteries are produced and used responsibly and sustainably, from mining to end-of-life. This requires collective efforts to address a variety of complex issues across the value chain from preventing human rights violations and ensuring safer working conditions, to lowering emissions and improving repurposing and recycling.[57]

*The Tropical Forest Alliance (TFA)*: TFA is a collective action platform hosted at the Forum that brings together over 170 organizations to encourage the global transition to sustainable rural development and deforestation-free supply chains for commodities using palm oil, soy, beef and paper/pulp.[58] Alliance partners include private sector representatives, governments, civil society organizations, Indigenous groups and multilateral organizations from across Latin America, West and Central Africa and Southeast Asia.[59]

### 3. Examples of the Forum Incubating an MSP

*The Platform for Accelerating the Circular Economy (PACE)*: PACE is a public-private partnership focused on accelerating the transition to a circular economy. The Platform connects leaders in the public and private sectors with innovative solutions to rapidly scale best practices and drive systemic change.[60] PACE is currently involved in scaling "circular economy action on plastics; electronics and capital equipment; food and agriculture; and textiles and fashion." It was established

*(continued)*

**Box 7.3 (continued)**

by the Forum in 2017[61] and is now located at the World Resources Institute's Center for Sustainable Business.[62]

*2030 Water Resources Group (2030 WRG)*: 2030 WRG is a public-private partnership hosted by the World Bank Group designed "to help countries close the gap between water demand and supply by 2030."[63] It currently engages 900 partners from across sectors, works in 14 countries around the world and has invested US\$893 million in water-management programmes. These investments have helped to eliminate the discharge of nearly 300 million cubic metres of untreated wastewater, avoid the abstraction of half a billion cubic metres of freshwater and increase cost-effective storage capabilities.[64] The Forum played a core role in establishing and incubating 2030 WRG, before it was spun-off to be hosted in the IFC and then the World Bank, and continues to be represented on the initiative's global governance and steering committee.

*The Global Alliance for Trade Facilitation*: This is a public-private partnership focused on "reducing the time and cost of conducting trade and to remove obstacles to the supply chain." The Alliance is led by WEF along with the Center for International Private Enterprise, the International Chamber of Commerce and Deutsche Gesellschaft fur Internationale Zusammenarbeit. The Alliance helps countries more easily trade by promoting digitization and facilitating dialogue to facilitate the sharing of best practices.[65] The programme has been or is currently involved in over 20 collaborative projects in South America, North and West Africa and Southeast Asia.[66]

Three of the most common objectives of multi-stakeholder platforms are to:

- Mobilize resources to make essential systems work better for people and for the planet, for example, health, food and energy systems
- Develop voluntary rules and standards to spread responsible business practices
- Advocate and campaign to change public policies and attitudes

The following section looks at a few leading examples in each of these three areas, although the most effective multi-stakeholder partnerships often focus on achieving several of these objectives at the same time.

## 7.3.1 Mobilize Resources to Make Essential Systems Work Better for People and the Planet

A growing number of multi-stakeholder coalitions are being established with the primary goal of leveraging the necessary resources, such as funding, research and development, technologies, logistics and distribution capabilities, marketing and public awareness platforms and so on, that are needed to overcome systemic obstacles to improving people's lives, livelihoods and learning or to make environmental ecosystems, large-scale landscapes and cities more resilient. These necessary resources and capabilities don't reside in any one company or even government. As such, multi-stakeholder platforms are required to help coordinate them, especially at scale. Such platforms have been particularly active in efforts to make essential systems such as food, health, energy, transport, finance and education more just and inclusive for people and more environmentally resilient.

In the area of food and agriculture, for example, large-scale multi-stakeholder partnerships include the Alliance for a Green Revolution in Africa; the Global Alliance for Improved Nutrition; the Sustainable Agriculture Initiative (SAI) Platform; the World Economic Forum's Food Systems Platform, including regional multi-stakeholder platforms such as Grow Asia; the Food and Land Use Coalition; the Global Agribusiness Alliance; the EAT Foundation; and a variety of commodity-specific value-chain coalitions, such as the World Cocoa Foundation, Aquaculture Stewardship Council, Better Cotton Initiative, Roundtable on Sustainable Biofuels, Global Roundtable on Sustainable Beef, Roundtable on Sustainable Soy and Bonsucro.

## 7.3.2  Develop Voluntary Rules and Standards to Spread Responsible Business Practices

Global frameworks agreed to by heads of state or their governments, such as the Universal Declaration on Human Rights, the ILO's International Labour Standards, the OECD's Guidelines for Multinational Enterprises, the Sustainable Development Goals, the Paris Climate Agreement and the UN Guiding Principles on Business and Human Rights, provide an essential foundation for promoting and implementing shared global values, norms and standards at national and local levels. Many companies use these to assess and improve their firm-level ESG policies and practices. Alongside global treaties negotiated and implemented by governments, there are a growing number of examples of multi-stakeholder platforms aimed at providing a voluntary mechanism for spreading more responsible practices by companies, civil society organizations and in certain cases governments. In some situations, these are a response to public governance gaps. In others, they are a complement to government efforts to regulate and incentivize systemic change in markets or to influence public behaviours on social and environmental issues.

Examples of a few multi-stakeholder platforms with these objectives include:

- *Improving natural resource governance*: The Extractives Industries Transparency Initiative; the Voluntary Principles on Security and Human Rights; the Marine and Forest Stewardship Councils; and a number of commodity-specific certification programmes in agriculture, forestry and minerals.
- *Tackling corruption and money laundering*: Transparency International's sector and country-based Integrity Pacts, especially in large-scale construction, infrastructure development and public procurement; the Partnering Against Corruption Initiative; and the Wolfsberg Group (a coalition of major banks focused on developing frameworks and guidance to tackle financial crimes).
- *Enhancing digital governance*: Establishing agile and multi-stakeholder global governance frameworks for disruptive digital technologies has become one of the most important and challenging global governance issues of recent years. Examples include the Centre for the Fourth Industrial Revolution, the Partnership for Responsible AI, the Partnership for Responsible Addressable Media and the Smart Cities Alliance, among others.
- *Respecting human rights in consumer goods, electronics and apparel supply chains*: Examples include the Better Work Program, the Fair Labor Association, the Ethical Trading Initiative, the Global Network Initiative, the Bangladesh Accord and Alliance initiatives and the ACT (Action, Collaboration, Transformation) initiative. Box 7.4 profiles two of these examples that have both been in existence for over a decade.

---

**Box 7.4 Improving Workers' Rights and Working Conditions Alongside Enterprise Productivity and Profitability**

Sixty million workers across the developing world rely on the garment industry for their livelihoods. Over 80% are women and many of them have migrated from rural areas—or even internationally—and garment work is their first entry into the job market. While factories are a valuable source of jobs and can help improve livelihoods of workers and their families, poor working conditions remain a pressing issue. Mechanisms to enforce labour laws are often poor and workers may not have a good understanding of their rights nor the skills to effectively realize them. Done differently, the global garment industry can potentially lift millions of people out of poverty by providing decent work, empowering women and driving inclusive economic growth and business competitiveness.

**The Better Work programme** was established in 2007 as a collaboration between the United Nations' International Labour Organization (ILO) and the International Finance Corporation (IFC), part of the World Bank Group. It brings

(continued)

**Box 7.4 (continued)**

together all levels of the garment industry to improve working conditions and respect of human rights for workers and to boost the competitiveness of apparel businesses. The programme is active in 1700 factories employing more than 2.4 million workers in nine countries. As well as advising factories, Better Work collaborates with governments to improve labour laws and with major retail brands to ensure progress is sustained. The programme also advises unions on how to give workers a greater say in their lives, and it works with donors to help achieve broader development goals. An independent impact assessment by a multidisciplinary team from Tufts University analysed nearly 15,000 survey responses from garment workers and 2000 responses from factory managers in Haiti, Indonesia, Jordan, Nicaragua and Vietnam. It found a causal effect of the programme on a range of working conditions in garment factories, including preventing abusive practices (forced labour, verbal abuse, sexual harassment), curbing excessive overtime and closing the gender pay gap. It also documented Better Work's impact on firm performance. For example, Supervisory Skills Training (SST), particularly among female supervisors, increased productivity by 22%; and factories experienced a rise in profitability (measured as the ratio of total revenue vs. total costs) due to their participation in the programme.[67]

**The Fair Labor Association (FLA)**: This alliance of companies, colleges and universities and civil society organizations was established in 1999 to implement a Workplace Code of Conduct in the apparel sector that defines labour standards aimed at achieving decent and humane working conditions. The Code's standards are based on International Labour Organization standards and internationally accepted good labour practices. Brands and companies affiliated with the FLA are expected to comply with all relevant and applicable laws and regulations of the country in which workers are employed and to implement the Workplace Code in their facilities, applying the highest standard when differences or conflicts arise. As of 2020, FLA and its participants were working to ensure respect for the rights of nearly 5 million workers in apparel and agriculture supply chains in 84 countries with company affiliates headquartered in 21 countries.[68] Over its two decades of operations, the FLA has recognized that conducting workplace audits, while useful for identifying and remedying immediate problems and the most egregious violations of labour rights, is not sufficient to drive sustainable and progressive improvements in working conditions. In response, it has developed a Sustainable Compliance Methodology, which is more consultative and focused on understanding and addressing root causes and driving more systemic solutions. The organization and its participants have also started to focus on the implementation of living wages. These offer two examples of how a collaborative approach and diverse perspectives are helping not only to address human rights abuses but also to improve working conditions and workers' voices, incomes and opportunities more broadly.

### 7.3.3 Advocate and Campaign to Change Public Policies and Attitudes

Multi-stakeholder coalitions focused on advocacy and campaigning are becoming increasingly important in efforts to accelerate and scale systemic change. These are coalitions where business leaders are joining forces with leaders in civil society, either in their individual or in institutional capacities, to advocate for progressive policy reforms or to change public attitudes and behaviours.

Ultimately, it will be unlikely to achieve large-scale and sustained impact on social and environmental issues without effective government interventions, whether in the form of policies, laws and regulations, fiscal incentives, or public sector investment and procurement vehicles. There is a growing need for companies, NGOs, academic institutions and where appropriate sub-national government entities to join forces to advocate for greater national government leadership on these issues.

Particularly in the current era of political polarization, populism and fake news, there is a need for leaders in business and civil society to step up and speak out publicly for the causes and the policies that they believe can make a positive impact on people's lives, especially on the lives of people who do not have the same public voice or ability to influence policymakers that business and civic leaders have. In some cases, there is a need to publicly challenge certain government policies or practices that undermine the core values of inclusion, diversity, social justice and environmental sustainability.

Such public advocacy positions can be difficult and politically risky for individual business leaders and even companies to undertake alone, no matter how influential they are. Working collectively and on a multi-stakeholder basis can offer great potential for helping participating companies and their partners to share the risks of public advocacy, to amplify the voices for such advocacy and to increase overall influence and impact.

There are examples of successful and long-term public advocacy alliances in the area of global health. The 30-year commitment to eradicate polio, led by Rotary International and supported by the United Nations and Gates Foundation, among many other public and private partners, is probably one of the best examples of a successful global advocacy campaign. Its success has depended not only on targeted advocacy with key national governments, ministers of health and intergovernmental organizations, but also on the fact that the advocacy campaign has been anchored by on-the-ground action and innovation and has been enabled by a network of tens of thousands of local

Rotary Clubs and hundreds of thousands of volunteers, many of them local business leaders, working in partnership with others.

Other global health coalitions that have strong public advocacy platforms, anchored by on-the-ground implementation programmes, include GAVI, the Vaccine Alliance, the Global Fund to Fight AIDS, Tuberculosis and Malaria, the Global Alliance for Improved Nutrition and the London Declaration for Neglected Tropical Diseases.

Over the past decade, a growing number of pioneering advocacy coalitions and campaigns with active business leadership have emerged to advocate for smart climate change policies and regulations. Box 7.5 illustrates a few of these climate advocacy coalitions that are playing a key role in advocating for both business action and government policies to increase the speed, scale and systemic impact of the response to the climate crisis.

---

**Box 7.5 Business Leadership Coalitions to Advocate for Climate Smart Policies and Practices**

No company can afford to ignore the growing momentum and business risks of climate change or the business opportunities associated with implementing effective mitigation and adaptation strategies. Simply put, sustainable enterprise value creation will be impossible without having a clear, science-based and data-driven roadmap for addressing the climate crisis.

Every company must start with their own business operations and value chain, focused on controlling what they can control. As the World Business Council for Sustainable Development and others have argued, companies must "[s]et an ambition to reach net zero greenhouse gas (GHG) emissions, no later than 2050 and have a science-informed plan to achieve it." They must also be able to disclose how they are governing and managing their climate risks and opportunities as recommended by the Task Force on Climate-Related Financial Disclosure (TCFD), with a focus on their climate governance, strategy, risk management, and metrics and targets. And, they should be able to demonstrate that they are identifying and managing some of the nexus risks and opportunities between their climate, water, biodiversity, land-use, circular economy and nature-based solutions and between their climate and human rights commitments, in terms of issues such as climate justice and just transition.

Yet, even the best voluntary performance that the largest companies can achieve in their own business operations and value chains is not sufficient. Tackling climate change is a quintessentially complex, cross-boundary, systems leadership challenge. The only way to achieve the speed, scale and systemic impact that is required is through collective business and investor action on a global, industry-wide or location-specific basis and substantial changes in public policies, regulations and market incentives. Over the past decade, one crucial area of collective action by companies and institutional investors has been the creation of business-led, policy advocacy alliances, calling for governments to ramp up specific public policies and incentives.

*(continued)*

**Box 7.5 (continued)**

There are a variety of advocacy coalitions that companies can join, both within their own industry sector, city or country of operation and beyond. Some of the most effective are based on a model whereby companies make their own specific, time-bound strategy, investment and operational climate commitments and targets, while at the same time, they also call on governments to implement specific, time-bound public policies, regulations and incentives to support the transition to a net-zero economy by 2050.

One long-standing example of this dual-track approach to collective action is **Ceres**. Established in 1989 following the Exxon Valdez disaster, Ceres has evolved into a global network of hundreds of leading institutional investors and corporations, focused on driving towards net-zero carbon emissions within their own enterprises and ecosystems as well as participating in other coalitions to drive large-scale transformation in markets and public policies. One of many "coalitions of coalitions" that Ceres has helped to spearhead is the **We Mean Business Coalition**. This platform was established in 2014 by the following business leadership organizations: Business for Social Responsibility, Carbon Disclosure Project (CDP), Ceres, The B Team, The Climate Group, Corporate Leader's Group and the World Business Council for Sustainable Development (WBCSD). It was created as a business-led coalition to mobilize joint business commitments, advocate for specific public policies and provide a common and constructive business voice to support negotiations for the Paris Climate Agreement.

In the lead up to COP26, the UN Climate Conference, in November 2021, We Mean Business, alongside its founding partners, and other recently established corporate and investor climate platforms, such as Race to Zero, Race to Resilience, the Net-Zero Asset Owner Alliance, the Net-Zero Asset Manager Initiative, the Paris Aligned Investment Initiative, Climate Action 100+ and the Science-Based Targets Initiative, continued to coordinate their activities and advocacy efforts. We Mean Business has identified the following four policy priorities as part of its "All In for 2030" campaign:

1. Commit to achieving economy-wide net-zero emissions by 2050 at the latest and reversing nature loss by 2030.
2. Put forward strengthened, high quality Nationally Determined Contributions (NDCs) in line with a 1.5°C trajectory to halve global emissions by 2030.
3. Develop policies, implementation plans and laws across the economy that reach NDC and net-zero targets and are nature positive.
4. Develop policies that ensure a just transition that is fair, respects the needs of all people and countries and builds a more inclusive economy.[69]

These business-led coalitions recognize that the urgency for collective leadership and partnerships has never been greater. Any company focused on creating sustainable enterprise value should participate in collective action and advocacy.

## 7.4 Be a Corporate Champion for Partnerships, Even When They Are Difficult

The leadership challenge is clear. Simply put, it will be impossible for companies to create sustainable enterprise value at the firm level without addressing some of the systemic, external obstacles they face and without being stakeholders themselves in the vitality and resilience of their operating context. Engaging in partnerships and collective action with other stakeholders will be essential to achieving this, and business leaders must become champions for such collaborative efforts.

Clearly, governments must do more on their own. New public policies, laws and regulations will play a crucial role in making the shift to more inclusive and sustainable growth, including new corporate disclosure requirements, changes in corporate law and taxation regimes, true cost accounting and pricing signals for social and environmental goods and negative externalities, and public investment in health, education, training, disaster preparedness and green infrastructure. Public sector procurement will also be a key driver of change. Equally essential will be demands from investors and changes in other capital market institutions, such as stock exchanges, rating agencies and reporting and accounting platforms. Shifts in public attitudes and mindsets and in customer and consumer behaviours and demands will be important. Some of these will happen in the absence of partnerships, but most of them will require concerted and collective action by stakeholders, including companies.

Partnerships among companies and between business and other stakeholders can help to address some of the resource constraints, governance gaps, market failures, and cultural and social norms and behaviours that undermine the acceleration and scaling of business engagement in sustainability. They can serve as a platform for facilitating "systems leadership" by convening and coordinating the diverse actions of numerous actors and for building mutually reinforcing linkages between different sectors and goals to achieve system-level change.[70]

Yet, they are not a panacea. Most partnerships are difficult to build and challenging to sustain and scale. They often entail high transaction costs, and there is a need in many cases to strengthen partnership governance and accountability, as well as operational efficiency and effectiveness. And the more complex, system-level alliances often need substantial time, years rather than months, to deliver results.

In deciding whether to allocate resources to building or participating in a partnership, companies should ask themselves the following questions:

- **Leverage**—will this partnership help us to increase the amount or diversity of resources (money, technologies, skills, expertise, capabilities, products, services, networks, facilities) to improve the scale or quality of our impact relative to what we could achieve acting alone?
- **Levelling the "playing field"**—will this partnership enable us to fairly share risks, costs and burdens with others, especially our peers and competitors, and/or help us to develop common standards and approaches that will enable fairer competition and the spread of more responsible business practices in a way that the market doesn't penalize us relative to competitors that don't adhere to the same level of standards and good practice?
- **Legitimacy**—will the partnership help us to build trust with key stakeholders, improve our social acceptance and licence to operate, enhance our reputation and/or extend our influence and voice in a credible and responsible manner?
- **Leadership**—will the partnership help our company to be more effective leaders than we could achieve on our own in terms of shaping the agenda and bringing about systemic change within our industry or our locations of operation around particular environmental, social, economic and governance issues that are material or salient to our business?

If a partnership has the potential to further one or more of these goals, it is usually worth investing in. Even the most effective partnerships, however, offer hard lessons in terms of how to design, implement and sustain them, to ensure mutual accountability for performance and results, and to build the flexibility and trust to adapt to changing circumstances. Throughout the life of a partnership, especially resource intensive and complex, system-level alliances, business leaders and their partners should be assessing whether it meets some or all of the "success factors" outlined in Box 7.6.

In conclusion, effective partnership building, especially among multiple stakeholders, requires new mindsets and skill sets on the part of individuals and new capabilities and incentives on the part of institutions. It requires patience, persistence and a long-term commitment in an era of short attention spans, accelerating and disruptive change and short-term performance pressures on companies and governments alike.

None of this is easy. Yet, it is essential work. The ability to galvanize and convene other stakeholders to co-create effective partnerships for achieving sustainable enterprise value at the level of the firm, and more inclusive and

## Box 7.6  Questions to Assess Partnership Viability and Success Factors

The following success factors are a synthesis of over 40 academic and practitioner studies exploring what works in building partnerships, ranging from global multi-stakeholder platforms and pre-competitive sector-based business alliances to more traditional public-private infrastructure and project-level partnerships.

| Key questions to ask | Key actions and practices to evaluate |
| --- | --- |
| **Do we have a shared purpose and understanding of the ecosystem and its stakeholders?** | 1. Have we got a compelling **agenda for change led by strong champions** who are leaders in their own organizations and are able to take decisions, allocate resources, motivate and mobilize others, and support a long-term commitment?<br>2. Have we jointly agreed on a set of **public commitments and a strategic plan** for achieving them, based on rigorous consultation and relevant baseline evidence, with clearly defined roles and responsibilities for participants?<br>3. Do we understand the **full value chain or ecosystem required for transformation** and our ability to either holistically coordinate activities or stakeholders across this system or target specific interventions that mutually reinforce those of others? |
| **Have we developed rigorous processes and operational alignment?** | 1. How effective is our **implementation capability?** Do we have dedicated and well-resourced "backbone support," committed practitioners from participant organizations who have the necessary authority and skills to engage, and effective communication and conflict resolution processes that enable regular and rigorous dialogue and feedback?<br>2. Is there strong alignment with and leverage of our own and our partners' **core competencies and interests?** |
| **Have we established good governance and mutual accountability for progress?** | 1. Do we have mutually agreed **metrics and governance mechanisms to track performance and ensure rigorous oversight and accountability**, both within the partnership itself and externally with relevant stakeholders, including beneficiaries and vulnerable groups where relevant?<br>2. Have we established **participatory monitoring and evaluation** approaches that facilitate shared learning and better decision-making in addition to ensuring transparency and accountability?<br>3. Have we "built in" enough flexibility to **"course correct" and be adaptive** based on evolving circumstances, disruptive events, failures, stakeholder feedback and lessons learned? |

Source: Adapted from Jane Nelson. *Partnerships for Sustainable Development: Collective Action by Business, Governments and Civil Society to Achieve Scale and Transform Markets.* Corporate Responsibility Initiative, Harvard Kennedy School with the Business and Sustainable Development Commission, 2017

sustainable growth in society more broadly, has become one of the essential leadership imperatives for the twenty-first century. One of the single most important lessons that has come out of 20 years of studying partnerships, especially complex, multi-stakeholder platforms, has been the crucial role played by corporate champions—by CEOs and senior executives either who are willing to do the hard work of partnership building themselves or who provide the space, resources and support for their teams to do so, including the long-time horizons often required to deliver results.[71]

## Notes

1. This chapter draws on other work by the author on building partnerships, including:

   * Jane Nelson, "Toward new models of leadership and partnership," in Nina Montgomery (ed), *Perspectives on Impact: Leading Voices on Making Systemic Change in the Twenty-First Century*. Routledge, 2019.
   * Jane Nelson. *Partnerships for Sustainable Development: Collective Action by Business, Governments and Civil Society to Achieve Scale and Transform Markets*. Corporate Responsibility Initiative, Harvard Kennedy School. Report commissioned by the Business and Sustainable Development Commission, 2017.
   * Jane Nelson, "Scaling Up Impact through Public–Private Partnerships," in L. Chandy, A. Hosono, H. Kharas, and J. Linn (eds), *Getting to Scale: How to Bring Development Solutions to Millions of Poor People*. Washington, DC: The Brookings Institution Press, 2013.
   * Lisa Dreier, David Nabarro and Jane Nelson. *Systems Leadership for Sustainable Development: Taking Action on Complex Challenges through the Power of Networks*. Cambridge, MA: Corporate Responsibility Initiative, Harvard Kennedy School, 2019.
   * Richard Gilbert and Jane Nelson. *Advocating Together for the SDGs: How Civil Society and Business Are Joining Voices to Change Policy, Attitudes and Practices*. Cambridge, MA: Corporate Responsibility Initiative, Harvard Kennedy School and Business Fights Poverty, 2018.

2. Jane Nelson and Beth Jenkins. *Tackling Global Challenges: Lessons in System Leadership from the World Economic Forum's New Vision for Agriculture Initiative*. Cambridge, MA: Corporate Responsibility Initiative, Harvard Kennedy School, 2016.

3. Nelson, Jane. *Building Partnerships: Cooperation between the United Nations system and the private sector*. United Nations, Department of Public Information, NY, 2002.

   See also:

   The Partnering Initiative. http://thepartneringinitiative.org

4. For more details and examples on each of these levels of partnership, see: Jane Nelson. *Partnerships for Sustainable Development: Collective Action by Business,*

*Governments and Civil Society to Achieve Scale and Transform Markets.* Corporate Responsibility Initiative, Harvard Kennedy School and Business and Sustainable Development Commission, 2017.

5. Grayson, David and Jane Nelson. *Corporate Responsibility Coalitions: The past, present and future of alliances for sustainable capitalism.* Greenleaf Publishing and Stanford University Press, 2013.

   See also:

   International Chamber of Commerce (ICC) and UN Global Compact (2015). Scaling Up Sustainability Collaboration: Contributions of Business Associations and Sector Initiatives to Sustainable Development.

   Flaherty, Margaret and Ann Rappaport (2015). *Agents of Change: Sustainability and Industry Trade Associations—An Evolving Value Proposition.* Business School Lausanne and Tufts University.

6. Keidanren. "About Keidanren." Accessed July 12, 2021. https://www.keidanren.or.jp/en/profile/pro001.html

7. "Society 5.0: Co-creating the Future," n.d. https://www.keidanren.or.jp/en/policy/2018/095_booklet.pdf

8. Nakanishi, Hiroaki. "Keidanren: Toward the Realization of Society 5.0 for SDGs (2019-01-01)." Keidanren. Accessed July 12, 2021. https://www.keidanren.or.jp/en/speech/2019/0101.html

9. Keidanren. "Keidanren's Initiatives and Efforts on Environment | Policy Proposals." Accessed July 12, 2021. https://www.keidanren.or.jp/en/policy/env.html

10. Confederation of British Industry. "About Us." Accessed July 12, 2021. https://www.cbi.org.uk/about-us/

11. Confederation of British Industry. "What We Do." Accessed July 12, 2021. https://www.cbi.org.uk/what-we-do/

12. Confederation of British Industry. "Race to Zero: Driving the UK's Sustainable Future." Accessed July 12, 2021. https://www.cbi.org.uk/our-campaigns/race-to-zero-delivering-the-uk-s-sustainable-future/

13. Lucian A. Bebchuk and Roberto Tallarita. *Will corporations deliver value to all stakeholders?* Draft of August 4, 2021. https://papers.ssrn.com/sol3/papers.cfm?abstract_id=3899421

14. Business Roundtable. Updated Statement Moves Away from Shareholder Primacy, and Includes Commitment to All Stakeholders. "Business Roundtable Redefines the Purpose of a Corporation to Promote 'An Economy That Serves All Americans,'" August 19, 2019. https://www.businessroundtable.org/business-roundtable-redefines-the-purpose-of-a-corporation-to-promote-an-economy-that-serves-all-americans

15. Business Roundtable—Opportunity Agenda. "Our Commitment to Our Employees and Communities." Accessed July 12, 2021. https://opportunity.businessroundtable.org/

16. Confederation of Indian Industry. "About Us." Accessed July 12, 2021. https://www.cii.in/About_Us.aspx?enc=ns9fJzmNKJnsoQCyKqUmaQ==

17. Confederation of Indian Industry. "Initiatives." Accessed July 12, 2021. https://www.cii.in/aboutUs_Initiatives.aspx?enc=ns9fJzmNKJnsoQCyKqUmaQ==

18. Confederation of Indian Industry. "CSR & Community Development." Accessed July 12, 2021. https://www.cii.in/sectors.aspx?enc=prvePUj2bdMtgTmvPwvisYH+5EnGjyGXO9hLECvTuNugJuO9h/k9vnVi/+uRQjYe

19. Confederation of Indian Industry. "Environment." Accessed July 12, 2021. https://www.cii.in/sectors.aspx?enc=prvePUj2bdMtgTmvPwvisYH+5EnGjyGXO9hLECvTuNtI5sIDkU3GehZCDzrCfdL4

20. Confederation of Indian Industry. "Building a Low Carbon Indian Economy." Accessed July 12, 2021. https://www.cii.in/PolicyAdvocacyDetails.aspx?enc=YrraYHcDGMmfDSl4agaorxHnD+XFz203oCjNYS4dbbrHfEU6GqxV4qp6luOgEYtM

21. Confederation of Indian Industry. "Disaster Management." Accessed July 12, 2021. https://www.cii.in/Sectors.aspx?enc=prvePUj2bdMtgTmvPwvisYH+5EnGjyGXO9hLECvTuNsAsLi8AXCEZ1JIiB0wtPeN

22. The Consumer Goods Forum. "Overview." Accessed July 12, 2021. https://www.theconsumergoodsforum.com/who-we-are/overview/

23. The Consumer Goods Forum. "Who Are the Members of The Consumer Goods Forum?" Accessed July 12, 2021. https://www.theconsumergoodsforum.com/who-we-are/our-members/

24. The Consumer Goods Forum. "The Board of Directors of The Consumer Goods Forum." Accessed July 12, 2021. https://www.theconsumergoodsforum.com/who-we-are/our-board-of-directors/

25. The Consumer Goods Forum. "Address Challenges." Accessed July 12, 2021. https://www.theconsumergoodsforum.com/what-we-do/address-challenges/

26. The Consumer Goods Forum. "Global Social Compliance Programme." Accessed July 12, 2021. https://www.theconsumergoodsforum.com/social-sustainability/sustainable-supply-chain-initiative/key-projects/benchmarking-recognition/global-social-compliance-programme/

27. "Responsible Care." Accessed July 12, 2021. https://icca-chem.org/focus/responsible-care/

28. "Innovation Is the Key to Sustainability." Accessed July 12, 2021. https://icca-chem.org/

29. "Technology Roadmap." International Energy Agency, n.d. https://icca-chem.org/wp-content/uploads/2020/05/Technology-Roadmap.pdf

30. IFPMA. "Companies." Accessed July 12, 2021. https://www.ifpma.org/who-we-are/our-membership/full-members/companies/

31. IFPMA. "Associations." Accessed July 12, 2021. https://www.ifpma.org/who-we-are/our-membership/full-members/associations/

32. IFPMA. "IFPMA Code of Practice (2019)." Accessed July 12, 2021. https://www.ifpma.org/subtopics/new-ifpma-code-of-practice-2019/
33. GSMA. "About Us." Accessed July 12, 2021. https://www.gsma.com/aboutus/
34. "2016 Mobile Industry Impact Report: Sustainable Development Goals." GSMA, n.d. p. 12 https://www.gsma.com/betterfuture/wp-content/uploads/2016/09/_UN_SDG_Report_FULL_R1_WEB_Singles_LOW.pdf
35. GSMA. *2020 Mobile Industry Impact Report: Sustainable Development Goals.* GSMA Association, September 2020. https://www.gsma.com/betterfuture/2020sdgimpactreport/
36. Mobile for Development. "Mobile for Development." Accessed July 12, 2021. https://www.gsma.com/mobilefordevelopment/
37. Flaherty, Margaret and Ann Rappaport (2015). *Agents of Change: Sustainability and Industry Trade Associations—An Evolving Value Proposition.* Business School Lausanne and Tufts University.
38. Grayson, David and Jane Nelson. *Corporate Responsibility Coalitions: The past, present and future of alliances for sustainable capitalism.* Greenleaf Publishing and Stanford University Press, 2013.
39. WBCSD. "Our history, 25th Anniversary". https://www.wbcsd.org/Overview/Our-history
40. WBCSD. "About Us". https://www.wbcsd.org/Overview/About-us
41. Ibid.
42. Kofi Annan's Address to the World Economic Forum in Davos, 1 February 1999. https://www.un.org/sg/en/content/sg/speeches/1999-02-01/kofi-annans-address-world-economic-forum-davos
43. The United Nations Global Compact, "Participation". https://www.unglobalcompact.org/participation Accessed August 24th, 2021.
44. The UN Principles for Responsible Investment, "About the PRI." https://www.unpri.org/pri/about-the-pri Accessed August 24th, 2021.
45. Grayson, David and Jane Nelson. *Corporate Responsibility Coalitions: The past, present and future of alliances for sustainable capitalism.* Greenleaf Publishing and Stanford University Press, 2013. Page 64.
46. The World Economic Forum. *Stakeholders for a Cohesive World: The Role of Lighthouse Projects.* Briefing paper, January 2020, p. 11 http://www3.weforum.org/docs/WEF_Lighthouse_Project_Report.pdf
47. "About Our Alliance." Accessed July 13, 2021. https://www.gavi.org/our-alliance/about
48. World Economic Forum. "This Is How the World Economic Forum Is Supporting COVID-19 Vaccination," December 2, 2020. https://www.weforum.org/agenda/2020/12/this-is-how-were-supporting-the-development-and-delivery-of-covid-19-vaccines/
49. "About Our Alliance." Accessed July 13, 2021. https://www.gavi.org/our-alliance/about

50. Gavi The Vaccine Alliance, "What is Covax?" Accessed August 24, 2021. https://www.gavi.org/covax-facility#what
51. "Global Fund Overview." Accessed July 13, 2021. https://www.theglobal-fund.org/en/overview/
52. "Results & Impact." The Global Fund. Accessed July 13, 2021. https://www.theglobalfund.org/en/impact/
53. World Economic Forum. "Global Fund Aims to Defeat the Deadliest Infectious Diseases." Accessed July 13, 2021. https://www.weforum.org/our-impact/global-fund-fights-three-of-the-deadliest-infectious-diseases-ever-known/
54. World Economic Forum. "Food Action Alliance." Accessed July 13, 2021. https://www.weforum.org/projects/food-action-alliance/
55. World Economic Forum. "About the Center for the Fourth Industrial Revolution." Accessed July 13, 2021. https://www.weforum.org/centre-for-the-fourth-industrial-revolution/about/
56. World Economic Forum. "Projects." Accessed July 13, 2021. https://www.weforum.org/centre-for-the-fourth-industrial-revolution/areas-of-focus/
57. World Economic Forum, "Global Battery Alliance: Batteries Powering Sustainable Development". Accessed August 24, 2021. https://www.weforum.org/global-battery-alliance/home
58. Tropical Forest Alliance. "Home." Accessed July 13, 2021. https://www.tropicalforestalliance.org/
59. World Economic Forum. "TFA 2020." Accessed July 13, 2021. https://www.weforum.org/projects/tfa-2020/
60. World Resources Institute. "Platform for Accelerating the Circular Economy (PACE)." Accessed July 13, 2021. https://www.wri.org/initiatives/platform-accelerating-circular-economy-pace
61. World Economic Forum. "Circular Economy." Accessed July 13, 2021. https://www.weforum.org/projects/circular-economy/
62. World Resources Institute. "Platform for Accelerating the Circular Economy (PACE)."
63. World Bank Group. "Vision and Mission—2030 Water Resources Group." Accessed July 13, 2021. https://www.2030wrg.org/about-us/vision-mission/
64. World Bank Group. "2030 Water Resources Group." Accessed July 13, 2021. https://www.2030wrg.org/
65. "Global Alliance for Trade Facilitation | World Economic Forum." Accessed July 13, 2021. https://www.weforum.org/projects/global-alliance-for-trade-facilitation
66. Global Alliance for Trade Facilitation. "Global Alliance for Trade Facilitation." Accessed July 13, 2021. https://www.tradefacilitation.org/
67. ILO and IFC. *Better Work: Progress and Potential—Findings from an Independent Impact Assessment.* https://betterwork.org/wp-content/uploads/2016/09/BW-ProgressAndPotential-Highlights.pdf
68. Fair Labor Association. *2019 Annual Report*, p. 3.

69. We Mean Business. *All In for 2030. Accelerating Action. Halving Emissions.*
    https://www.wemeanbusinesscoalition.org/building-a-net-zero-world/
70. Lisa Dreier, David Nabarro and Jane Nelson. *Systems Leadership for Sustainable Development: Taking Action on Complex Challenges through the Power of Networks.* Cambridge, MA: Corporate Responsibility Initiative, Harvard Kennedy School, 2019.
71. Ibid.

# 8

# Conclusion: Towards Integrated Business Leadership

This book has presented a navigational guide for boards and management teams desiring to take a fully integrated approach to running their companies in order to capture the greatest possible synergy between shareholder and other stakeholder interests, which is to say between business and societal value creation, short- and long-term performance, and strong operational and financial performance, on the one hand, and diligent stewardship of environmental, social, governance and data (ESG&D) risks and opportunities, on the other. It is a handbook for turning the directional *principles* of stakeholder capitalism into the concrete *practices* that drive stronger sustainable enterprise value creation.

The book has presented an action agenda for implementing this more integrated approach to corporate governance and oversight, corporate strategy and implementation, corporate reporting and accountability, and corporate partnerships and systemic change. This is a business leadership agenda for the twenty-first century, a period in which profound changes in the technological, economic, environmental, social and political context in which firms operate are compelling such integration. In this concluding chapter, we look at what this implementation agenda means for the craft of business leadership itself.

## 8.1 Integrated Thinking and Decision-Making

Creating sustainable enterprise value through the rigorous practice of stakeholder capitalism requires three principal additional aspects of leadership from C-suite executives and board directors, especially the CEO and

© The Author(s) 2022
R. Samans, J. Nelson, *Sustainable Enterprise Value Creation*,
https://doi.org/10.1007/978-3-030-93560-3_8

chairperson. The first is organizational, how they institutionalize the integration of ESG&D considerations within the company. The second is systemic, how they understand, engage with and build effective external coalitions to achieve large-scale change in the broader system in which they operate. And the third, which underpins everything else, is personal, how they approach their individual decision-making responsibilities in an increasingly complex, disruptive and multi-stakeholder operating context.

First, creating stronger sustainable enterprise value through stakeholder capitalism requires the board and C-suite to institutionalize the integration of ESG&D considerations into their firm's core governance, purpose, strategy, resource allocation, operations, performance metrics, reporting and corporate culture. This is the terrain covered by Chaps. 4, 5 and 6 in Part II of this book. Organizational leadership of this nature is needed to ensure the disciplined identification and balancing of financial and non-financial, shareholder and other stakeholder, short- and long-term considerations in decision-making at all levels of the organization. It requires leaders to establish or enhance relevant policies, processes and management systems, ranging from oversight and compliance mechanisms to incentive and accountability structures. These need to be robust enough that changes will endure after the current leaders have left, while also being capable of adaptation to changes in external trends, risks, opportunities and societal expectations of business.

Second, creating sustainable enterprise value through stakeholder capitalism requires systems leadership. As illustrated throughout the book, companies are part of a complex ecosystem of stakeholders who need to be engaged, balanced and aligned with the firm's strategic direction. Firms are also stakeholders themselves in the vitality and resilience of their operating context. Company executives, especially the Chair and CEO, have a key role to play in this regard in partnership with leaders of other companies, governments and civil society organizations to help overcome some of the governance gaps, market failures and norms that impede progress towards more inclusive and sustainable growth. As such, they increasingly need to be coalition-builders, ambassadors and open collaborators who are capable of inspiring and achieving system-level change beyond their own companies' operations and value chains.[1] As outlined in Chap. 7, effective systems leadership requires individual leaders and their institutions to be able to cultivate a shared vision for change, empower widespread innovation and action, and enable mutual accountability for progress, through regular stakeholder engagement, metrics and credible governance structures.[2]

Third, underpinning both organizational and systems leadership is the crucial importance of personal leadership and good judgement. Leading a company in today's increasingly complex, multi-issue and multi-stakeholder operating context is massively challenging. So-called win-win choices and opportunities to effectively manage shared risks to the company and its stakeholders or create shared value for the company and its stakeholders are not always the reality that leaders face. Trade-offs between financial and non- or pre-financial considerations or between different stakeholder interests will inevitably arise that are not resolved by the governance processes, policies and management systems that have been installed. These trade-offs will require personal judgements and decisions to be made at the C-suite and board levels. If full integration of ESG&D considerations through the institutionalization of governance processes and management systems represents the science of business leadership for sustainable enterprise value creation, then how CEOs, executive teams and boards approach these difficult, complex decisions represents its art. An art that must be based fundamentally on leaders having and living by a clear set of values, a sense of purpose, and good judgement.

CEOs, executive teams and boards need to demonstrate, day in and day out, that their company's values and purpose statements are not simply words on paper. They must demonstrate by their own behaviours, actions and decisions that the *how* of sustainable enterprise value creation is as important as the *what*, that it's not only important what a company does with the profits it generates, but how it makes them in the first place. They must be willing to take decisive action and hold individuals to account, for example, when one of their number or other managers in the firm do not adhere to these values, even if the person in question is a top financial or operational performer. They must be prepared to take responsibility, both internally and externally, when things go wrong, especially when poor decisions or a crisis negatively affect the resilience and reputation of the company and people's lives or the planet.

Some of the greatest and most understandable mistrust and cynicism among employees and other internal and external stakeholders results from CEOs, senior managers and directors failing to "walk the talk" on the values they espouse and the public commitments they make. Having rigorous compliance systems in place and integrating ESG&D considerations into performance metrics and incentive structures are essential, but they can only go so far. To achieve widespread integrity beyond compliance and a fully integrated approach to business leadership requires influencing behaviours and corporate culture more broadly. It requires business leaders who will not compromise on their responsibility as role models for integrity and integrated approaches, who recognize the challenges of cognitive bias and the importance of including and listening to diverse perspectives, and who are well prepared to be held personally accountable for delivering a more integrated approach to performance and value creation.

Of course, judgement and decision-making are the essence of leadership. CEOs, executive teams and boards are routinely called upon to balance short- and long-term considerations in business strategy and financial planning. The art of business leadership as it relates to sustainable enterprise value creation begins with recognizing that difficult decisions weighing financial against non- or pre-financial considerations and shareholder versus other stakeholder interests, while often more complex, are no different in principle from traditional business decisions that require balancing long- and short-term considerations, for example, whether to approve a big investment in a new plant, major acquisition, promising new technology or novel marketing campaign to establish or strengthen a brand. All of these decisions require estimating and balancing the prospects of higher immediate profitability versus stronger medium- to long-term enterprise value.

That said, the practice of stakeholder capitalism—the careful weighing of diverse stakeholder interests and of financial priorities with material and salient ESG&D considerations—may often require judgements to be made regarding the relative value of preserving or strengthening certain of the firm's intangible assets—for example, its reputation with customers, standing with regulators and communities, the rights, capabilities, well-being and loyalty of its employees or the basic social and environmental viability of its enabling environment, upon which business continuity ultimately rests. These intangible considerations are often difficult to reduce to numbers—to discounted cash flows—and thus to an apples-to-apples comparison with the near-term financial cost and opportunity of the other side of the decision. However, they are no less material or significant for it. There is no getting around weighing them in a rigorous fashion against more immediate and financially quantifiable considerations and taking such an integrated approach to decision-making.

Integrated thinking means that a CEO, executive team and board always and simultaneously conceptualize their firm's plans and decisions for creating value in tangible and intangible, financial and non- or pre-financial, short term and long term, and shareholder and other stakeholder dimensions. Integrated decision-making means not only institutionalizing governance processes and management systems that routinely and rigorously mediate such potential trade-offs but also creating a decision-making culture at the top that embraces complexity and diverse perspectives and that makes debate and considered judgements about ESG&D-related trade-offs a core part of the C-suite's and board's duties, carving out the necessary time in their agendas to do so when such matters are referred to them. As chief stewards of the company's values and value protection and creation, the CEO, executive team and board must fully internalize these matters in their own thinking and decision-making agendas. They cannot be segmented from "core business" decisions and subordinated through their delegation to communications, stakeholder relations and other functional officers. At the same time, these officers need to be engaged directly in the thinking and decision-making of chief executive, financial and operating officers.

In summary, the integrated thinking that is inherent in sustainable enterprise value creation requires an expanded set of skills in business leaders and a more complex approach to their preparation and execution of decisions. ESG&D-related priorities and trade-offs presented to the CEO, executive team or board for decision may often hinge on a judgement about the relative value of intangible and more tangible assets and investments. The science of valuing intangible assets, particularly those related to ESG&D factors, is in its infancy. Initiatives like the Value Balancing Alliance[3] and the Impact-Weighted Accounts Project[4] at Harvard Business School, and the Impact Management Project,[5] are doing important but still early stage work in this area. Thus, for the time being, integrated decision-making is mainly concerned with drawing qualitative—which is to say human—judgements rather than making quantitative calculations.

## 8.2    Developing Future Business Leaders

As outlined in the previous section, stakeholder capitalism places a special premium on the ability of business leaders to integrate the financial and non- or pre-financial, the short and long term, the tangible and intangible, and the shareholder and stakeholder dimensions of a decision. As such, the art of sustainable enterprise value creation is the art of integrated thinking and decision-making, as well as systems leadership.

The education, training and development of business leaders must therefore expose students and young executives far more to ESG&D business issues and the transformational trends and human, social and political contexts that give rise to them. Examples include the intersection of climate change, water scarcity and enterprise value creation; the intersection of workers' rights, protections and voice and enterprise value creation; the intersection of anti-corruption and enterprise value creation; the intersection of algorithmic bias and transparency and enterprise value creation, and so on. Similarly, experiences of students and young executives need to incorporate opportunities to cultivate the craft of facilitating dialogue, debate and decisions involving the types of trade-off that are outlined above.

This cultivation of integrated thinking and decision-making and systems leadership in the next generation of business leaders requires three practical changes:

- First, exposure to ESG&D issues, business-and-society dilemmas and stakeholder relations must begin well before ascension to the C-suite, starting with vocational, academic or professional education and training, and continuing in the journey through the company ranks. This is currently the exception rather than the rule in many contemporary training and education institutions and business cultures.

- Second, the type of stakeholder mapping and engagement discussed in Part II must become routine and interactive for current and aspiring managers and business leaders. Since ESG&D matters often cannot be reduced to quantitative, like-for-like comparisons with the financial data of profit and loss projections, the quality of information about them will depend on the depth of not only desk analysis but also stakeholder conversations. On particularly strategic or sensitive matters, these conversations will need to be direct, that is, conducted face to face by top executives and board members themselves. All future business leaders must be equipped with the tools for effective multi-stakeholder mapping and engagement.

- Third, since such decisions can have major direct and indirect implications for people's rights and dignity and the quality of their lives and livelihoods, they may evoke an unusually strong personal sense of investment in them by colleagues within the firm and by external stakeholders. Effective leadership in such circumstances means not only arriving at a considered judgement by allocating sufficient time for analysis, discussion and debate *ex ante* but also creating adequate space for explanation, ongoing feedback and possible adjustment, *ex post*. As such, future business leaders also require training and experiential exposure to understand how their decisions might impact people, for better or worse, and how to develop appropriate institutional and personal accountability mechanisms.

In summary, the rigorous practice of stakeholder capitalism requires an integrated form of business leadership—what we've referred to as integrated thinking and decision-making—to achieve the integrated approach to corporate governance, strategy, reporting and partnerships outlined in Part II. These are the essential raw ingredients of sustainable enterprise value creation. They are the means through which stakeholder capitalism is expressed by firms. As such, they should be a core component of business education, training and talent development processes as well as a key requirement in vocational, academic and professional qualifications. Above all, they should be gained through on-the-ground experiential learning and feedback, and as such, they should be an essential element of job assignments and assessments, and of mentoring and championing high potential managers at all levels of an organization.

What does this leadership and integration of sustainable enterprise value creation look like in firms that are in the vanguard of implementing stakeholder capitalism? We conclude with a summary of some of the priority ESG&D issues that all companies should consider and a summary of the practical leadership actions that were outlined in Part II and are relevant for any company.

## 8.3    Summary of Leadership Actions for Creating Sustainable Enterprise Value

As we have outlined throughout the book, there are now countless research studies, management frameworks, reporting guidelines and "agendas for action" that are available for companies to draw on in their journey towards creating sustainable enterprise value. Some of these are broad, generic guidelines, and others are focused on specific industry sectors, countries or ESG&D issues.

Despite industry and geographic differences, it is increasingly clear that every chairperson, CEO, board and executive team should set targets for their company to address climate change mitigation and adaptation priorities as well as goals to manage other major environmental risks and opportunities, establish policies and due diligence processes to respect human rights, including core and other labour standards, and support for diversity, equity and inclusion, and engage transparently with stakeholders on their progress against these. Appendices A, B and C provide more in-depth guidance on some of the specific ESG&D risks and opportunities that have been identified for cross-industry reporting by the Measuring Stakeholder Capitalism initiative, industry-specific reporting by the Sustainability Accounting Standards Board (SASB) Materiality Map and climate change reporting by the preliminary prototype of a climate-related financial disclosure standard developed by a group of leading voluntary standard-setting organizations.

The following table summarizes the leadership actions that we identified in Part II of the book as being important for any company aiming to create sustainable enterprise value, regardless of industry sector, geography or ownership structure. They provide a set of leadership criteria that all boards and executive teams can assess themselves against in the areas of corporate governance and oversight, corporate strategy and implementation, corporate reporting and accountability, and corporate partnerships and systemic change.

**Box 8.1 Summary of Leadership Actions for Creating Sustainable Enterprise Value**

| CORPORATE GOVERNANCE AND OVERSIGHT | |
|---|---|
| Revise governance principles and guidelines to include stakeholders and ESG&D priorities | • Explicitly recognize the board's responsibility for oversight of management in determining corporate purpose and strategy for creating long-term value for stakeholders, including but not only shareholders<br>• Provide language on the board's responsibility for oversight of ESG&D risks, opportunities and performance in addition to financial and operational risks, opportunities and performance |
| Enhance board oversight on aligning the company's purpose, strategy and capital allocation with creating sustainable enterprise value | • Support management as stewards of corporate purpose<br>• Provide robust and regular guidance on corporate strategy (spend more time on strategy; align strategy with corporate purpose; integrate the company's sustainability and other stakeholder-oriented strategies with corporate strategy)<br>• Review ESG&D implications of capital allocation and investment decisions |
| Expand oversight of risks to include material and salient ESG&D risks | • Ensure oversight of material and salient ESG&D risks<br>• Strengthen preparedness for and resilience to systemic shocks and crises (improve preparedness; support crisis management and response; strengthen recovery and future resilience) |
| Focus on diverse succession planning, talent development and an inclusive culture | • Integrate ESG&D into oversight of CEO and executive performance, compensation and succession<br>• Provide guidance on corporate culture<br>• Serve as champions of inclusion and diversity<br>• Review and support long-term talent development |
| Integrate ESG&D priorities into oversight of executive performance, incentives and accountability | • Integrate ESG&D priorities into business planning and performance oversight<br>• Align incentives to corporate purpose and hold executives accountable<br>• Commit to integrated reporting of the company's performance and prospects |

(continued)

## Box 8.1 (continued)

| | |
|---|---|
| **Enhance board organization, composition and engagement** | • Integrate ESG&D into board organization and structure (at the full board and in board committee charters)<br>• Ensure board composition is fit for the complex operating environment<br>• Enhance board engagement with internal and external stakeholders |

### CORPORATE STRATEGY AND IMPLEMENTATION

| | |
|---|---|
| **Embed purpose, values and ESG&D priorities into corporate strategy and operations** | • Ensure stakeholder consultation, especially with employees in defining or revising purpose and identifying priorities<br>• Identify and prioritize the social and environmental issues most material to the company's core business and salient to its stakeholders<br>• Communicate purpose and ESG&D priorities clearly and consistently, accompanied by measurable goals and targets and supported by policies, standards and incentives<br>• Commit to measuring and accounting for performance on a regular and consistent basis |
| **Strengthen management of material and salient ESG&D risks** | • Invest time to engage stakeholders in rigorous materiality analysis and due diligence<br>• Integrate ESG&D risks into enterprise risk management and risk appetite frameworks<br>• Commit to dynamic reviews and stress-testing of risks<br>• Leverage technology to improve risk management—and manage the tech risk<br>• Address both acute risks and broader business model or systemic risks<br>• Combine quantifiable metrics and science-based targets with qualitative insights and stakeholder surveys |

(*continued*)

**Box 8.1 (continued)**

| | |
|---|---|
| **Invest in innovation to drive inclusive and sustainable growth** | • Invest in breakthrough technologies, products and services to deliver scalable and/or "leap-frog" solutions to global challenges such as improving access to more affordable and sustainable energy, food, health and financial inclusion<br>• Develop innovative business models (inclusive business models; circular economy and regenerative models; shared use and omni-channel models) and innovative financing mechanisms, such as internal venture capital funds and innovation award programmes as well as external partnerships or joint, blended funding mechanisms with other private or public sector financiers<br>• Participate in innovation coalitions and accelerator platforms |
| **Promote employee well-being, talent, diversity and inclusion** | • Invest in employee health, safety and well-being<br>• Make diversity and inclusion a priority<br>• Invest in employees' future skills and opportunities<br>• Enable employee engagement and participation |
| **Establish robust and accountable mechanisms for external stakeholder engagement** | • Understand and map key stakeholders and issues<br>• Establish external advisory councils |

**CORPORATE REPORTING AND ACCOUNTABILITY**

| | |
|---|---|
| **Implement integrated reporting in the firm** | • Embrace ESG&D materiality and design it into the annual report, including by reporting against the IFRS **climate change** standard; the 21 WEF/IBC *measuring stakeholder capitalism* **cross-industry** core metrics and recommended disclosures, which are a baseline best-practice composite of GRI, CDSB, TCFD and SASB elements; and the SASB **industry-specific** metrics that pertain to the firm's main business lines as per its materiality map<br>• Assemble the building blocks of the integrated annual report<br>• Review, assure and approve for issuance |

*(continued)*

**Box 8.1 (continued)**

| | |
|---|---|
| **Accelerate the creation of an international reporting standard through collective business leadership** | • Support the International Organization of Securities Commissions (IOSCO) and the International Financial Reporting Standards Foundation (IFRS) initiatives to develop a baseline global sustainability reporting standard<br>• Encourage national regulators to adopt this standard outright or build on top of it, in order to ensure the global comparability of a substantial base of such reporting |

**CORPORATE PARTNERSHIPS AND SYSTEMIC CHANGE**

| | |
|---|---|
| **Develop a holistic, multi-level strategy for engaging in partnerships** | • Empower numerous project-level, financing and operational partnerships<br>• Strategically leverage key industry-level, pre-competitive business alliances<br>• Prioritize a small number of multi-stakeholder institutions, platforms and networks |
| **Support pre-competitive business alliances to scale industry-wide progress** | • Leverage the reach and influence of representative business organizations<br>• Establish targeted corporate responsibility leadership coalitions within specific countries, locations, industries or focus on specific challenges |
| **Participate in multi-stakeholder platforms to drive system-wide change** | • Mobilize resources to make essential systems work better for people and the planet<br>• Establish shared rules and standards to spread responsible business practices<br>• Advocate and campaign for changes in public policies and attitudes |
| **Be a corporate champion for partnerships, even when they are difficult** | • Assess the value of each partnership in terms of its leverage, ability to "level the playing field," legitimacy and leadership impact<br>• Ask the right questions—do we have a shared purpose and understanding of the ecosystem and its stakeholders; have we developed rigorous processes and operational alignment; have we established good governance and mutual accountability for progress |

As we have outlined throughout the book, disruptive and often transformational changes in the operating environment for most companies and industry sectors continue to accelerate and gather momentum in terms of their complexity and their materiality to business risks and opportunities. No business is immune from these changes. In this dynamic new operating context, no firm's ability to create and sustain value can be taken for granted. There is simply no room for complacency or insularity in management teams and boards. The boards, executives and companies that will lead in the twenty-first century will be those that are integrating priority ESG&D issues and stakeholder interests into their corporate governance, strategy, reporting and partnerships, through the set of actions described in this book. These are the companies that will help to shape the pathway towards sustainable enterprise value creation and, ultimately, towards stakeholder capitalism and more just, inclusive and sustainable growth.

## Notes

1. Jane Nelson, "Toward new models of leadership and partnership," Chapter 3 in Nina Montgomery ed. "Perspectives on Impact: Leading Voices in Making Systemic Change in the Twenty-First Century." Routledge, Taylor and Francis Group, 2019.
2. Jane Nelson and Beth Jenkins. *Tackling Global Challenges: Lessons in System Leadership from the World Economic Forum's New Vision for Agriculture Initiative.* Harvard Kennedy School, Corporate Responsibility Initiative, 2016. https://www.hks.harvard.edu/sites/default/files/centers/mrcbg/programs/cri/files/NVAReport.pdf. See also: Lisa Dreier, David Nabarro, and Jane Nelson. *Systems Leadership for Sustainable Development: Taking Action on Complex Challenges through the Power of Networks.* Harvard Kennedy School, Corporate Responsibility Initiative, 2019. https://www.hks.harvard.edu/sites/default/files/centers/mrcbg/files/Systems%20Leadership.pdf
3. The Value Balancing Alliance. https://www.value-balancing.com/
4. Impact-Weighted Accounts. https://www.hbs.edu/impact-weighted-accounts/Pages/default.aspx
5. The Impact Management Project. https://impactmanagementproject.com/impact-management/impact-management-norms/

# Appendix A. Prototype IFRS Sustainability Disclosure Standard for Climate-Related Disclosures

Developed by the Technical Readiness Working Group, chaired by the IFRS Foundation, to provide recommendations to the International Sustainability Standards Board for consideration.

November 2021

R. Samans, J. Nelson, *Sustainable Enterprise Value Creation*,
https://doi.org/10.1007/978-3-030-93560-3

# Objective

1 The objective of these disclosure requirements is to require an entity to disclose information about its exposure to *climate-related risks* and *opportunities*, enabling users of an entity's general purpose financial reporting:

(a) to determine the effects of climate-related risks and opportunities on the entity's financial position, financial performance and cash flows and to assist users in their assessment of the entity's future cash flows and their value, timing and certainty, over the short, medium and long term and, therefore, assist users in their assessment of the entity's enterprise value;

(b) to understand how management's use of resources and corresponding inputs, activities, outputs and outcomes support the entity's response to and strategy for managing its climate-related risks and opportunities; and

(c) to evaluate the ability of the entity to adapt its planning, *business model* and operations in response to climate-related risks and opportunities.

2 An entity shall apply this [draft] Standard in preparing and disclosing climate-related disclosures in accordance with the IFRS Sustainability Disclosure Standard: General Requirements for the Disclosure of Sustainability-Related Financial Information.

# Scope

3 This Standard applies to:

(a) climate-related risks that the entity is exposed to, including but not restricted to:

　(i) physical risks from climate change (*physical risks*); and
　(ii) risks associated with the transition to a lower-carbon economy (*transition risks*); and

(b) climate-related opportunities available to and considered by the entity.

# Governance

4 An entity shall disclose information that enables users of general purpose financial reporting to understand the governance processes, controls and procedures used to monitor and manage climate-related risks and opportunities. To achieve this objective, the entity shall disclose a description of the governance body or bodies (which can include a board, committee or equivalent body charged with governance) with oversight of climate-related risks and opportunities, and of management's role with respect to climate-related risks and opportunities, including:

(a) the identity of the body or individual within a body responsible for climate-related risks and opportunities;

(b) how the body's responsibilities for climate-related risks and opportunities are reflected in terms of reference, board mandates and other relevant entity policies;

(c) how the body ensures that the correct skills and competencies are available to oversee strategies designed to respond to climate-related risks and opportunities;

(d) the processes and frequency by which the body and its committees (audit, risk or other committees) are informed about climate-related matters and the associated climate-related risks and opportunities;

(e) how the body and its committees consider climate-related risks and opportunities when overseeing the entity's strategy, decisions on major transactions and risk management policies, including any assessment of trade-offs and analysis of sensitivity to uncertainty that may be required;

(f) how the body oversees the setting of climate-related targets and monitors progress towards them, including whether and how related performance metrics are incorporated into remuneration policies; and

(g) a description of management's role in assessing and managing climate-related risks and opportunities (e.g., whether climate-related responsibilities have been assigned to specific management-level positions or committees, and that appropriate controls have been put in place by management to monitor climate-related matters, including ways in which climate-related risks and opportunities are considered and coordinated across different internal functions) and how the body oversees management in that role.

## Strategy

5 An entity shall disclose information that enables users of general purpose financial reporting to understand its strategy for addressing climate-related risks and opportunities, including the entity's assessment of:

(a) the significant climate-related risks and opportunities that it reasonably expects could affect its business model, strategy and cash flows over the short, medium or long term (see paragraph 6);

(b) the impact of significant climate-related risks and opportunities on its business model (see paragraph 7);

(c) the impact of significant climate-related risks and opportunities on management's strategy and decision-making (see paragraph 8);

(d) the impact of significant climate-related risks and opportunities on its financial position, financial performance and cash flows at the reporting period end and the *anticipated* effects over the short, medium and long term (see paragraph 9); and

(e) the *resilience* of the entity's strategy to significant climate-related risks associated with the physical impacts of climate change and the transition to a lower-carbon economy (see paragraph 10).

6 An entity shall disclose information that enables users of general purpose financial reporting to understand the significant climate-related risks and opportunities that are reasonably expected to affect the entity's business model, strategy and cash flows over the short, medium or long term. Specifically, the entity shall disclose:

(a) a description of the processes in place to identify climate-related risks and opportunities that it reasonably expects could positively or negatively affect its business model, strategy and cash flows;

(b) how it defines the short, medium and long term and how the definitions are linked to the entity's strategic planning horizons and capital allocation plans;

(c) a description of significant climate-related risks or opportunities and the time horizon over which each could reasonably be expected to have a financial effect on the entity; and

(d) whether the risks identified are physical risks or transition risks. For example, acute physical risks could be increased severity of extreme weather events, such as cyclones and floods, and chronic physical risks could include rising sea levels or rising mean temperatures. Transition risks could include regulatory, technological, market, legal or reputational risks.

7 An entity shall disclose information that enables users of general purpose financial reporting to understand its assessment of the impact of significant climate-related risks and opportunities on its business model. Specifically, the entity shall disclose:

(a) a description of the current and anticipated effects of significant climate-related risks and opportunities on its value chain for producing goods or services (e.g., supply chains, operations, workforce, marketing and distribution channels); and

(b) where in its value chain significant climate-related risks or opportunities are concentrated (e.g., geographical areas, facilities or types of assets, inputs, outputs or distribution channels).

8 An entity shall disclose information that enables users of general purpose financial reporting to understand its assessment of the impact of significant climate-related risks and opportunities on management's strategy and decision-making, including its *transition plans*. Specifically, the entity shall disclose:

(a) how it is responding to significant climate-related risks and opportunities including but not restricted to:

(i) how it plans to achieve any climate-related targets it has set, including how these plans will be resourced, the processes in place for review of those targets and assumptions about the use of *carbon offsets* in achieving the target, including minimum quality or certification thresholds for the offsets;

(ii) how it is advancing research and development related to climate change mitigation, adaptation or opportunities;

(iii) whether it is adopting new technologies;

(iv) what direct adaptation and mitigation efforts it is undertaking (e.g., through workforce, changes in materials used or product specifications or introduction of efficiency measures);

(v) what indirect adaptation and mitigation efforts it is undertaking (e.g., through working with customers and supply chains or use of certification schemes [e.g., an internationally recognized scheme providing certification for the sustainability of a commodity such as lumber or palm oil]); and

(vi) the extent to which mitigation efforts rely on offsetting strategies and the factors affecting the choice of any offsetting strategy; for example, following an assessment of multiple schemes, a technology company has decided to offset residual emissions within its value chain via an afforestation programme to meet its strategic commitment to mitigate climate risk. The company selected offset programmes because they led to permanent and additional outcomes and met an accredited verification standard. The entity described each project, the geography in which the projects operate, the number of metric tonnes of offsets, the cost per metric tonne, the year in which the emission reduction occurred and the verification standard applying to the scheme.

(b) plans and critical assumptions for *legacy assets*, including strategies to manage carbon-, energy- and water-intensive operations and to decommission carbon-, energy- and water-intensive assets.

(c) quantitative and qualitative information about the progress of plans previously disclosed in accordance with paragraphs 8(a) and 8(b).

(d) how significant climate-related risks and opportunities are included in the entity's financial planning decision-making (e.g., in relation to investment decisions and funding).

9 An entity shall disclose information that enables users of general purpose financial reporting to understand the impact of significant climate-related risks and opportunities on its financial position, financial performance and cash flows at the reporting period end, and the anticipated effects over the short, medium and long term. Specifically, the entity shall disclose qualitatively and quantitatively when feasible:

(a) how significant climate-related risks and opportunities have affected its most recently reported financial performance, financial position and cash flows;

(b) how management expects the entity's financial position to change over time in line with its strategy to address significant climate-related risks and opportunities, reflecting:

(i) the entity's current and committed capital allocation plans and their anticipated impact on the financial position (e.g., major acquisitions and divestments, joint ventures, business transformation, innovation, new business areas and asset retirements); and

(ii) the entity's planned sources of funding to implement the strategies; and

(c) how management expects the entity's financial performance to change over time given its strategy to address significant climate-related risks and opportunities (e.g., increased revenue from or costs of products and services aligned with a lower-carbon economy, consistent with the Paris Agreement; physical damage to assets from climate events; and the total costs of climate adaptation or mitigation); and

(d) how the entity's assessment of significant climate-related risks and opportunities has affected judgements made or present sources of estimation uncertainty in the financial statements.

10 An entity shall disclose an analysis of the resilience of the entity's strategy to significant climate-related risks (physical and transition), including:

(a) how the analysis has been conducted, including:

(i) whether it has been conducted by comparing a diverse range of *climate-related scenarios* and whether it has used a *Paris-aligned scenario* and scenarios consistent with increased physical climate-related risks;

(ii) which scenarios were used for the assessment and the sources of the scenarios used (e.g., Network for Greening the Financial System Net Zero 2050 scenarios, the International Energy Agency Net Zero 2050 scenario and the Intergovernmental Panel on Climate Change Representative Concentration Pathway 1.9 and 2.6);

(iii) an explanation of why the entity believes the chosen scenarios are relevant to assessing its resilience to climate-related risks and opportunities;

(iv) the time horizons over which the analysis has been conducted;

(v) the inputs into the scenario analysis, including but not limited to the scope of risks (e.g., the scope of physical risks included in the scenario analysis), the scope of operations covered (e.g., the operating locations used) and the level of detail in the assumptions (e.g., geospatial coordinates specific to company locations or national- or regional-level broad assumptions); and

(vi) management's assumptions about the way the transition to a lower-carbon economy will affect the entity, including policy assumptions for the jurisdictions in which the entity operates, macroeconomic trends, energy usage and mix and technology assumptions; and

(b) the results of the analysis together with an assessment demonstrating how the entity's financial position and financial performance support the resilience of the entity's strategy and business model over the short, medium and long term, including:

  (i) how assets and investments are aligned with or are sufficiently flexible to be reallocated, decommissioned, repaired and upgraded, in the event of physical disruption or chronic changes in weather patterns resulting from climate change; and

  (ii) the current or planned investment in lower-carbon alternatives (and what proportion that represents overall investment), reskilling the workforce and the degree of capital flexibility available to withstand the physical effects of climate change.

## Risk Management

11 An entity shall disclose information that enables users of general purpose financial reporting to understand how climate-related risks are identified, assessed, managed and mitigated. To achieve this objective the entity shall describe:

(a) the process by which climate-related risks are identified;

(b) the process, or processes, by which the entity assesses the significance of climate-related risks, including, where relevant:

  (i) how it determines the likelihood and impact of such risks (such as the qualitative factors or quantitative thresholds used);

  (ii) how it prioritizes climate-related risks relative to other types of risks, including the use of risk assessment tools (e.g., science-based risk assessment tools or other sources);

  (iii) which significant input parameters it uses (e.g., data sources, the scope of operations covered and the level of detail used in assumptions); and

  (iv) whether it has changed the processes used compared to the prior reporting period;

(c) for each significant climate-related risk, information that enables an understanding of how the risk is being monitored, managed and mitigated, including related policies; and

(d) the extent to which, and how, these climate-related risk identification, assessment and management processes are integrated into the entity's overall risk management process.

# Metrics and Targets

12 An entity shall disclose information that enables users of general purpose financial reporting to understand the entity's performance in managing significant climate-related risks and opportunities. To achieve this objective, an entity shall disclose:

(a) cross-industry metrics (see paragraph 13);

(b) industry-based metrics (see Appendix B);

(c) targets set by management to mitigate or adapt to climate-related risks or maximize climate-related opportunities; and

(d) other key performance indicators used by the board or management to measure progress towards the targets identified in paragraph 12(c).

13 An entity shall disclose the following cross-industry metrics:

(a) *greenhouse gas emissions*—in terms of absolute gross *Scope 1*, *Scope 2* and *Scope 3*, expressed as metric tonnes of $CO_2$ *equivalent*, in accordance with the Greenhouse Gas Protocol and emissions intensity;

(b) transition risks—the amount and percentage of assets or business activities vulnerable to transition risks;

(c) physical risks—the amount and percentage of assets or business activities vulnerable to physical risks;

(d) climate-related opportunities—the proportion of revenue, assets or other business activities aligned with climate-related opportunities, expressed as an amount or as a percentage;

(e) capital deployment—the amount of capital expenditure, financing or investment deployed towards climate-related risks and opportunities, expressed in the reporting currency;

(f) internal *carbon prices*—the price for each metric tonne of greenhouse gas emissions used internally by an entity, including how the entity is applying the carbon price in decision-making (e.g., investment decisions, transfer pricing and scenario analysis), expressed in the reporting currency per metric tonne of $CO_2$ equivalent; and

NOTE: Included in the TRWG's recommendations for consideration by the ISSB is the suggestion to develop (as a priority and building on existing content where possible) detailed technical protocols for the cross-industry metrics listed in paragraph 13, to ensure consistency and comparability across reporting entities (e.g., the consolidation and disclosure of Scope 3 emissions and denominators for intensity disclosures). As it stands, some of the cross-industry metrics listed in paragraph 13 represent categories that need to be built upon further to become metrics. The TRWG also recommends that further guidance be developed regarding the relationship between cross-industry disclosures and industry-based disclosures.

(g) remuneration—the proportion of executive management remuneration affected by climate-related considerations in the current period (also see paragraph 4(f)), expressed in a percentage, weighting, description or amount in reporting currency.

14 For Scope 3 greenhouse gas emissions, the entity shall provide an explanation of the activities included within the disclosed metric. For example, an online retailer may be exposed to risks or opportunities related to the greenhouse gas emissions arising out of third-party transportation and distribution services purchased by the reporting entity for outbound logistics of products sold to customers. The retailer may determine that information about such emissions is material to the users of its general purpose financial reports in their assessment of its enterprise value. Therefore, the retailer will explain how the emissions information provided by entities in its supply chain has been included in the determination of Scope 3 greenhouse gas emissions.

15 The entity shall disclose its climate-related targets, and:

(a) the objective of the targets (e.g., mitigation, adaptation and conformance with sector and science-based initiatives);

(b) whether the target is *absolute* or *intensity-based*;

(c) whether the target is *science-based*, and if so, whether it has been validated by a third party;

(d) whether the target was derived using a sectoral decarbonization approach;

(e) the time frame over which the target applies;

(f) the base year from which progress is measured;

(g) any milestones or interim targets; and

(h) metrics used to assess progress towards reaching targets and achieving strategic goals.

# Effective Date

16  [IFRS SX] was issued in [Month, Year]. An entity shall apply [IFRS SX] for annual reporting periods beginning on or after 1 January 20XX. Earlier application is permitted. If an entity applies [IFRS SX] earlier, it shall disclose that fact.

17  An entity is not required to provide the disclosures specified in paragraphs [4–15] for any period before the date of initial application if it is impracticable to do so.

# Appendix B. Measuring Stakeholder Capitalism Core Metrics: World Economic Forum International Business Council

| Theme | Governance: Core metrics and disclosures | Sources |
|---|---|---|
| Governing purpose | **Setting purpose**<br>The company's stated purpose, as the expression of the means by which a business proposes solutions to economic, environmental and social issues. Corporate purpose should create value for all stakeholders, including shareholders. | The British Academyand Colin Mayer, GRI 102-26, Embankment Project for Inclusive Capitalism (EPIC) andothers |
| Quality of governing body | **Governance body composition**<br>Composition of the highest governance body and its committeesby: competencies relating to economic, environmental and socialtopics; executive or non-executive; independence; tenure on the governance body; number of each individual's other significant positions and commitments, and the nature of the commitments; gender; membership of under-represented social groups; stakeholder representation. | GRI 102-22, GRI 405-1a, IR 4B |
| Stakeholder engagement | **Material issues impacting stakeholders**<br>A list of the topics that are material to key stakeholders andthe company, how the topics were identified and how the stakeholders were engaged. | GRI 102-21, GRI 102-43, GRI 102-47 |
| Ethical behaviour | **Anti-corruption**<br>1. Total percentage of governance body members, employees and business partners who have received training on the organization's anti-corruption policies and procedures, brokendown by region.<br>a) Total number and nature of incidents of corruption confirmed during the current year, but related to previous years; and<br>b) Total number and nature of incidents of corruptionconfirmed during the current year, related to this year.<br>2. Discussion of initiatives and stakeholder engagement to improve the broader operating environment and culture, inorder to combat corruption. | GRI 205-2, GRI 205-3 |
| | **Protected ethics advice and reporting mechanisms**<br>A description of internal and external mechanisms for:<br><br>1. Seeking advice about ethical and lawful behaviour and organizational integrity; and<br><br>2. Reporting concerns about unethical or unlawful behaviour and lack of organizational integrity. | GRI 102-17 |
| Risk and opportunity oversight | **Integrating risk and opportunity into business process**<br>Company risk factor and opportunity disclosures that clearly identify the principal material risks and opportunities facing the company specifically (as opposed to generic sector risks), the company appetite in respect of these risks, how these risks and opportunities have moved over time and the response to those changes. These opportunities and risks should integrate material economic, environmental and social issues, including climate change and data stewardship. | EPIC, GRI 102-15, World Economic Forum Integrated Corporate Governance, IR 4D |

**Fig. B.1** Summary overview of core metrics and disclosures. Source: World Economic Forum International Business Council (reproduced by permission)

R. Samans, J. Nelson, *Sustainable Enterprise Value Creation*,
https://doi.org/10.1007/978-3-030-93560-3

Planet

| Theme | Planet: Core metrics and disclosures | Sources |
|-------|--------------------------------------|---------|
| Climate change | Greenhouse gas (GHG) emissions<br>For all relevant greenhouse gases (e.g. carbon dioxide, methane, nitrous oxide, F-gases etc.), report in metric tonnes of carbon dioxide equivalent (tCO2e) GHG Protocol Scope 1 and Scope 2 emissions.<br><br>Estimate and report material upstream and downstream (GHGProtocol Scope 3) emissions where appropriate. | GRI 305:1-3,<br>TCFD,<br>GHG Protocol |
| | TCFD implementation<br>Fully implement the recommendations of the Task Force on Climate-related Financial Disclosures (TCFD). If necessary, disclose a timeline of at most three years for full implementation. Disclose whether you have set, or have committed to set, GHG emissions targets that are in line with the goals of the Paris Agreement – to limit global warming to well below 2°C above pre-industrial levels and pursue efforts to limit warming to 1.5°C – and to achieve net-zero emissions before 2050. | Recommendation sof the TCFD;<br>CDSB R01, R02, R03, R04 and R06;<br>SASB 110;<br>Science Based Targets initiative |
| Nature loss | Land use and ecological sensitivity<br>Report the number and area (in hectares) of sites owned, leased or managed in or adjacent to protected areas and/or keybiodiversity areas (KBA). | GRI 304-1 |
| Freshwater availability | Water consumption and withdrawal in water-stressed areas<br>Report for operations where material: megalitres of water withdrawn, megalitres of water consumed and the percentage ofeach in regions with high or extremely high baseline water stress, according to WRI Aqueduct water risk atlas tool.<br><br>Estimate and report the same information for the full value chain(upstream and downstream) where appropriate. | SASB CG-HP-140a.1,<br>WRI Aqueduct waterrisk atlas tool |

People

| Theme | People: Core metrics and disclosures | Sources |
|-------|--------------------------------------|---------|
| Dignity and equality | Diversity and inclusion (%)<br>Percentage of employees per employee category, by age group, gender and other indicators of diversity (e.g. ethnicity). | GRI 405-1b |
| | Pay equality (%)<br>Ratio of the basic salary and remuneration for each employee category by significant locations of operation for priority areas of equality: women to men, minor to major ethnic groups, and other relevant equality areas. | Adapted from GRI 405-2 |
| | Wage level (%)<br>Ratios of standard entry level wage by gender compared to local minimum wage.<br><br>Ratio of the annual total compensation of the CEO to the median of the annual total compensation of all its employees, except the CEO. | GRI 202-1,<br>Adapted from Dodd-Frank Act, US SEC Regulations |
| | Risk for incidents of child, forced or compulsory labour<br>An explanation of the operations and suppliers considered to have significant risk for incidents of child labour, forced or compulsory labour. Such risks could emerge in relation to:<br><br>a) type of operation (such as manufacturing plant) and type ofsupplier; and<br>b) countries or geographic areas with operations and suppliersconsidered at risk. | GRI 408-1b,<br>GRI 409-1 |

**Fig. B.1** (continued)

| Theme | People: Core metrics and disclosures | Sources |
|---|---|---|
| Health and well- being | Health and safety (%)<br>The number and rate of fatalities as a result of work-related injury;high-consequence work-related injuries (excluding fatalities); recordable work-related injuries; main types of work-related injury;and the number of hours worked.<br><br>An explanation of how the organization facilitates workers' accessto non-occupational medical and healthcare services, and the scope of access provided for employees and workers. | GRI:2018 403-9a&b,<br><br>GRI:201 8403-6a |
| Skills for the future | Training provided (#, $)<br>Average hours of training per person that the organization's employees have undertaken during the reporting period, by gender and employee category (total number of hours of trainingprovided to employees divided by the number of employees).<br><br>Average training and development expenditure per full time employee (total cost of training provided to employees divided bythe number of employees). | GRI 404-1,<br><br>SASB HC 101-15 |

| Theme | Prosperity: Core metrics and disclosures | Sources |
|---|---|---|
| Employment and wealth generation | Absolute number and rate of employment<br>1. Total number and rate of new employee hires during the reporting period, by age group, gender, other indicators ofdiversity and region.<br><br>2. Total number and rate of employee turnover during the reporting period, by age group, gender, other indicators ofdiversity and region. | Adapted, to includeother indicators of diversity, from GRI 401-1a&b |
|  | Economic contribution<br>1. Direct economic value generated and distributed (EVG&D), on an accruals basis, covering the basic components for theorganization's global operations, ideally split out by:<br>– Revenues<br>– Operating costs<br>– Employee wages and benefits<br>– Payments to providers of capital<br>– Payments to government<br>– Community investment<br>2. Financial assistance received from the government: total monetary value of financial assistance received by the organization from any government during the reporting period. | GRI 201-1,<br><br>GRI 201-4 |
|  | Financial investment contribution<br>1. Total capital expenditures (CapEx) *minus* depreciation, supported by narrative to describe the company's investmentstrategy.<br><br>2. Share buybacks *plus* dividend payments, supported by narrative to describe the company's strategy for returns ofcapital to shareholders. | As referenced in IAS7 and US GAAP ASC 230 |
| Innovation of better products and services | Total R&D expenses ($)<br>Total costs related to research and development. | US GAAP ASC 730 |
| Community and social vitality | Total tax paid<br>The total global tax borne by the company, including corporateincome taxes, property taxes, non-creditable VAT and other sales taxes, employer-paid payroll taxes, and other taxes that constitute costs to the company, by category of taxes. | Adapted from GRI201-1 |

Prosperity

**Fig. B.1** (continued)

# Appendix C. Sustainability Accounting Standards Board Materiality Map

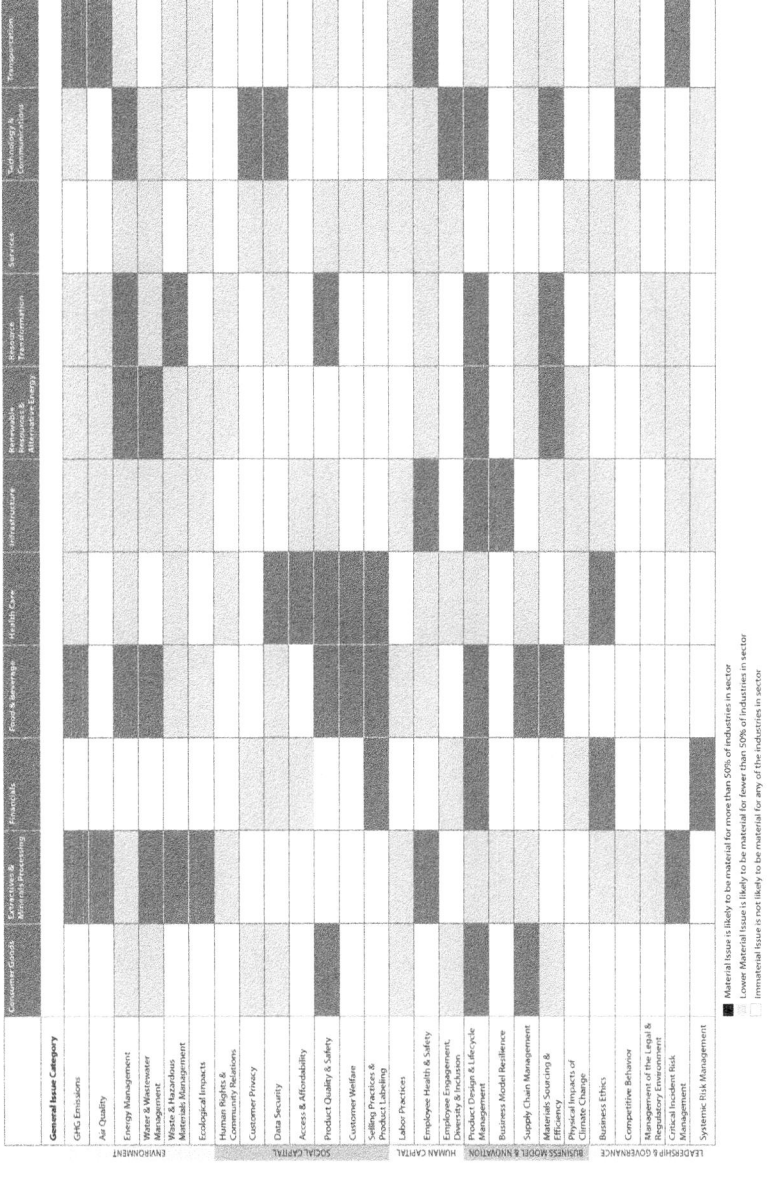

Source: Value Reporting Foundation (reproduced by permission)

# Index[1]

---

[1] Note: Page numbers followed by 'n' refer to notes.

© The Author(s) 2022
R. Samans, J. Nelson, *Sustainable Enterprise Value Creation*,
https://doi.org/10.1007/978-3-030-93560-3

The manufacturer's authorised representative in the EU is Springer
Nature Customer Service Centre GmbH, Europaplatz 3, 69115 Heidelberg,
Germany. If you have any concerns regarding our products, please
contact ProductSafety@springernature.com

Printed and bound by CPI Group (UK) Ltd, Croydon, CR0 4YY
05/05/2026
02102981-0008